W9-BZP-504

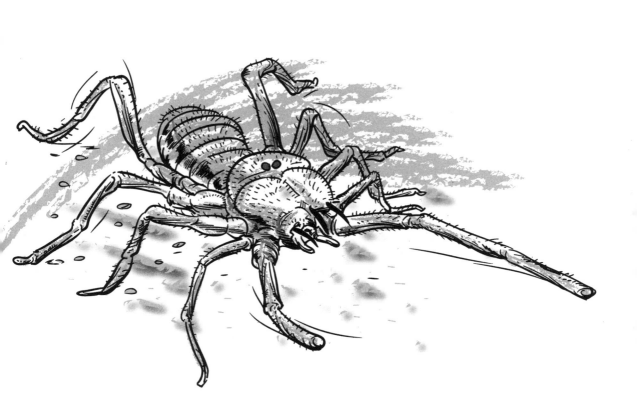

I dedicate this book with love to
Craig Yoe,
for listening patiently to an unending litany of gross bug facts.

Con amore a **Giovanna Anzaldi** e **Nerio Gussoni,**
grazie per le mille attenzioni e dedizione.

—Clizia Gussoni

Dedicated with love to **Carole,**
Logan, and **Gabriel.**

—Luke McDonnell

The Awesome Book of BUGS!

by
Clizia Gussoni

Illustrated by
Luke McDonnell

RP | KIDS
PHILADELPHIA • LONDON

Italian born and trained, Clizia Gussoni is co-founder and Creative Director of Gussoni-Yoe Studio, Inc., an innovative design firm housed in a mountaintop castle overlooking the Hudson River. Her clients are among the top names in corporate America: Disney, Warner Bros., Cartoon Network, MTV, Nickelodeon, Mattel, and Microsoft, to name but a few.

Clizia specializes in innovative design and creations and has garnered several awards in recognition of her accomplishments, including a Mobius and two Addys. She has been featured in various publications including *The New York Times, Li©ense! Magazine,* and *The Women's Business Journal.*

©2008 by Gussoni-Yoe Studio, Inc.
All rights reserved under the Pan-American and International Copyright Conventions

Printed in the United States

*This book may not be reproduced in whole or part, in any form or by any means,
electronic or mechanical, including photocopying, recording, or by any information storage
and retrieval system now known or hereafter invented, without written permission from the publisher.*

9   8   7   6   5   4   3   2   1
Digit on the right indicates the number of this printing

Library of Congress Control Number: 2007941959

ISBN 978-0-7624-3234-9

Published by Running Press Kids, an imprint of
Running Press Book Publishers
2300 Chestnut Street
Philadelphia, PA 19103-4371

Visit us on the web!
www.runningpress.com

A myriad of thank-yous to the following people who, with their creativity, patience, and dedication have made this book possible: Jon Anderson, Teresa Bonaddio, Craig Yoe, the Maestro Luke McDonnell, Jayne Antipow, Mike Hill, Joy Court, Alfeo Tancioni, Linda Salsedo, and Mom and Dad.

— *Clizia Gussoni*

Thanks to all the bugs who posed for these pictures!

— *Luke McDonnell*

What do you imagine when you think of the word "bug"? You can use it to refer to a centipede, a spider, or even a snail. But centipedes, spiders, and snails don't look at all like one another and belong to very different groups of animals.

I tried to imagine what the word "bug" meant for me, and I came up with all the animals described in this book. As you can see, some have six legs, some have eight, some have one thousand, and some have none. But what they all have in common is the power to give us a creepy feeling and be a source of fascination.

IN THIS **AWESOME BOOK,** YOU WILL FIND MANY **BUG DESCRIPTIONS.** THERE IS STILL MUCH THAT IS **NOT KNOWN** ABOUT BUGS AND HOW THEY **INTERACT** WITH **EACH OTHER,** WITH **NATURE,** AND WITH **US. HUNDREDS** OF **THOUSANDS** OF BUGS ARE YET TO BE **DISCOVERED,** MAYBE **YOU'LL** BECOME AN **ENTOMOLOGIST** AND **DISCOVER** SOME!

FOR DIFFICULT TERMS, CHECK OUT THE **GLOSSARY** AT THE END OF THE BOOK.

GLOSSARY

WHAT IS A BUG?

BUGS ARE PART OF THE ANIMAL KINGDOM LIKE MAMMALS, REPTILES, AND BIRDS. BUGS ARE DIVIDED INTO MANY GROUPS DEPENDING ON THEIR SHARED CHARACTERISTICS. BUT NO MATTER WHAT GROUPS THEY BELONG TO, ALL BUGS HAVE ONE THING IN COMMON: THEY ARE ALL INVERTEBRATES. THIS MEANS THAT THEY LACK A BACKBONE.

INSECTS DON'T HAVE A BACKBONE, BUT THEY HAVE AN EXOSKELETON. AN EXOSKELETON IS A HARD COVERING THAT WRAPS UP THE SOFT AND DELICATE INSIDES OF THE INSECT TO PROTECT THEM.

ALL THE BUGS DESCRIBED IN THIS BOOK ARE ARTHROPODS, WHICH MEANS THAT THEY ALL HAVE JOINTED LEGS.

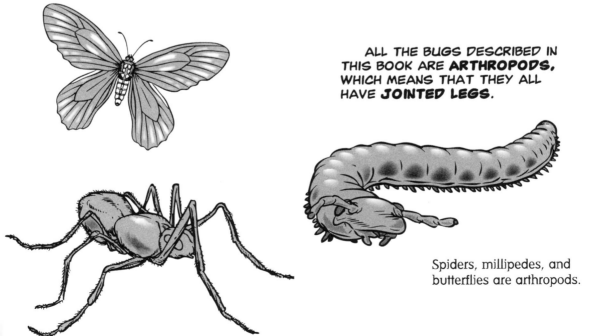

Spiders, millipedes, and butterflies are arthropods.

WHAT IS AN
ARTHROPOD?

Animals with jointed legs

TO BE CALLED AN **ARTHROPOD,** AN ANIMAL MUST HAVE THE FOLLOWING **FOUR CHARACTERISTICS. . .**

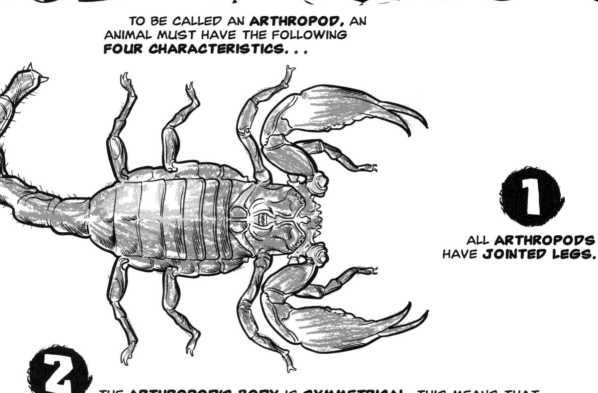

1

ALL **ARTHROPODS** HAVE **JOINTED LEGS.**

2

THE **ARTHROPOD'S BODY** IS **SYMMETRICAL.** THIS MEANS THAT **HALF** OF THE BODY IS **IDENTICAL** TO THE **OTHER HALF.** IN COMPARISON, **NATURAL SPONGES** ARE **ASYMMETRICAL** ANIMALS. YOU CAN DRAW A LINE THROUGH A SPONGE AND YOU CAN SEE THAT THE **LEFT HALF** OF THE BODY **DOESN'T RESEMBLE** THE **RIGHT ONE.**

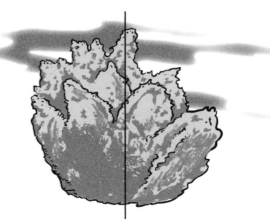

Natural sponges are animals, but they are not arthropods.

3 ARTHROPODS HAVE SEGMENTED BODIES, OFTEN ARRANGED IN GROUPS. FOR EXAMPLE, THE END SECTION OF A HONEYBEE IS FORMED OF SEVEN SEGMENTS, GROUPED TOGETHER IN A LARGER UNIT, CALLED THE ABDOMEN. EXCEPT FOR SMALL CHANGES, ALL SEGMENTS ARE PRETTY MUCH A COPY OF ONE ANOTHER; BOTH IN THEIR EXTERNAL APPEARANCE AND IN THE INTERNAL ORGANS THEY CARRY.

4 ALL ARTHROPODS HAVE AN EXOSKELETON, AN ARMOR-LIKE COVERING THAT PROTECTS THE INTERNAL ORGANS.

ARTHROPODS ARE THE **BIGGEST GROUP** OF ANIMALS IN THE WORLD. THEY INCLUDE A **VARIETY** OF **LIVING ANIMALS**, LIKE **ARACHNIDS** (SCORPIONS, SPIDERS, MITES, ETC.), **INSECTS** (FLIES, BUTTERFLIES, ANTS, ETC.), **MYRIAPODS** (CENTIPEDES, MILLIPEDES, ETC.), AND **CRUSTACEANS** (CRABS, LOBSTERS, SHRIMP, ETC.).

ARTHROPODS

HEXAPODS (INSECTS, OR ANIMALS WITH SIX FEET)

ANTS

FLIES

MITES

BUTTERFLIES

CHELICERATA (ARACHNIDS, OR ANIMALS WITH FANGS)

SPIDERS

SCORPIONS

HORSESHOE CRABS

SEA SPIDERS

MYRIAPODS (ANIMALS WITH A GREAT NUMBER OF FEET)

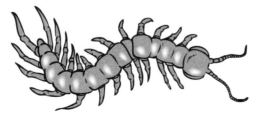
CENTIPEDES

MILLIPEDES

SHRIMP

CRABS

BARNACLES

BRINE SHRIMP
(KNOWN AS
SEA MONKEYS)

WOODLICE

LOBSTER

ARTHROPODS HAVE **ADAPTED** TO LIVE IN **EVERY ENVIRONMENT** ON **EARTH**, FROM THE **SEA**, TO THE **AIR**, TO THE **LAND**. SPECIES OF ARTHROPODS CAN **SURVIVE** IN PLACES WITH **EXTREME CLIMATES**, LIKE THE **POLES** AND THE **EQUATOR**.

THERE ARE MANY OTHER **NON-LIVING ARTHROPODS**. FOR EXAMPLE, **TRILOBITES** AND **SEA SCORPIONS** BELONG TO THIS GROUP, BUT THEY ARE **EXTINCT**.

THERE ARE **MORE ARTHROPODS** THAN **ALL THE OTHER ANIMALS COMBINED**. OVER **75%** OF ALL KNOWN LIVING ANIMALS BELONG TO THIS GROUP. BUT THERE ARE MANY MORE **SPECIES** OF **ARTHROPODS** SCIENTISTS HAVEN'T YET **DISCOVERED**. SCIENTISTS SUSPECT THAT THEY ONLY KNOW ABOUT **10%** OF THE SPECIES BELONGING TO THIS GROUP.

Arthropods

Mammals, Fish, Reptiles,
Birds, People

BUG BITES

The word **arthropod** combines two Greek words, *arthron* and *podos*, meaning "jointed foot." All animals in this group have jointed legs.

THE EXOSKELETON

THE **EXOSKELETON** IS A **HARD SKIN,** ALMOST LIKE AN **ARMOR,** THAT **PROTECTS** THE SOFT **ORGANS** OF **ARTHROPODS. HUMANS** HAVE AN **ENDOSKELETON,** OR A SKELETON **INSIDE** THEIR **BODIES.** ARTHROPODS HAVE AN **EXOSKELETON,** OR A SKELETON **WRAPPED AROUND** THEIR **BODIES.**

Bugs have
exoskeletons.

Humans have
endoskeletons.

THE **EXOSKELETON** IS
MADE UP OF **THREE LAYERS.**

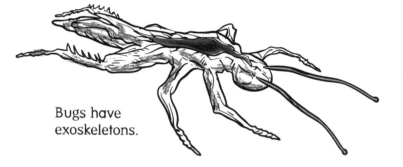

EPIDERMIS

CUTICLE

BASEMENT
MEMBRANE

BUG BITES

The exoskeleton keeps the internal organs from drying up and from coming in contact with toxins and moisture.

JUST LIKE A KNIGHT'S ARMOR, THE **EXOSKELETON** IS MADE UP OF **DIFFERENT PARTS** TO **ALLOW** FOR **MOVEMENT.** BUT SOMETIMES THE ARTHROPOD NEEDS TO **GROW LARGER** THAN ITS EXOSKELETON. WHEN THIS HAPPENS, THE ARTHROPOD **REPLACES** ITS **SKELETON** WITH A **BIGGER ONE.** THIS PROCESS IS CALLED **ECDYSIS,** OR **MOLTING.**

DURING **MOLTING,** THE **CUTICLE** DETACHES ITSELF FROM THE **EPIDERMIS.** THE OLD EXOSKELETON **CRACKS** ALONG THE **BACK** AND THE ARTHROPOD **CRAWLS** OUT OF IT.

MOLTING IS A **DANGEROUS** MOMENT IN THE LIFE OF THE ARTHROPOD. DURING THIS TIME, THE ARTHROPOD BECOMES **MOTIONLESS,** AND IT **CAN'T DEFEND ITSELF** AGAINST PREDATORS.

1. During molting, the exoskeleton cracks along the back.

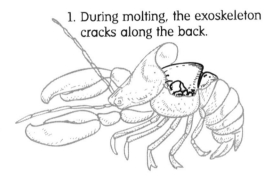

2. The lobster pulls itself out of the old exoskeleton.

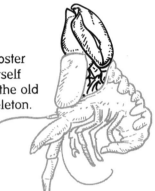

3. The legs are free too.

4. Once the old exoskeleton is discarded, the lobster lets its new exoskeleton get hard.

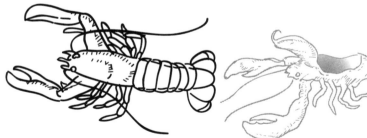

THE NEW **EXOSKELETON** IS **SOFT** AND **LIGHT COLORED,** BUT WITHIN A SHORT TIME IT BECOMES **HARD** AND **DARKENS.** THIS PROCESS IS CALLED **SCLEROTIZATION.**

DURING **SCLEROTIZATION,** THE ARTHROPOD **ENLARGES** ITS **BODY** EITHER WITH **AIR** OR **WATER,** SO THAT THE **EXOSKELETON HARDENS** AT A **LARGER** SIZE. THIS ENSURES THAT THE **NEW EXOSKELETON** IS **BIG** ENOUGH TO **ALLOW** FOR **GROWTH.**

BUG BITES

If they lose a limb, some arthropods, like crabs, can grow a new one. But it might take several molts before a complete new limb is formed.

WHAT IS AN
INSECT?

Hexapods, or animals with six legs

INSECTS ARE ONE OF THE **GROUPS** OF **ANIMALS** BELONGING TO THE **ARTHROPODS.** SCIENTISTS THINK THAT THERE COULD BE **TEN MILLION SPECIES** OF **INSECTS** ON EARTH. SO FAR, ONLY ABOUT **ONE MILLION SPECIES** HAVE BEEN STUDIED, SO THE **MAJORITY** OF **INSECTS** ARE YET TO BE **DISCOVERED!**

TO BE CALLED AN **INSECT,** AN ANIMAL **MUST HAVE FOUR CHARACTERISTICS...**

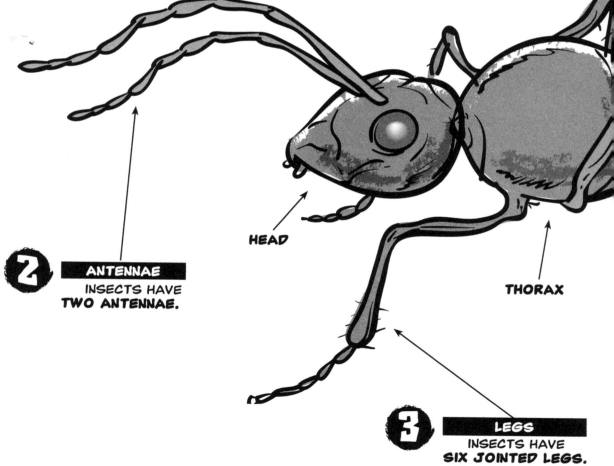

1

THE BODY
THE **BODY** OF AN INSECT IS DIVIDED INTO **THREE PARTS:** THE **HEAD,** THE **THORAX,** AND THE **ABDOMEN.**

HEAD

2 **ANTENNAE**
INSECTS HAVE **TWO ANTENNAE.**

THORAX

3 LEGS
INSECTS HAVE **SIX JOINTED LEGS.**

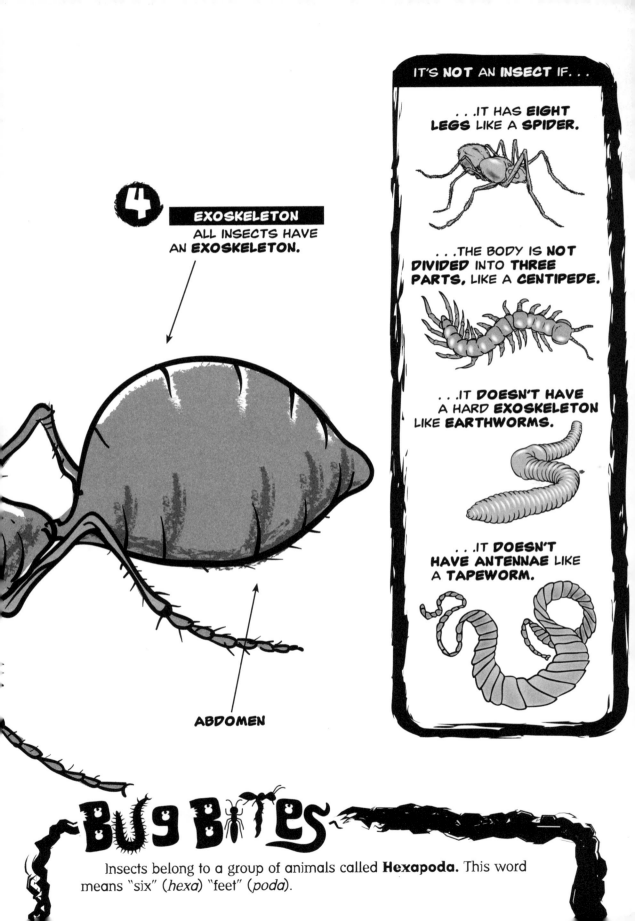

4

EXOSKELETON
ALL INSECTS HAVE
AN **EXOSKELETON.**

ABDOMEN

IT'S NOT AN INSECT IF...

. . .IT HAS **EIGHT
LEGS** LIKE A **SPIDER.**

. . .THE BODY IS **NOT
DIVIDED** INTO **THREE
PARTS,** LIKE A **CENTIPEDE.**

. . .IT **DOESN'T HAVE**
A HARD **EXOSKELETON**
LIKE **EARTHWORMS.**

. . .IT **DOESN'T
HAVE ANTENNAE** LIKE
A **TAPEWORM.**

BUG BITES

Insects belong to a group of animals called **Hexapoda.** This word
means "six" (*hexa*) "feet" (*poda*).

INSECT DETAILS

THE TERM **INSECT** COMES FROM THE LATIN WORD **INSECTUM,** WHICH MEANS **"CUT INTO SECTIONS."** THIS NAME IS VERY **APPROPRIATE** BECAUSE THE **BODY** LOOKS LIKE IT'S **DIVIDED** INTO **THREE PARTS: THE HEAD,** THE **THORAX,** AND THE **ABDOMEN.**

OCELLI

MOST INSECTS HAVE **THREE OCELLI** POSITIONED ON TOP OF THEIR HEADS. THE **OCELLI** ARE VERY **SIMPLE EYES.** JUST LIKE REGULAR EYES, THE OCELLI **PERCEIVE LIGHT.** UNLIKE REGULAR EYES, THE OCELLI **CANNOT** PERCEIVE **IMAGES.**

ANTENNAE

EVERY INSECT HAS A **PAIR** OF **ANTENNAE** ON ITS HEAD. ANTENNAE ARE **SENSORY ORGANS.** AN INSECT USES ITS **ANTENNAE** TO **SENSE, TOUCH,** AND **FEEL** ITS SURROUNDING **ENVIRONMENT.**

EYES

INSECTS GENERALLY HAVE A **PAIR** OF **COMPOUND EYES.** COMPOUND EYES ARE MADE UP OF **MANY SMALL EYES.**

THORAX

THE **THORAX** IS WHERE THE **WINGS** AND THE **LEGS** ARE LOCATED.

WINGS

SOME INSECTS HAVE **ONE PAIR** OF **WINGS,** OTHERS HAVE **TWO PAIRS** OF **WINGS.** MANY INSECTS **DON'T HAVE WINGS** AT ALL.

WINGS ARE **ATTACHED** TO THE **THORAX,** NEVER TO THE **ABDOMEN.**

ABDOMEN

ON THE ABDOMEN, THE **EXOSKELETON** IS MADE UP OF **SEGMENTS** THAT **VARY IN NUMBER** DEPENDING ON THE INSECT SPECIES. THE **GRASSHOPPER** HAS THE MOST WITH **ELEVEN.** THE **SPRINGTAIL** HAS ONLY **SIX.** THE **HONEYBEE** HAS **SEVEN.**

LEGS

ALL **SIX LEGS** OF AN INSECT ARE **ATTACHED** TO THE **THORAX.** THERE ARE **NO INSECTS** THAT HAVE THEIR **LEGS ATTACHED** TO THE **ABDOMEN.**

BUG BITES

Scientists who study insects are called **entomologists.** This word comes from the Greek *entomos,* and has the same meaning as the Latin word *insectum:* "cut into sections."

INSECTS HAVE **TWO COMPOUND EYES,** MADE UP OF **SMALL EYES** CALLED **OMMATIDIA.** SOME SPECIES OF INSECTS, LIKE **ANTS,** HAVE ONLY A **FEW HUNDRED OMMATIDIA.** OTHERS HAVE THOUSANDS. **DRAGONFLIES,** FOR EXAMPLE, HAVE **30,000** OMMATIDIA. THEY NEED **BETTER VISION** THAN ANTS BECAUSE MANY **DRAGONFLIES HUNT** AT **NIGHT.**

BECAUSE THE **COMPOUND EYES** ARE SO **BIG** AND **ROUND,** THEY ARE **BETTER** ABLE TO **DETECT MOVEMENT** THAN **HUMAN EYES.** ON THE OTHER HAND, INSECTS ARE **SHORTSIGHTED** AND CAN'T PUT THINGS IN FOCUS UNLESS THEY ARE VERY CLOSE BY. **BUMBLEBEES** CAN ONLY SEE A **COUPLE** OF **FEET** AHEAD OF THEM, AND **ANTS** ONLY A **FEW INCHES.**

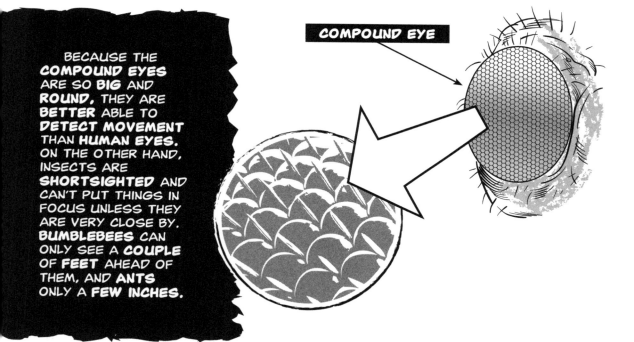

COMPOUND EYE

EACH **OMMATIDIUM** SENDS **ONE PICTURE** TO THE **BRAIN.** EACH PICTURE IS AT A **DIFFERENT ANGLE,** BECAUSE EACH OMMATIDIUM POINTS IN A **DIFFERENT DIRECTION.**

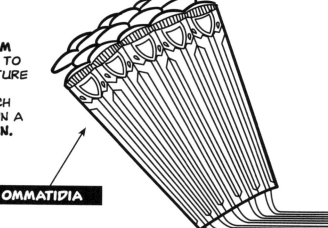

OMMATIDIA

SOME INSECTS CAN SEE **POLARIZED LIGHT**, A PHENOMENON THAT THE HUMAN EYE IS NOT ABLE TO PERCEIVE. POLARIZED LIGHT **CHANGES** DURING THE DAY IN **RELATION** TO THE **SUN**. BY BEING ABLE TO SEE POLARIZED LIGHT, INSECTS **NEVER** GET **DISORIENTED**, AND ARE **ABLE** TO **RETURN** TO THEIR **NESTS**.

SOME INSECTS CAN **DISTINGUISH COLORS** AND CAN SEE **ULTRAVIOLET LIGHT**. ULTRAVIOLET LIGHT IS INVISIBLE TO THE HUMAN EYE. INSECTS THAT **FEED** ON **FLOWER POLLEN**, LIKE HONEYBEES, ARE ABLE TO PERCEIVE ULTRAVIOLET LIGHT.

BUG BITES

Insects can't move their eyes around like we do. Also, insects don't have eyelids, and they have to rest with their eyes open.

THE **HEAD** IS WHERE THE INSECT'S **SENSORY RECEPTORS** ARE LOCATED. SENSORY RECEPTORS ARE **SPECIALIZED BODY PARTS** THAT **RECEIVE INFORMATION** ABOUT THE **ENVIRONMENT**, AND SEND THEM TO THE BRAIN. **COMPOUND EYES, OCELLI,** AND **ANTENNAE** ARE SENSORY RECEPTORS.

OCELLUS

ANTENNA

COMPOUND EYE

INSECTS HAVE **TWO ANTENNAE**. ANTENNAE ARE SENSORY ORGANS. THEY ARE USED FOR **TOUCHING, SMELLING, HEARING,** AND EVEN TO **COMMUNICATE** WITH **OTHER INSECTS** OF THE **SAME SPECIES**.

ANTENNAE CAN BE **FILIFORM,** OR **THREAD-LIKE**.

ANTENNAE CAN BE **SERRATED,** LOOKING LIKE A SAW.

THEY CAN BE **MONILIFORM,** OR SHAPED WITH LITTLE **BUMPS** THAT LOOK **LIKE A STRAND OF PEARLS**.

THEY CAN BE **CAPITATE,** OR LOOKING LIKE THEY HAVE A HEAD, OR A **BIG BUMP,** AT THE END.

ANTENNAE CAN BE **CLAVATE,** OR IN THE SHAPE OF A **CLUB**.

THEY CAN BE **PECTINATE,** OR RESEMBLE A **COMB**.

ANTENNAE CAN BE **LAMELLATE,** MADE UP OF LAMELLAE, OR **SMALL, FLAT PLATES**.

THEY CAN BE **PLUMOSE,** OR FEATHER-LIKE.

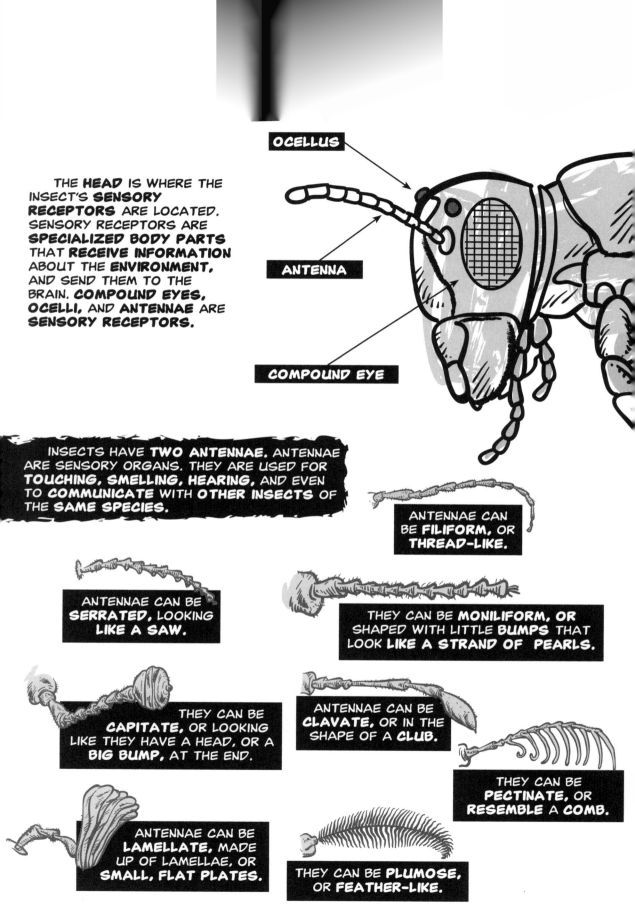

INSECTS HAVE DIFFERENT KINDS OF MOUTHS SO THEY CAN EAT THEIR FAVORITE FOODS.

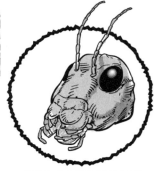

GRASSHOPPERS FEED ON **PLANTS** THAT THEY CHEW WITH THEIR **POWERFUL JAWS.**

FEMALE MOSQUITOES PIERCE AND THEN SUCK THE **BLOOD** OF **ANIMALS,** INCLUDING **PEOPLE,** WITH THEIR **SHARP PROBOSCIS.**

FLIES USE THEIR MOUTH TO **SPONGE UP** THEIR **FOOD.**

BUTTERFLIES HAVE A **PROBOSCIS,** TOO. THEY USE IT TO **SIPHON** THE **NECTAR** FROM **FLOWERS.**

HORSEFLIES DON'T BITE. THEY ARE ABLE TO **CUT THROUGH** THE **HIDE** OF A **HORSE** WITH THEIR MOUTH. THEN THEY **SPONGE** THE **BLOOD.**

WASPS CAN **CHEW** ON OTHER **INSECTS** OR **FRUIT,** BUT THEY CAN ALSO **LAP UP** THEIR FOOD.

BUG BITS

THE **THORAX** IS **DIVIDED** INTO **THREE SEGMENTS: PROTHORAX, MESOTHORAX,** AND **METATHORAX.** EACH SEGMENT BEARS A **COUPLE** OF **LEGS.**

THE **FOREWINGS** ARE ATTACHED TO THE **MESOTHORAX,** WHILE THE **HIND WINGS** ARE ATTACHED TO THE **METATHORAX.**

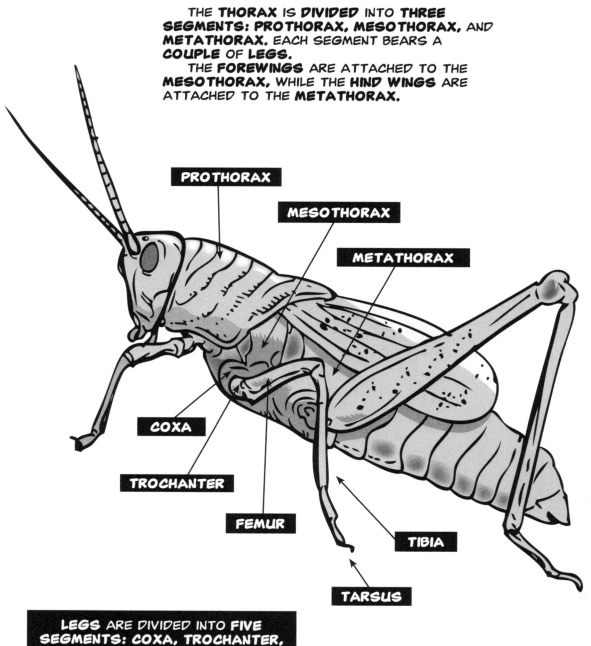

PROTHORAX

MESOTHORAX

METATHORAX

COXA

TROCHANTER

FEMUR

TIBIA

TARSUS

LEGS ARE DIVIDED INTO **FIVE** SEGMENTS: **COXA, TROCHANTER, FEMUR, TIBIA,** AND **TARSUS.**

LEGS ARE **DIFFERENT** IN EACH INSECT SPECIES. THEY HAVE **ADAPTED** TO SUPPORT **VARIOUS KINDS** OF **LIFESTYLES.**

POWERFUL, LONG LEGS MAKE CRICKETS JUMP.

SKINNY, LONG LEGS MAKE COCKROACHES RUN FAST.

PRAYING MANTIDS HAVE **LONG FOREARMS** TO BETTER **GRASP** THEIR **PREY.**

HONEYBEES HAVE **HAIRY LEGS** THAT **COLLECT POLLEN.**

NOT ALL INSECTS CAN FLY. THE ONES THAT DO CAN HAVE EITHER **ONE** OR **TWO PAIRS** OF **WINGS,** DEPENDING ON THEIR SPECIES. WINGS ARE **ATTACHED** TO THE **MESOTHORAX** AND THE **METATHORAX.** EACH SEGMENT BEARS A COUPLE OF WINGS.

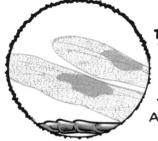

WINGS CAN BE **THIN** AND **TRANSPARENT,** WITH **VEINS** RUNNING THROUGH THEM. THESE ARE THE WINGS OF A **DRAGONFLY.**

WINGS CAN BE **THICK** AND COVERED BY **COLORFUL SCALES.** THESE ARE THE WINGS OF A **BUTTERFLY.**

BEETLES HAVE **TWO PAIRS** OF **WINGS.** THE **TOP** ONE IS **HARD** AND **PROTECTS** THE **WINGS UNDERNEATH.**

BUG BITES

Insects' feet have one or more claws, and a pad called the arolium or pulvillus, depending on the species. Some species of insects, like flies, can ooze a sticky substance from their feet. This substance helps them walk on the ceiling or on very smooth surfaces like glass.

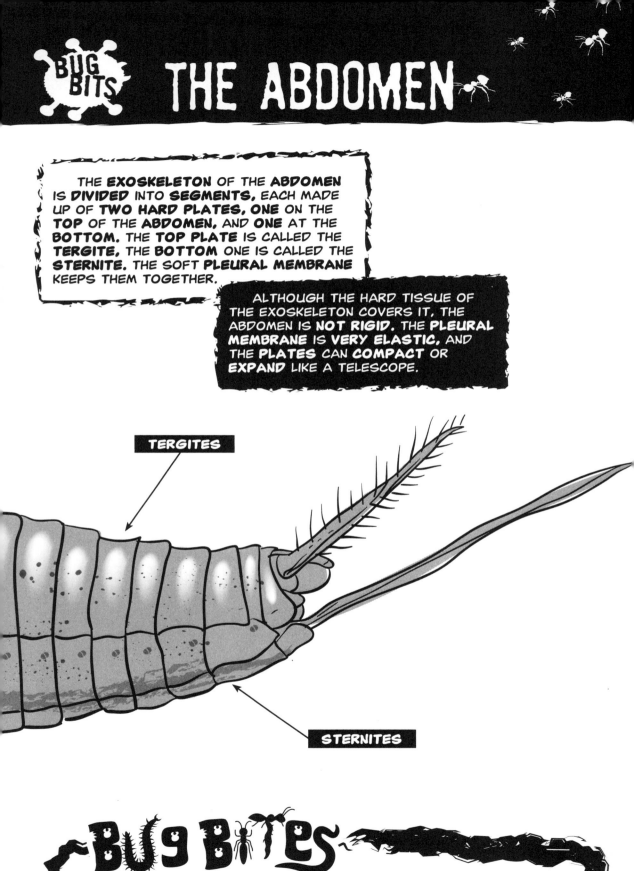

BUG BITS

THE ABDOMEN

THE **EXOSKELETON** OF THE **ABDOMEN** IS **DIVIDED** INTO **SEGMENTS,** EACH MADE UP OF **TWO HARD PLATES, ONE** ON THE **TOP** OF THE **ABDOMEN,** AND **ONE** AT THE **BOTTOM.** THE **TOP PLATE** IS CALLED THE **TERGITE,** THE **BOTTOM** ONE IS CALLED THE **STERNITE.** THE SOFT **PLEURAL MEMBRANE** KEEPS THEM TOGETHER.

ALTHOUGH THE HARD TISSUE OF THE EXOSKELETON COVERS IT, THE ABDOMEN IS **NOT RIGID.** THE **PLEURAL MEMBRANE** IS **VERY ELASTIC,** AND THE **PLATES** CAN **COMPACT** OR **EXPAND** LIKE A TELESCOPE.

TERGITES

STERNITES

BUG BITES

The abdomen houses the insect's digestive and reproductive systems.

INSECTS HAVE **SPIRACLES** ALONG THE **UPPER PLATES** OF THEIR **ABDOMEN.** THE **SPIRACLES** ARE **SMALL OPENINGS** THROUGH WHICH THE INSECT **BREATHES. MUSCLES** ALONG THE ABDOMEN MAKE THE SPIRACLES **OPEN** OR **CLOSE,** FORCING THE **AIR IN** AND **OUT.**

SPIRACLE

INSECTS **DON'T** HAVE **LUNGS** LIKE HUMANS. INSTEAD, THEY HAVE **MANY TRACHEAE,** A SYSTEM OF **TINY TUBES** FILLED WITH FLUID. THE **TRACHEAE** CARRY THE OXYGEN FROM THE SPIRACLES **EVERYWHERE** INTO THE BODY OF THE **INSECT.**

WHILE HUMANS **PUMP AIR IN** AND **OUT** OF THEIR **BODIES** THROUGH THEIR **NOSES,** INSECTS **DIFFUSE** AIR THROUGH THE SPIRACLES. **DIFFUSION** IS **NOT** A **VERY EFFICIENT** WAY OF **BREATHING,** AND CAN ONLY WORK IN **SMALL ANIMALS** LIKE **INSECTS.** THAT'S WHY INSECTS **NEVER GROW** VERY **LARGE.**

IN **PREHISTORIC TIMES** THERE WAS **MORE OXYGEN** IN THE ATMOSPHERE THAN THERE IS TODAY. THIS ALLOWED INSECTS TO GROW **BIGGER.** THERE ARE **FOSSILS** OF **DRAGONFLIES** LIVING **300 MILLION YEARS AGO** THAT HAD A **WINGSPAN** OF **TWO** AND A **HALF FEET!**

BUG BITES

Scientists tested the theory that insects can grow bigger in the presence of more oxygen. They bred fruit flies in an oxygen-rich environment. The more oxygen, the bigger the fruit flies grew!

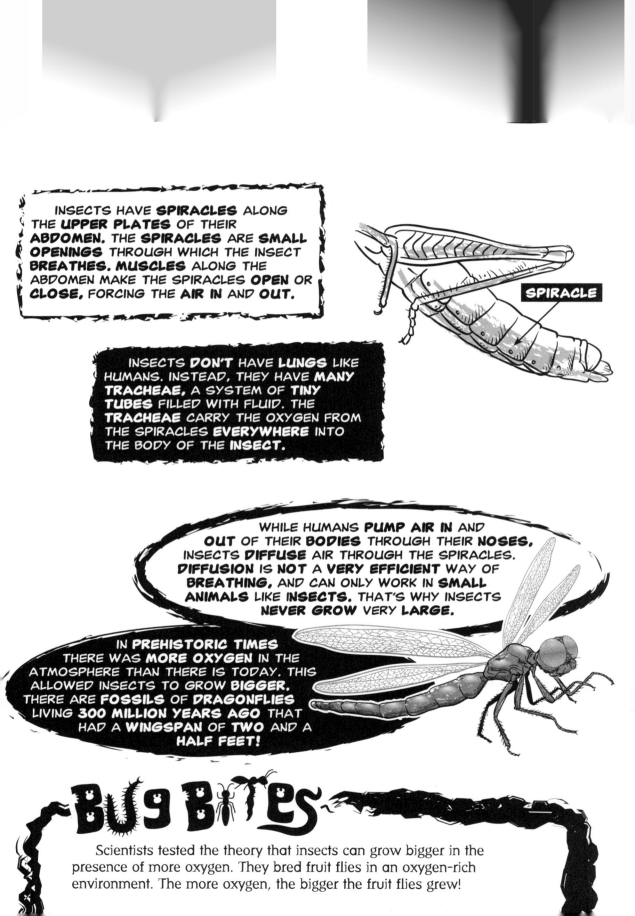

BUG BITS

AT THE VERY **TIP** OF THEIR **ABDOMEN,** MANY INSECTS HAVE A **PAIR** OF **RECEPTORS** CALLED **CERCI** (THE SINGULAR IS **CERCUS).** CERCI ARE **SENSORY ORGANS.** JUST LIKE WITH ITS ANTENNAE, AN INSECT CAN **FEEL** AND **TOUCH** THE **SURROUNDING ENVIRONMENT** WITH ITS **CERCI.** SOME INSECTS, LIKE **WASPS** AND **BEES,** DON'T HAVE **CERCI.**

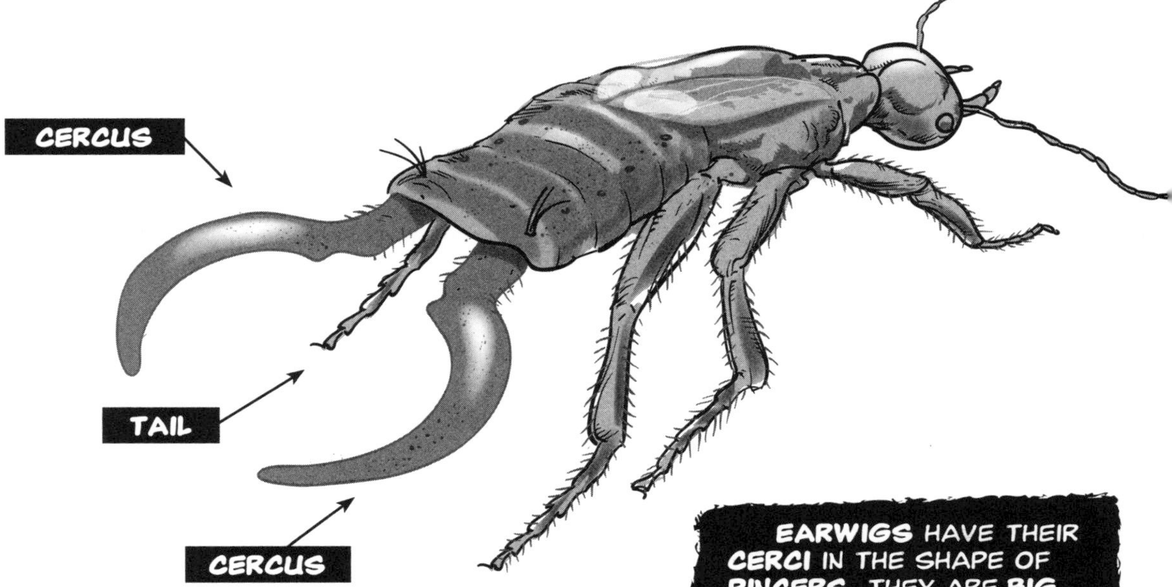

CERCUS

TAIL

CERCUS

EARWIGS HAVE THEIR **CERCI** IN THE SHAPE OF **PINCERS.** THEY ARE **BIG** AND **HARD.** EARWIGS USE THEM FOR **DEFENSE.**

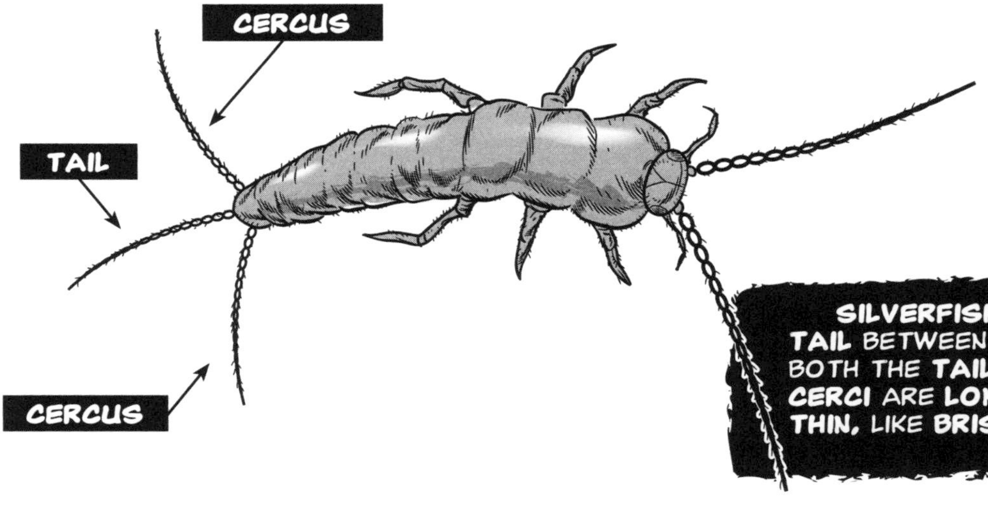

CERCUS

TAIL

CERCUS

SILVERFISH HAVE A **TAIL** BETWEEN THE **CERCI.** BOTH THE **TAIL** AND THE **CERCI** ARE **LONG** AND **THIN,** LIKE **BRISTLES.**

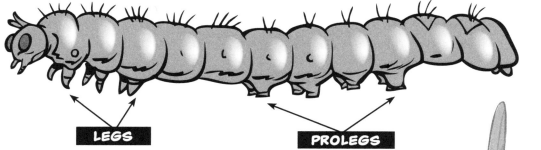

LEGS

PROLEGS

BUTTERFLIES CAN HAVE UP TO TEN APPENDAGES CALLED PROLEGS. PROLEGS ARE LEG-LIKE APPENDAGES, BUT THEY ARE NOT TRUE LEGS BECAUSE THEY DON'T HAVE JOINTS. PROLEGS ARE PRESENT ONLY WHEN THE BUTTERFLY IS IN ITS LARVAL STATE, WHEN IT IS STILL A CATERPILLAR. BUTTERFLIES DON'T HAVE PROLEGS ONCE THEY BECOME ADULTS.

CORNICLES

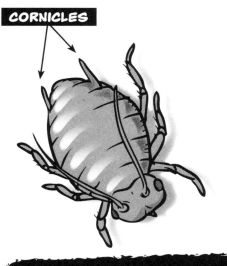

STINGER

THIS IS THE ABDOMEN OF AN APHID. THE TWO APPENDAGES ARE NOT CERCI. THEY ARE CALLED CORNICLES AND OOZE A FLUID THAT REPELS THE APHID'S PREDATORS.

WASPS AND BEES HAVE EVOLVED THEIR REPRODUCTIVE ORGAN INTO A STINGER, WHICH CARRIES VENOM. THEY USE IT TO CHASE AWAY THEIR ENEMIES.

METAMORPHOSIS

THE **DEVELOPMENT** OF AN **INSECT**, FROM THE **EGG** TO THE **ADULT STAGE**, IS CALLED **METAMORPHOSIS**. METAMORPHOSIS IS THE **PROCESS** DURING WHICH THE **EGG HATCHES** AND, IN TIME, THE **NEWBORN LARVAE** BECOME **ADULTS**.

SOME INSECTS GO THROUGH **COMPLETE METAMORPHOSIS;** OTHERS GO THROUGH **GRADUAL METAMORPHOSIS;** AND SOME **DON'T GO THROUGH METAMORPHOSIS** AT ALL.

COMPLETE METAMORPHOSIS

THE **SCIENTIFIC NAME** OF INSECTS THAT GO THROUGH A **COMPLETE METAMORPHOSIS** IS **ENDOPTERYGOTA**. THIS IS A GREEK WORD THAT MEANS "INTERNAL WING DEVELOPMENT."

THEY WERE GIVEN THIS NAME BECAUSE MANY OF THESE INSECTS ARE **WINGED**, BUT THE **WINGS** ARE ONLY **VISIBLE** WHEN THE INSECT BECOMES **ADULT**. THE **DEVELOPMENT** OF THE **WINGS** IS **INTERNAL**.

Caterpillars are immature butterflies. Unlike their adult counterparts, caterpillars don't have any visible wings.

SOME SPECIES ARE **NOT WINGED,** BUT THEIR **ANCESTORS WERE.** FOR THIS REASON THEY ARE STILL KNOWN AS **ENDOPTERYGOTA.**

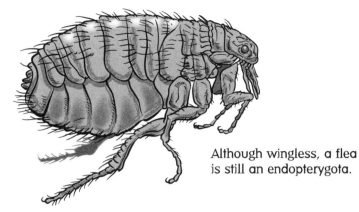

Although wingless, a flea is still an endopterygota.

DURING THEIR **METAMORPHOSIS,** ENDOPTERYGOTE INSECTS **CHANGE** THEIR BODY APPEARANCE **FOUR TIMES** DURING THEIR TRANSFORMATION FROM AN EGG TO AN ADULT. OFTEN THE **NEWBORN INSECTS** ARE **EXTREMELY DIFFERENT** FROM THE **ADULTS.**

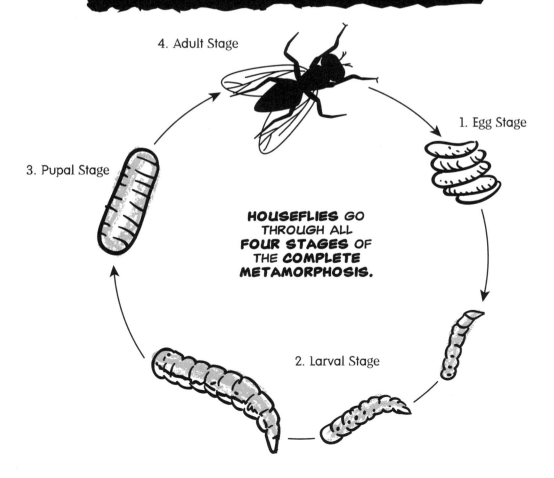

4. Adult Stage

1. Egg Stage

3. Pupal Stage

HOUSEFLIES GO THROUGH ALL **FOUR STAGES** OF THE **COMPLETE METAMORPHOSIS.**

2. Larval Stage

METAMORPHOSIS

COMPLETE METAMORPHOSIS IN THE **LIFE** OF AN **INSECT** INCLUDES **FOUR STAGES**. EACH TIME THE **IMMATURE INSECT** GOES THROUGH A STAGE, IT CAN LOOK **VERY DIFFERENT** FROM THE WAY IT LOOKED IN THE **PREVIOUS STAGE**, AND FROM THE WAY THE INSECT WILL LOOK IN THE **NEXT STAGE**.

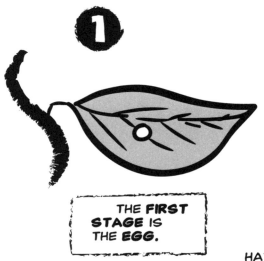

THE **FIRST STAGE** IS THE **EGG**.

THE **SECOND STAGE** IS THE **LARVA**, WHICH HATCHES FROM THE EGG. IN SOME SPECIES THE **LARVA** IS NAMED **DIFFERENTLY**. FOR EXAMPLE, THE **LARVA** OF A **BUTTERFLY** IS CALLED A **CATERPILLAR**, THE **LARVA** OF A **BEETLE** IS CALLED A **GRUB**, AND THE **LARVA** OF A **FLY** IS CALLED A **MAGGOT**. LARVAE BECOME **BIGGER**, **MOLTING SEVERAL TIMES**.

INSECTS THAT GO THROUGH A COMPLETE METAMORPHOSIS ARE:

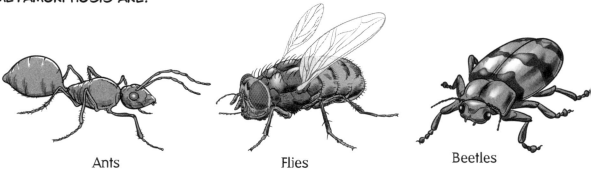

Ants   Flies   Beetles

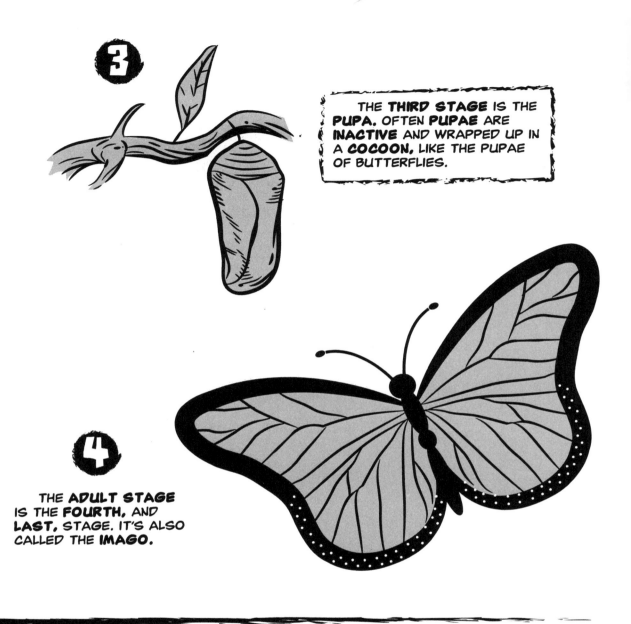

3

THE **THIRD STAGE** IS THE **PUPA.** OFTEN **PUPAE** ARE **INACTIVE** AND WRAPPED UP IN A **COCOON,** LIKE THE PUPAE OF BUTTERFLIES.

4

THE **ADULT STAGE** IS THE **FOURTH,** AND **LAST,** STAGE. IT'S ALSO CALLED THE **IMAGO.**

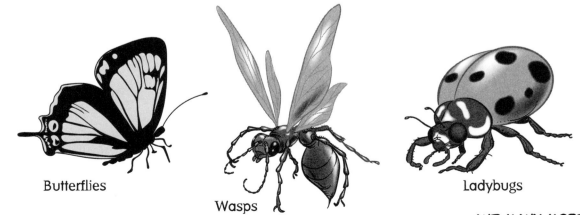

Butterflies

Wasps

Ladybugs

. . .AND MANY MORE

METAMORPHOSIS

GRADUAL METAMORPHOSIS

THE **SCIENTIFIC NAME** OF THOSE INSECTS THAT GO THROUGH A GRADUAL METAMORPHOSIS IS **EXOPTERYGOTA.** THIS IS A GREEK WORD THAT MEANS **"EXTERNAL WING DEVELOPMENT."** THEY WERE SO NAMED BECAUSE THESE INSECTS ARE **WINGED,** AND EVEN IN THEIR **IMMATURE STAGE,** WING BUDS ARE VISIBLE.

THE **NYMPH** HATCHES FROM THE **EGG.** THE **NYMPH** LOOKS **VERY SIMILAR** TO THE **ADULT,** EXCEPT FOR **LACKING** THE **WINGS** AND BEING **UNABLE TO LAY EGGS. . .**

THE **FIRST STAGE** IS THE **EGG.**

INSECTS THAT GO THROUGH A **GRADUAL METAMORPHOSIS** ARE:

Cicadas

Cockroaches

Praying Mantids

Dragonflies

Stoneflies

. . .AND MANY MORE.

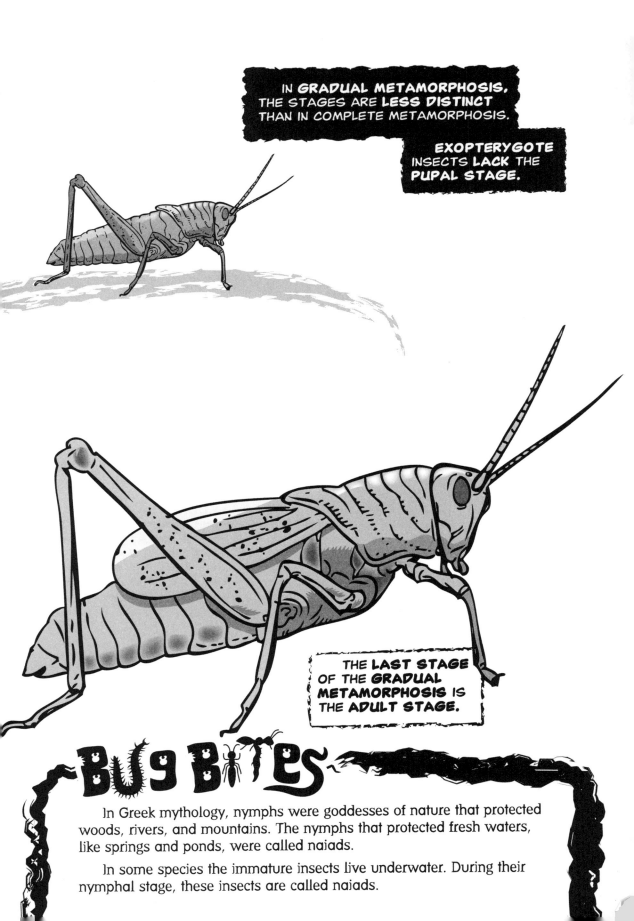

IN **GRADUAL METAMORPHOSIS,** THE STAGES ARE **LESS DISTINCT** THAN IN COMPLETE METAMORPHOSIS.

EXOPTERYGOTE INSECTS **LACK** THE **PUPAL STAGE.**

THE **LAST STAGE** OF THE **GRADUAL METAMORPHOSIS** IS THE **ADULT STAGE.**

BUG BITES

In Greek mythology, nymphs were goddesses of nature that protected woods, rivers, and mountains. The nymphs that protected fresh waters, like springs and ponds, were called naiads.

In some species the immature insects live underwater. During their nymphal stage, these insects are called naiads.

NO METAMORPHOSIS

THE **SCIENTIFIC NAME** OF THOSE WINGLESS INSECTS THAT DON'T GO THROUGH METAMORPHOSIS IS **APTERYGOTA.** THIS IS A GREEK WORD THAT MEANS **"WITHOUT WING DEVELOPMENT."**

THE **FIRST STAGE** IS THE **EGG.**

THE **IMMATURE INSECTS LOOK** LIKE THE **ADULTS,** ONLY THEY ARE **SMALLER** AND **CAN'T REPRODUCE.**

THE LAST
STAGE IS THE
ADULT INSECT.

INSECTS THAT **DON'T** GO
THROUGH **METAMORPHOSIS** ARE:

Telsontails

Silverfish

. . . AND A FEW MORE.

Types of Insects

THIS IS HOW INSECTS ARE GROUPED, BASED ON THEIR SHARED CHARACTERISTICS.

APTERYGOTA
(WINGLESS INSECTS)
THESE ARE INSECTS THAT **DON'T** GO THROUGH **METAMORPHOSIS.**

ENDOPTERYGOTA
(INSECTS WITH INTERNAL WING DEVELOPMENT)
THESE INSECTS GO THROUGH A **COMPLETE METAMORPHOSIS.**

PTERYGOTA
(WINGED INSECTS)

EXOPTERYGOTA
(INSECTS WITH EXTERNAL WING DEVELOPMENT)
THESE INSECTS GO THROUGH A **GRADUAL METAMORPHOSIS** THAT **LACKS** THE **PUPAL STAGE.**

- **PROTURA** TELSONTAILS
- **THYSANAURA** SILVERFISH

- **COLEOPTERA** BEETLES
- **DIPTERA** TRUE FLIES
- **HYMENOPTERA** BEES, WASPS, AND ANTS
- **LEPIDOPTERA** BUTTERFLIES
- **MECOPTERA** SCORPIONFLIES
- **MEGALOPTERA** DOBSONFLIES
- **SIPHONAPTERA** FLEAS
- **STREPSIPTERA** TWISTED-WINGED PARASITES
- **TRICHOPTERA** CADDISFLIES

- **ANOPLURA** LICE
- **DERMAPTERA** EARWIGS
- **DICTYOPTERA** COCKROACHES AND MANTIDS
- **EMBIOPTERA** WEB SPINNERS
- **EPHEMEROPTERA** MAYFLIES
- **GRYLLOBLATTODEA** ROCK CRAWLERS
- **HEMIPTERA** TRUE BUGS
- **HOMOPTERA** APHIDS, SCALES, AND CICADAS
- **ISOPTERA** TERMITES
- **MALLOPHAGA** BITING LICE
- **ODONATA** DRAGONFLIES AND DAMSELFLIES
- **ORTHOPTERA** CRICKETS AND GRASSHOPPERS
- **PHASMATODAE** STICK INSECTS AND LEAF INSECTS
- **PLECOPTERA** STONEFLIES
- **PSOCOPTERA** BOOKLICE AND BARKLICE
- **THYSANOPTERA** THRIPS
- **ZORAPTERA** ANGEL INSECTS

goin' buggy!!

1. HOW DOES A **BUTTERFLY BUILD** ITS **HOUSE?**

–IT USES **CATER-PILLARS!**

2. DID YOU KNOW THAT THE **SPIDERS** HAD A **POP QUIZ** AT **SCHOOL** TODAY?

–YEAH, THEY ALL GOT **BEES!**

3. WHAT DOES THE **SPIDER SPREAD** ON ITS **TOAST?**

–A LITTLE **BUTTER-FLY!**

BUURRP

4.

DID YOU HEAR ABOUT THAT
BUG THAT **BURPS** DURING **LUNCH?**

-YEAH, SHE'S NO **LADYBUG!**

5.

HOW DO **TWO BEES**
GREET EACH OTHER?

-THEY GIVE EACH OTHER
A **HIVE** FIVE!

6.

WHAT DOES THE **MOM**
SPIDER SAY TO HER **KID?**

-"YOU ARE THE APPLE
OF MY **EIGHT EYES!"**

CATERPILLARS HAVE **4,000 MUSCLES** (PEOPLE ONLY HAVE ABOUT **630**).

SOME **MALE SPIDERS** PLUCK A **FEMALE'S WEB** LIKE A **GUITAR** TO **COURT** HER. EACH MALE SPECIES **"PLAYS"** ITS OWN **SPECIFIC SONG,** AND FEMALES ARE ABLE TO **RECOGNIZE** THEIR **MATE** IN THIS WAY. SOME OTHER SPECIES OF SPIDERS **IMITATE** THE MALE SPIDER'S **PLUCKING.** THE FEMALE **THINKS** HE'S A **MATE,** BUT WHEN SHE APPROACHES HIM, **HE EATS HER** INSTEAD!

MOTHS AND SOME **NOCTURNAL BUTTERFLIES** HAVE **EARS** ON THEIR **FOREWINGS.** THEY CAN DETECT THE **ULTRASOUNDS** EMITTED BY **BATS** AND, IN THIS WAY, **AVOID** BECOMING THEIR **PREY.**

IN 2005, **QUENTIN WHEELER** AND **KELLY MILLER**, TWO ENTOMOLOGISTS FROM CORNELL UNIVERSITY, NAMED TWO **SLIME-MOLD BEETLES** IN HONOR OF PRESIDENT GEORGE W. BUSH AND **VICE-PRESIDENT DICK CHENEY**. THE **SCIENTIFIC NAMES** ARE *AGATHIDIUM BUSHI* AND *AGATHIDIUM CHENEYI*.

GOLIATH BEETLES ARE THE **BIGGEST BEETLES** AND THE **BIGGEST INSECTS** IN THE **WORLD**. THEY ARE **FIVE INCHES LONG** AND WEIGH **3.5 OUNCES!**

THE WORD **ENTOMOLOGY**, OR THE **STUDY** OF **INSECTS**, IS OFTEN CONFUSED WITH **ETYMOLOGY**, OR THE **STUDY** OF THE **ORIGIN** OF **WORDS**.

TELSONTAILS

Apterygota (wingless insects)
Proturans (insects with a primitive tail)

TELSONTAILS BELONG TO A GROUP OF INSECTS CALLED **PROTURANS.** THE WORD PROTURAN MEANS **"PRIMITIVE TAIL,"** AND REFERS TO THE FACT THAT ANIMALS IN THIS GROUP HAVE **NO CERCI** ON THEIR **TAILS.**

TELSONTAILS HAVE **THREE PAIRS** OF **APPENDAGES** HANGING FROM THEIR **ABDOMEN.** THESE ARE **NOT LEGS.**

TELSONTAILS DON'T HAVE **EYES** OR **ANTENNAE.** IN ORDER TO FEEL THEIR WAY AROUND, THEY USE THEIR **FORELEGS.** THEIR FORELEGS ARE IN FACT **MUCH BIGGER** THAN THE OTHER TWO SETS OF LEGS. ON THE TIP OF THEIR FORELEGS, TELSONTAILS HAVE **TARSAL SENSILLA,** OR **SENSORY HAIRS.** TELSONTAILS AND ALL THE OTHER PROTURANS USE THESE SENSORY ORGANS TO **FIND FOOD** AND **AVOID PREDATORS.**

TELSONTAILS ARE **VERY SMALL INSECTS,** JUST A LITTLE MORE THAN **1/16** OF AN **INCH** LONG. THEY MAINLY LIVE IN THE TOP **THREE INCHES** OF **SOIL,** ESPECIALLY WHERE THERE ARE **DEAD LEAVES, MOSS,** AND **ROTTING BARK.**

TELSONTAILS EAT **FUNGI** AND **DEAD MITES.**

THESE LITTLE INSECTS GO THROUGH AN **ANAMORPHIC DEVELOPMENT.** THIS MEANS THAT WHEN THEY HATCH, THE **NEWBORNS** LOOK LIKE THE **ADULTS,** EXCEPT FOR HAVING **FEWER SEGMENTS.** LARVAE HAVE ONLY **NINE,** WHILE ADULTS HAVE **TWELVE.**

WITH EVERY **MOLTING,** TELSONTAILS ADD **MORE SEGMENTS** TO THEIR **ABDOMEN,** UNTIL THEY HAVE **TWELVE.**

BUG BITES

In the winter, when the topsoil becomes cold, telsontails migrate from the higher part of the soil to ten inches deeper, where the soil is not as cold. In the summer, telsontails move back to the upper part of the soil, where it is warmer.

SILVERFISH

Apterygota (wingless insects)
Thysanura (insects with a bristle-like tail)

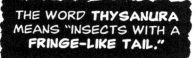

THE WORD **THYSANURA** MEANS "INSECTS WITH A **FRINGE-LIKE TAIL.**"

THESE INSECTS CAN BE A **MINOR PEST** BECAUSE THEY EAT THE **GLUE** AND **PAPER** OF **BOOKS, MAGAZINES, COMIC BOOKS,** AND **PRINTS.** IN THE **WILD,** SILVERFISH EAT **VEGETATION** AND **MOLDS.**

SILVERFISH HAVE
**THREE CAUDAL
FILAMENTS.** THESE ARE
THREE **BRISTLE-LIKE
HAIRS** AT THE **END** OF THE
ABDOMEN. IN FACT,
SILVERFISH ARE ALSO
CALLED **BRISTLETAILS.**

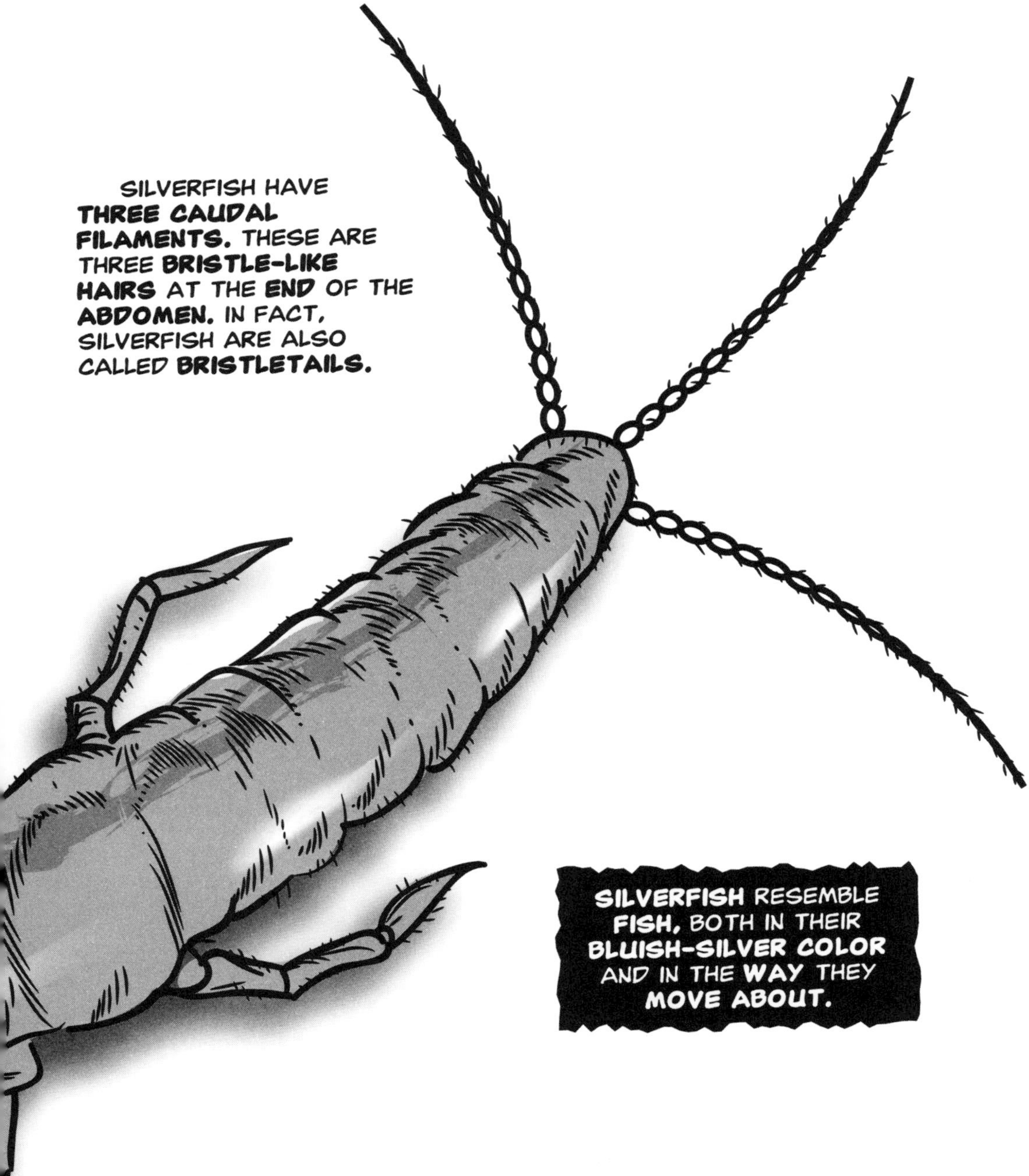

SILVERFISH RESEMBLE
FISH, BOTH IN THEIR
BLUISH-SILVER COLOR
AND IN THE **WAY** THEY
MOVE ABOUT.

SILVERFISH LIKE **DARK** AND **HUMID**
PLACES, LIKE **CAVES** OR PILES OF
ROTTING LEAVES. THEY ARE OFTEN
FOUND AROUND THE **HOUSE** IN THE
ATTIC OR THE **BASEMENT.** SILVERFISH
ARE **SHY** AND **NOCTURNAL.**

SILVERFISH CAN GO
FOR **ONE YEAR**
WITHOUT EATING.

YOU EAT INSECTS!
YUM! BUGS!

Despite the great lengths food manufacturers go to ensure the cleanliness of what we eat, some bugs are still able to sneak through. The Food and Drug Administration issues guidelines on the amount of bugs that it is safe to have in our food. Here are some examples. . .

Pasta: 454 insect fragments for every pound of product.

Raisins: 20 insects and 75 insect eggs for every pound of product.

Frozen Broccoli: 272 aphids and mites for every pound of product.

Apple Butter: 28 insects for every pound of product.

Ground Cinnamon: 1816 insect fragments for every pound of product.

Chocolate: 408 insect fragments for every pound of product.

Peanut Butter: 136 insect fragments for every pound of product.

Canned Corn: 2 corn ear worms or corn bores and larva skin fragments every 24 pounds of product.

Scientists have been reporting that insects are a great source of protein. Once the hard-to-digest exoskeleton is removed, the proteins in bees and crickets contain more nutrients and less fats than those in beef. Also, insects are cheaper and easier to raise than cows.

SOME PEOPLE LIKE TO EAT BUGS!

In Australia, Aborigines look for honey pot ants. To eat the sweet nectar these ants store in their abdomen, they squeeze them into their mouth. Another native Australian delicacy is the witchetty grub. Witchetty grubs are the larvae of moths and are about three inches long. Aborigines eat them alive.

In Japan you can buy canned bee pupae in soy sauce and order fried rice with grasshoppers at a restaurant.

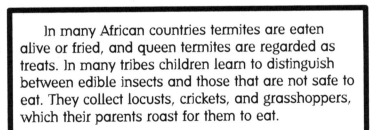

In Thailand it's common to buy fried giant water bugs and scorpions from street food vendors.

In many African countries termites are eaten alive or fried, and queen termites are regarded as treats. In many tribes children learn to distinguish between edible insects and those that are not safe to eat. They collect locusts, crickets, and grasshoppers, which their parents roast for them to eat.

What's on the dessert menu? Chocolate-covered ants from Mexico!

Ewww! Bugs in Food!

Cochineal dye is a powder made with cochineal scales. It's a red pigment used in the food industry to color food red and, in cosmetics, for lipsticks and powders. Cochineal dye is found in many fruit drinks, frozen ice treats, candies, and yogurt, to name a few.

Although not a vegetarian product, cochineal dye is a good alternative to synthetic red food colorings, which have proved to be carcinogenic.

Aztecs used cochineal dye to color garments. When the Spanish brought this pigment back to Europe, it became in such demand that it was almost as expensive as gold.

Ewww! Bugs in Drinks!

Kermes dye was a deep red coloring made from a scale insect in ancient Persia. The Persian word *kermes* means "produced by insects" and is the origin of the English words "carmine" and "crimson."

In the 1500s, Tuscan monks used kermes dye to make a red, Italian drink called *alkermes*. The Medici family called it the "Elixir of Long Life," as it was erroneously thought to have medicinal properties.

These scale insects are parasites of the kermes oak tree.

Ewww! Ewww! More Bugs in Food!

Lac insects are small Asian scales that suck tree juices. To hold onto the tree, lac scales secrete a substance that creates a protective cocoon. People harvest the cocoons and, after a purifying process, make them into shellac, a substance similar to plastic. It takes 100,000 lac scales to make one pound of shellac.

In the past, shellac was used to make everyday objects like boxes, combs, and picture frames, and, as a wax, to finish furniture. The first 78 rpm records that played on phonographs were made of shellac, before the invention of vinyl.

Today shellac is used as a wax to coat fruits to prevent them from rotting. Because it is produced from insects, fruits treated with shellac are not considered part of a truly vegetarian diet. Shellac is also used to coat candy and candy bars, and, in medicine, pills.

Yuck! Bugs in Inks!

Oak trees form a growth, called gall, when a gall wasp deposits an egg into the wood. People used to collect the galls and make them into a dark, purple ink. The galls that made the most durable ink came from the city of Aleppo, in Syria. For this reason they were called Aleppo galls.

Until a few years ago, Aleppo galls were used to print currency and important documents. This is because these inks didn't wear out over time.

Aleppo gall was also used to make "invisible ink."

BEETLES

Endopterygota (insects with internal wing development)
Coleoptera (insects with sheathed wings)

BEETLES BELONG TO A **GROUP** CALLED **COLEOPTERA.** THIS WORD MEANS **"SHEATHED WINGS."** THIS REFERS TO THE **BEETLES' FOREWINGS,** CALLED **ELYTRA,** WHICH ARE **VERY HARD.** THE ELYTRA **PROTECT** THE BEETLES' **THIN HIND WINGS,** IN THE SAME WAY AS A **SHEATH** PROTECTS A **SWORD.**

BEETLES GO THROUGH A **COMPLETE METAMORPHOSIS.**

THE **OLDEST FOSSILS** OF COLEOPTERA ARE ALMOST **300 MILLION YEARS OLD, 50 MILLION YEARS OLDER** THAN **DINOSAURS!** COLEOPTERA FIRST APPEARED AT THE **END** OF THE **PALEOZOIC ERA.**

THERE ARE **OVER 350,000 SPECIES** OF BEETLES.

BUG BITES

Beetles don't use their elytra for flying, but only to protect the soft hind wings. Only the soft hind wings are used for flying.

TIGER BEETLES

Endoptergota (insects with internal wing development)
Coleoptera (insects with sheathed wings)

TIGER BEETLES CAN BE A VERY COLORFUL METALLIC GREEN, BLUE, OR ORANGE. OTHERS HAVE BEAUTIFUL BLACK AND WHITE DESIGNS ON THEIR BACKS. THE COLORS AND THE DESIGNS HELP THESE BEETLES TO CAMOUFLAGE IN THEIR ENVIRONMENT.

THE AVERAGE TIGER BEETLE IS ABOUT 1/2 OF AN INCH LONG. THERE ARE OVER 2,000 SPECIES OF TIGER BEETLES KNOWN. THEY LIVE ON THE SHORES OF LAKES, RIVERS, AND SEAS.

TIGER BEETLES ARE **CARNIVOROUS** AND HAVE A **TIGER-LIKE ABILITY** TO **HUNT.** TIGER BEETLES HAVE **VERY BIG EYES** PROTRUDING FROM THEIR HEADS TO **BETTER DETECT** THEIR **PREY.** ONCE THEY ZERO IN ON A POSSIBLE VICTIM, THEY CHASE IT UNTIL THEY CATCH IT WITH THEIR **POWERFUL, CURVED JAWS.** WHILE HOLDING ON TO THEIR PREY, TIGER BEETLES **OOZE DIGESTIVE JUICES** ON IT. THEN, THEY **SQUEEZE** THEIR PREY, WHILE **SUCKING** IN THE **PRE-DIGESTED PARTS.**

TIGER BEETLES HAVE **VERY LONG ANTENNAE** AND **LEGS.** THEY CAN RUN **VERY FAST,** AND **QUICKLY FLY AWAY** FROM THEIR **PREDATORS.**

TIGER BEETLES CAN REMAIN IN THEIR **LARVAL STAGE** FOR UP TO **TWO YEARS.** AN ADULT TIGER BEETLE LIVES FOR ABOUT **SIX WEEKS.** IN SOME SPECIES, THE ADULTS **BURROW** TO **HIBERNATE.**

BUG BITES

Tiger beetles love light and are very active on sunny days. On cloudy days, tiger beetles are sluggish, even lethargic.

When they feel attacked, some species of tiger beetle give off a bad smell from their anal glands. The smell keeps predators away.

TIGER BEETLE

TIGER BEETLES GO THROUGH A **COMPLETE METAMORPHOSIS**.

Hook

EGG STAGE

THE **FEMALE** TIGER BEETLE **DEPOSITS** HER **EGGS** INTO THE **GROUND**, THEN COVERS THEM UP WITH **DIRT**.

EVEN THE **TIGER BEETLES LARVAE** ARE ABLE **PREDATORS**, ALTHOUGH THEY **CANNOT FLY**. THE **LARVA** SUDDENLY POPS FROM ITS BURROW TO **LUNGE** AT AN **UNSUSPECTING PREY**. TO STAY PUT, LARVAE ANCHOR THEMSELVES TO THE **GROUND** USING A **HOOK**, WHICH GROWS ON THEIR BODIES.

LARVAL STAGE

THE **LARVA** EMERGES FROM THE **EGG**. LARVAE **DIG** THEIR **BURROWS** INTO THE GROUND AS THEY **GROW**. THE BURROW CAN BE EVEN **ONE FOOT DEEP**. LARVAE DON'T LEAVE THEIR BURROWS UNTIL THEY BECOME **ADULTS**.

IF THE **BURROW** GETS ACCIDENTALLY **BLOCKED**, THE **TRAPPED TIGER BEETLE LARVA** CAN SURVIVE IN IT FOR **THREE WEEKS**.

PUPAL STAGE

WHEN THE **PUPAL STAGE APPROACHES**, THE LARVA DIGS A **NEW BURROW** AND THEN IT **SEALS IT**. SOME SPECIES REMAIN IN THE PUPAL STAGE **ALL WINTER LONG**, HIBERNATING, WHILE OTHERS STAY FOR LESS THAN A **MONTH**.

ADULT STAGE

IT MIGHT TAKE AN ADULT TIGER BEETLE **TWO DAYS** TO BECOME **FULLY ACTIVE** AFTER EMERGING FROM THE **PUPAL STAGE**.

BOMBARDIER BEETLES

Endopterygota (insects with internal wing development)
Coleoptera (insects with sheathed wings)

AS A **DEFENSE MECHANISM,** THIS BEETLE **SHOOTS** ITS **ENEMIES** WITH A **TOXIC MIX** OF **CHEMICALS.** THE NAME **BOMBARDIER** COMES FROM THE FACT THAT THE CHEMICALS ARE **FIRED** WITH A **LOUD POP** FROM THE BEETLE'S **ABDOMEN.** ONCE FIRED, THE CHEMICALS ARE **HOT** AND **HIGHLY IRRITATING,** EVEN FOR **PEOPLE.**

CHARLES DARWIN WAS AN **ENGLISH NATURALIST** WHO FIRST THOUGHT UP THE **IDEA** THAT **ALL CREATURES** DESCEND FROM A **COMMON ANCESTOR.** HE WAS AN **AVID COLLECTOR** OF **BEETLES** AND DESCRIBES HIS **ENCOUNTER** WITH A **BOMBARDIER:**

"ONE DAY, ON TEARING OFF SOME OLD BARK, I SAW TWO RARE BEETLES, AND SEIZED ONE IN EACH HAND; THEN I SAW A THIRD AND NEW KIND, WHICH I COULD NOT BEAR TO LOSE, SO THAT I POPPED THE ONE WHICH I HELD IN MY RIGHT HAND INTO MY MOUTH. ALAS! IT EJECTED SOME INTENSELY ACRID FLUID, WHICH BURNT MY TONGUE SO THAT I WAS FORCED TO SPIT THE BEETLE OUT, WHICH WAS LOST, AS WAS THE THIRD ONE."

STAG BEETLES

Endopterygota (insects with internal wing development)
Coleoptera (insects with sheathed wings)

THE **STAG BEETLE** GETS ITS NAME FROM THE FACT THAT ITS **MANDIBLES** RESEMBLE THE **ANTLERS** OF A **MALE DEER.** IN ADDITION, THE MALE STAG BEETLE **FIGHTS** OVER **TERRITORY** AND **FEMALES** IN A WAY **SIMILAR** TO THAT OF A STAG: THEY **CROSS** THEIR **HORNS** AND **HEAD BUTT** ONE ANOTHER. DESPITE THE IMPRESSIVE MANDIBLES, MALE STAG BEETLES **CAN'T BITE** VERY **HARD.**

FEMALE STAG BEETLES DON'T HAVE SUCH **OVERSIZED MANDIBLES,** BUT THEIR **BITE** IS MUCH **MORE PAINFUL** THAN THE MALES'.
THE BIG MANDIBLES ARE **USELESS** FOR **FEEDING,** BECAUSE STAG BEETLES **EAT TREE SAP.**

ALTHOUGH THEIR **LIFE CYCLE** CAN LAST FOR **FIVE YEARS,** THE **ADULTS** LIVE FOR ONLY A **FEW MONTHS.** ADULTS **EMERGE** FROM PUPAE IN **MAY** OR **JUNE.** MALES **DIE** RIGHT AFTER MATING, AT THE **END** OF **JULY.** FEMALES DIE AFTER **LAYING** THEIR **EGGS,** IN **AUGUST.**

RHINO BEETLES

Endopterygota (insects with internal wing development)
Coleoptera (insects with sheathed wings)

THE **RHINO BEETLE** BELONGS TO THE **SAME GROUP** AS THE **STAG BEETLE**. THE RHINO BEETLE'S **MANDIBLES** RESEMBLE THE **HORNS** OF A **RHINO**. JUST LIKE THE STAG BEETLE, THE RHINO BEETLE USES ITS **MANDIBLES** DURING **FIGHTS**.

THE RHINO BEETLE IS SO **POWERFUL** THAT IT CAN **LIFT** ALMOST **900 TIMES** ITS **OWN WEIGHT!**

BESS BEETLES

Endopterygota (insects with internal wing development)
Coleoptera (insects with sheathed wings)

JUST LIKE RHINO BEETLES, **BESS BEETLES** HAVE A **HORN** ON THEIR **HEADS,** BUT IT'S **MUCH SMALLER** THAN THE ONE ON THE RHINO BEETLES' HEADS. BESS BEETLES **STRIDULATE,** WHICH MEANS THAT THEY MAKE **SOUNDS** BY **STROKING** THEIR **ELYTRA.** THEY STRIDULATE TO **COMMUNICATE** WITH **EACH OTHER.** SCIENTISTS HAVE RECOGNIZED **14 DISTINCTIVE SOUNDS,** EACH INDICATING A **SPECIFIC ACTIVITY.** THE BESS **LARVAE,** WHICH DON'T HAVE ELYTRA, STRIDULATE BY **STROKING** THEIR **LEGS.**

BESS BEETLES LIVE IN **COLONIES** AND **BOTH MALES** AND **FEMALES REAR** THEIR **YOUNG.** THE **COLONY** IS **CARVED** IN **ROTTING WOOD,** WHICH THE BEETLES EAT, CREATING **CHAMBERS** AND **GALLERIES. EGGS, LARVAE,** AND **PUPAE** ARE KEPT IN **SEPARATE AREAS** OF THE **COLONY.** WHEN A LARVA **HATCHES,** AN ADULT **CARRIES** IT TO THE **PROPER PLACE.** THE SAME HAPPENS WHEN A **LARVA PUPATES.**
THE ADULTS **FEED** THE LARVAE **CHEWED WOOD** AND THEIR OWN **FECES. FECES** CONTAIN **BENEFICIAL BACTERIA** AND **ENZYMES** LARVAE NEED TO **DIGEST WOOD.**

JEWEL BEETLES

Endopterygota (insects with internal wing development)
Coleoptera (insects with sheathed wings)

THE **BEETLES** OF THIS GROUP ARE **THINNER** AND **LONGER** THAN OTHERS. THEY ARE **BRIGHTLY COLORED** AND **IRIDESCENT**. FOR THIS REASON THEY ARE CALLED JEWEL BEETLES. THE IRIDESCENT EXOSKELETON IS OFTEN COVERED WITH **COMPLEX** AND **MULTI-COLORED PATTERNS**.

THE JEWEL BEETLE **LARVAE** BORE **HOLES** INTO THE **BRANCHES** OF **TREES**, EATING THE **WOOD**. SOME SPECIES ARE CONSIDERED **PESTS** BECAUSE THEY CAN KILL **TREES**. THE ADULTS FEED ON **NECTAR** FROM **FLOWERS**.

A JEWEL BEETLE CALLED THE **FIREBUG** IS ABLE TO FIND **FOREST FIRES** EVEN WHEN THEY ARE OVER **40 MILES AWAY**. THIS IS BECAUSE **PORES** LOCATED IN THE FIREBUG'S **THORAX** CAN DETECT **INFRARED RADIATION** FROM FIRE. BEETLES IMMEDIATELY **FLY TOWARD IT** AND THEY **LAY** THEIR **EGGS** IN THE **BURNT WOOD**. FIRES GET RID OF ALL ANIMALS, INCLUDING JEWEL BUGS' **PREDATORS**. BY **LAYING EGGS** IN A **BURNT FOREST**, FIREBUGS **PROTECT** THEIR **OFFSPRING** FROM **BIRDS** AND **FROGS**. UNLIKE MANY JEWEL BEETLE SPECIES, **FIREBUGS** ARE JUST **PLAIN BLACK**.

CLICK BEETLES

Endopterygota (insects with internal wing development)
Coleoptera (insects with sheathed wings)

AS A **DEFENCE MECHANISM**, **CLICK BEETLES** HAVE A **SPINE UNDER** THEIR **THORAX** THAT **SNAPS** INTO A **SOCKET**. WHEN THIS HAPPENS, THE **SPINE CLICKS** AND THE BEETLE **JUMPS** IN THE **AIR**.

THIS **SIMPLE**, BUT **STARTLING**, MECHANISM IS PERFECT FOR **DEFENSE**. IF A **BIRD** TRIES TO **EAT** A CLICK BEETLE, FIRST THE BEETLE **FAKES** BEING **DEAD**. IT **LIES** ON THE **GROUND** WITH ITS **LEGS FOLDED** ON ITS **BELLY**. THEN, ALL OF A SUDDEN, THE BEETLE **CLICKS** AND **JUMPS, STARTLING** THE **BIRD** SO IT **FLIES AWAY**.

ALTHOUGH **ADULT** CLICK BEETLES FEED ON **NECTAR** FROM **FLOWERS**, THEIR **LARVAE**, CALLED **WIREWORMS**, ARE ONE OF THE **WORST PESTS** OF **CROPS** AND GARDENS. THESE INSECTS CAN **REMAIN IN THEIR** LARVAL STAGE FOR **FOUR YEARS**, EATING **ROOTS, TUBERS, BUDS**, AND **SEEDS**.

IF A CLICK BEETLE FINDS ITSELF **BELLY UP** ON THE **GROUND**, IT JUST NEEDS TO **JUMP UP** WITH ITS REMARKABLE **CLICK**.

CARPET BEETLES

Endopterygota (insects with internal wing development)
Coleoptera (insects with sheathed wings)

CARPET BEETLES ARE CALLED SO BECAUSE THEY FEED ON ALL KINDS OF SUBSTANCES, INCLUDING CARPETS, BUT ALSO FEATHERS, SKIN, AND HAIR. SCIENTISTS WHO STUDY THE BONE STRUCTURE OF ANIMALS KNOW THAT CARPET BEETLES CAN CLEAN A CARCASS VERY EFFICIENTLY, LEAVING THE BONES INTACT.

NATURAL HISTORY MUSEUMS HAVE BEEN USING THESE BEETLES FOR THIS PURPOSE SINCE THE 1800S.

DUNG BEETLES

Endopterygota (insects with internal wing development)
Coleoptera (insects with sheathed wings)

AS THEIR NAME SUGGESTS, **DUNG BEETLES** FEED ON **DUNG** (POOP), MAKING THEM THE **ULTIMATE RECYCLERS.** DEPENDING ON THE SPECIES, THESE BEETLES DON'T FEED **EXCLUSIVELY** ON DUNG, ADDING TO THEIR DIET **ROTTING MUSHROOMS, LEAVES, CARRION,** AND **DECAYING FRUITS.**

WHEN THE **EGG HATCHES,** THE NEWBORN **LARVA** FEEDS ON THE **DUNG** UNTIL IT PUPATES. THE **ADULT** EMERGES FROM THE PUPA WHILE **STILL INSIDE** THE **DUNG BALL.** THE ADULT BEETLE HAS TO **DIG ITSELF OUT** FROM UNDERGROUND, AND, ONCE **OUTSIDE,** IT WILL GO IN **SEARCH** OF **FRESH MANURE.**

DUNG BEETLES CAN **LOCATE** FRESH **MANURE** FROM **FAR AWAY.** THEY FLY TO IT, **FOLLOWING** THE **SMELL** USING THEIR ANTENNAE, WHICH WORK LIKE A **NOSE.**

WHEN THEY **ARRIVE** AT THE **SOURCE** OF THE **SMELL,** SOME DUNG BEETLES **MANIPULATE** THE **MANURE** INTO A **BALL,** USING THEIR **FORELEGS** LIKE **RAKES.** THESE BEETLES ARE CALLED **ROLLERS.** A **MALE** AND A **FEMALE** BEETLE **ROLL** THE **BALL** TO A PLACE WHERE IT CAN BE **BURIED.** ALONG THE WAY, **ANOTHER MALE** BEETLE MIGHT **TRY** TO **STEAL** THEIR **BALL** OF DUNG, AND THE **TWO MALES FIGHT** IT OUT. BEFORE BURYING THE BALL, THE **FEMALE LAYS ONE EGG** INSIDE IT.

DUNG BEETLES

Endopterygota (insects with internal wing development)
Coleoptera (insects with sheathed wings)

DUNG BEETLES ARE **BENEFICIAL INSECTS.** THEY PROVIDE **THREE EFFECTIVE WAYS** OF **IMPROVING** THE **ENVIRONMENT** IN WHICH THEY LIVE:

1. DUNG BEETLES ARE A **NATURAL PEST CONTROL.** THEY **BURY MANURE,** THE **BREEDING GROUND** FOR MANY **FLIES** THAT **CARRY DISEASES** TO **CATTLE.** EVEN IF THE FLIES HAVE ALREADY DEPOSITED THEIR **EGGS** IN THE MANURE, THEIR **LARVAE DIE** WHEN THE DUNG BEETLES **ROLL** AWAY OR **BURY** THE **MANURE.**

2. DUNG BEETLES **IMPROVE** THE **SOIL** BY **DIGGING** TUNNELS, ALLOWING **AIR** TO PENETRATE IT. **OXYGEN** IS **NECESSARY** FOR THE **GOOD DEVELOPMENT** OF **PLANT ROOTS.**

3. THEY **FERTILIZE** THE **SOIL** BY BURYING MANURE.

SOMETIMES THE BALL OF ROLLER DUNG IS BIGGER THAN THE BEETLE ITSELF.

IN **ANCIENT EGYPT** DUNG BEETLES WERE **SACRED** AND PEOPLE THOUGHT THEY WERE THE INCARNATION OF **KHEPRI**, THE **GOD** OF THE **SUN**. JUST LIKE DUNG BEETLES ROLL DUNG, KHEPRI **ROLLED** THE **SUN**.

EVERY **MORNING**, KHEPRI ROLLED THE SUN TO THE **WORLD** OF THE **LIVING**. THEN EVERY **EVENING**, KHEPRI **ROLLED** THE SUN **AWAY** FROM THE **EARTH**, TO THE **WORLD** OF THE **DEAD**. FOR THE ANCIENT EGYPTIANS THIS **UNSTOPPABLE CYCLE** MEANT **REGENERATION** AND **ETERNAL LIFE**.

FOR THIS REASON, ANCIENT EGYPTIANS PLACED **STONES** CARVED TO LOOK LIKE **DUNG BEETLES** ON THE **CHESTS** OF THEIR **DEAD RELATIVES** BEFORE **BURYING** THEM. THESE STONES ARE CALLED **HEART SCARABS**. THEY WERE A **WISH** OF A **HAPPY ETERNAL LIFE** IN THE **WORLD** OF THE **DEAD**.

Egyptian heart scarab

OTHER SPECIES OF DUNG BEETLES ARE CALLED **TUNNELERS**. WHEN THEY **LOCATE** A PILE OF **FRESH MANURE**, THEY **DIG TUNNELS** UNDER IT. THEN, THE **MALE** BEETLE **COLLECTS** SOME **DUNG** AND **PASSES** IT TO THE **FEMALE**. THE FEMALE BEETLE **MAKES** IT INTO A **BALL**, DEPOSITS AN **EGG** IN IT, AND **PLACES** IT IN A **TUNNEL**.

JUST AS WITH ROLLERS, THE **LARVA** OF A **TUNNELER** EATS FROM **WITHIN** THE **BALL**, AND TURNS INTO A PUPA FROM WHICH THE ADULT EMERGES. ADULTS **DIG** THEMSELVES **OUT** TO **START** THE **CYCLE** ALL OVER **AGAIN**.

DUNG BEETLE **ADULTS** FEED ON THE **MANURE FLUIDS**, WHICH THEY SUCK. **LARVAE** ARE EQUIPPED WITH **FANGS** AND CAN **CHEW** THE **MANURE**, INCLUDING THE **HARD VEGETABLE FIBERS** IT **CONTAINS**.

BURYING BEETLES

Endopterygota (insects with internal wing development)
Coleoptera (insects with sheathed wings)

BURYING BEETLES ARE BLACK AND SHINY, WITH ORANGE SPOTS ON THEIR BACKS. THEY ARE SCAVENGERS, FEEDING ON CARCASSES OF SMALL BIRDS AND MAMMALS. BURYING BEETLES SMELL USING THEIR CLUB-LIKE ANTENNAE, WHICH CAN DETECT A DEAD ANIMAL EVEN IF IT IS THREE MILES AWAY.

BURYING BEETLES **WORK** IN **COUPLES, ONE MALE** AND **ONE FEMALE**, AND ARE **NOCTURNAL**. WHEN THEY **FIND** A **CARCASS**, THEY TRY TO **DRAG IT** TO A **PLACE** WHERE THE **SOIL** IS **SOFT ENOUGH** FOR BURIAL. IF THEY **CAN'T MOVE** THE CARCASS, THEY **BURY** IT **WHERE IT STANDS**.

BOTH BEETLES **DIG UNDER** THE **CARCASS** UNTIL THEY ARE **ABLE** TO BURY IT UNDER **SEVERAL INCHES OF DIRT**. IN THE MEANTIME, THEY TAKE THE **FUR** OR **FEATHERS** OFF THE CARCASS. THE BEETLES **SECRETE CHEMICALS** FROM THEIR **ANAL GLANDS** THAT **KEEP** THE CARCASS FROM **ROTTING**.

WHEN THE CARCASS IS READY, THE FEMALE **LAYS** HER **EGGS**. ONCE THEY HATCH, THE **LARVAE FEED** ON THE **CARCASS**. IF THE CARCASS **ISN'T BIG ENOUGH** FOR THE **WHOLE BROOD**, THE PARENTS **EAT** SOME OF THEIR **OFFSPRING**. IN THIS WAY, THE **REMAINING LARVAE** WILL HAVE **ENOUGH FOOD**.

LARVAE DON'T EAT THE CARCASS DIRECTLY. THEIR **PARENTS** FEED ON THE **CARCASS** AND THEN **REGURGITATE** IT FOR THEIR **YOUNG** TO EAT.

WHEN IT'S TIME TO **PUPATE**, THE **LARVAE MOVE AWAY** FROM THE CARCASS. **ADULTS** EMERGE FROM THE **PUPAE**.

BUG BITES

Parental care, like the burial beetles have for their larvae, is rare in the insect world.

FIREFLIES

Endopterygota (insects with internal wing development)
Coleoptera (insects with sheathed wings)

FIREFLIES, ALSO KNOWN AS **LIGHTNING BUGS,** ARE BEETLES ABLE TO PRODUCE **LIGHT,** A PROCESS CALLED **BIOLUMINESCENCE.** EVEN **FIREFLY LARVAE** PRODUCE **LIGHT,** AND THEY ARE CALLED **GLOWWORMS.**

FIREFLIES ARE **NOT FLIES.** TRUE FLIES ONLY HAVE **ONE PAIR** OF **WINGS.** FIREFLIES HAVE **ONE PAIR** OF **ELYTRA** AND **ONE PAIR** OF **WINGS.**

IN MOST SPECIES, **FIREFLY MALES FLY,** WHILE **FEMALES LIVE** ON THE **GROUND.** DURING **SUMMER NIGHTS,** IN ORDER TO FIND A **MATE,** A FIREFLY **MALE** FLIES AROUND **FLASHING** HIS **LIGHT.** THE **FEMALE RECOGNIZES** THE MALE OF THE **CORRECT SPECIES** BY THE WAY THE MALE **FLASHES** HIS **LIGHT.** SHE **RESPONDS,** FOLLOWING A SPECIFIC **LIGHT-FLASHING PATTERN.** THEIR **LIGHT-FLASHING COURTSHIP** BRINGS THEM **TOGETHER** TO MATE.

SOME FIREFLIES OF THE SAME SPECIES **CONGREGATE** IN A PLACE AND **RHYTHMICALLY FLASH** THEIR **LIGHTS** IN **UNISON**.

SOME FIREFLY FEMALES **MIMIC** THE **FLASHING** OF THE **FEMALES** OF **OTHER SPECIES**. WHEN THE MALE **FLIES** TO THEM TO MATE, THE FEMALE **EATS** HIM INSTEAD!

FIREFLIES PRODUCE **LIGHT** BY COMBINING **CHEMICALS** WITHIN THEIR **BODIES**. THE LIGHT IS **PRODUCED** IN A PART OF THEIR BODIES WHERE THE **EXOSKELETON** IS **TRANSLUCENT**.
THE **COLOR** OF THE FIREFLIES' LIGHT GOES FROM **BLUISH-YELLOW**, OR **GREENISH-YELLOW**, TO **ORANGE** AND **RED**, DEPENDING ON THEIR SPECIES.

A SPECIES OF **FIREFLY LARVAE** LIVE IN SOME **CAVES** IN **NEW ZEALAND**. THE LARVAE PRODUCE A **STICKY SILK** AND **HANG** FROM THE **CEILING, ILLUMINATING** THE ENTIRE **CAVE**. THE **STRANGE LIGHTS** ATTRACT **UNSUSPECTING INSECTS** THAT GET **CAUGHT** IN THE **SILK** AND **EATEN** BY THE **LARVAE**.

FIREFLY LARVAE EAT **EARTHWORMS**, OTHER **LARVAE, SNAILS**, AND **SLUGS**. THEY **INJECT** THEIR **PREY** WITH **DIGESTIVE** AND **PARALYZING FLUIDS** BEFORE **EATING THEM**.

LADYBUGS

Endopterygota (insects with internal wing development)
Coleoptera (insects with sheathed wings)

THE **SCIENTIFIC NAME** OF THE **LADYBUG** IS **COCCINELLIDAE,** WHICH MEANS **"LITTLE SPHERE,"** BECAUSE OF THE **ROUND SHAPE** OF THIS INSECT.

LADYBUGS' **ELYTRA** CAN BE **YELLOW, ORANGE, PINK,** OR **RED** WITH **BLACK SPOTS.** EACH LADYBUG SPECIES HAS A SPECIFIC NUMBER OF SPOTS. THERE ARE OVER **5,300 SPECIES** OF LADYBUGS IDENTIFIED SO FAR.

LADYBUGS ARE **VORACIOUS PREDATORS** OF **APHIDS.** ONE LADYBUG CAN **EAT 500 APHIDS** IN ONE **DAY!**

WHEN **DISTURBED**, LADYBUGS **OOZE FLUID** FROM THE JOINTS OF THEIR LEGS. THIS FLUID IS **HEMOLYMPH**, THE LADYBUG'S **BLOOD**. IT **STINKS** AND IT'S **HIGHLY TOXIC** TO THE LADYBUG'S **PREDATORS**, BUT NOT TO PEOPLE. THIS **DEFENSE MECHANISM** REPELS **ATTACKERS**.

OFTEN PREDATORS AVOID EATING LADYBUGS JUST BY LOOKING AT THE LADYBUG'S **ELYTRA**. THE **BRIGHT COLORS** ARE A **WARNING** THAT THIS BUG IS **TOXIC**. THIS PHENOMENON IS CALLED **APOSEMATIC COLORATION**, AND IT'S A **COMMON WAY** FOR **POISONOUS ANIMALS** TO COMMUNICATE TO THEIR **POTENTIAL PREDATOR**, "I'M **POISONOUS**, DON'T EAT ME!"

AS A **DEFENSE MECHANISM**, LADYBUGS CAN **HIDE** THEIR **HEADS** UNDER THEIR **PRONOTUM**. THE PRONOTUM IS THE **FIRST SEGMENT** OF THE **ABDOMEN**.

BUG BITES

Some ladybugs are just black or grey.

LADYBUGS

MANY SPECIES OF LADYBUGS ARE **BENEFICIAL INSECTS** BECAUSE THEY **EAT PESTS** THAT **DAMAGE CROPS** AND **GARDEN PLANTS**, LIKE **APHIDS, SCALES,** AND **MEALYBUGS.** BUT SOME LADYBUGS CAN BE **PESTS**, LIKE THE **MEXICAN BEAN LADYBUG,** WHICH **EATS SOYBEAN LEAVES,** AND THE **SQUASH LADY BEETLE.**

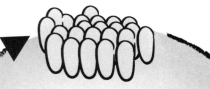

A LADYBUG CAN DEPOSIT **1,200 EGGS!** TO INSURE THAT ALL ITS **LARVAE** HAVE **PLENTY** TO **EAT**, LADYBUGS DEPOSIT THEIR EGGS WHERE THERE ARE **LOTS** OF **APHIDS.** IF THEY CAN'T FIND ENOUGH APHIDS, LADYBUGS **DEPOSIT** SOME **EGGS** THAT ARE **NOT FERTILIZED** FOR THEIR **LARVAE** TO **EAT.**

THE **ASIAN LADY BEETLE** IS A LADYBUG THAT WAS **INTRODUCED** TO THE UNITED STATES FROM **ASIA,** TO FIGHT CROP PESTS. BUT THIS BEETLE HAS BROUGHT SOME **NATIVE LADYBUG SPECIES** ALMOST TO **EXTINCTION.** THIS IS BECAUSE THE ASIAN LADY BEETLE IS MUCH **MORE TOXIC** THAN NATIVE SPECIES, AND HAS **FEWER PREDATORS.**

ALTHOUGH FEEDING ON HARMFUL INSECTS, ASIAN LADY BEETLES ARE CONSIDERED **PESTS** BECAUSE THEY INVADE PEOPLE'S **HOUSES** IN THE **FALL.** THEY DO SO TO SPEND THE **WINTER** IN A **WARM PLACE,** PROTECTED FROM THEIR **PREDATORS.**

WHIRLIGIG BEETLES

Endopterygota (insects with internal wing development)
Coleoptera (insects with sheathed wings)

WHEN THE **WHIRLIGIG BEETLE** LANDS ON **WATER, IT RESTS** ON THE **SURFACE. IT SWIMS** WITH ITS **FOUR PADDLE-LIKE LEGS,** AND USES ITS **TWO FRONT LEGS** TO CATCH **SMALL INSECTS** TO **EAT.** IF THE WHIRLIGIG BEETLE FEELS **THREATENED, IT SWIMS** IN **QUICK CIRCLES,** A HABIT THAT GAINED IT ITS **NAME.**

Eye to see above the water.

Water

Eye to see below the water.

THE **WHIRLIGIG BEETLE** SEES **ABOVE** AND **BELOW** THE **WATER** AT THE **SAME TIME.** IF A **PREDATOR** FROM **ABOVE** TRIES TO **CATCH IT,** THE WHIRLIGIG BEETLE **DIVES** IN TO THE **WATER.**

TRUE FLIES

Endopterygota (insects with internal wing development)
Diptera (insects with two wings)

MANY **INSECTS** HAVE THE WORD **"FLY"** IN THEIR **NAME**, LIKE **BUTTERFLIES** AND **DRAGONFLIES**, BUT THEY ARE **NOT FLIES**. ONLY THE INSECTS IN THIS **GROUP** ARE **REAL FLIES**, AND THAT'S WHY THEY ARE COMMONLY NAMED **TRUE FLIES**.

THE SCIENTIFIC NAME **DIPTERA** MEANS **"TWO WINGS,"** AND ALL TRUE FLIES HAVE **ONLY TWO WINGS**. THE **ANCESTORS** OF TRUE FLIES HAD **FOUR WINGS**, BUT THE **SECOND PAIR** HAS BECOME **SMALLER** WITH EVOLUTION. IN **MODERN TRUE FLIES**, THE SECOND PAIR OF WINGS HAVE BECOME **SMALL ORGANS** THAT INSECTS USE TO **BALANCE** THEMSELVES WHILE **FLYING**. THEY'RE CALLED **HALTERES**.

TRUE FLIES ARE DIVIDED INTO **TWO GROUPS**, DEPENDING ON THEIR **SHARED CHARACTERISTICS**. ONE GROUP IS CALLED **LONG-HORNED FLIES**, OR **NEMATOCERA**, AND INCLUDES **MOSQUITOES** AND **DANCE FLIES**. FLIES OF THE NEMATOCERA GROUP HAVE **LONG ANTENNAE**.

THE OTHER GROUP IS CALLED **SHORT-HORNED FLIES**, OR **BRACHYCERA**, AND INCLUDES **ROBBER FLIES, HUNCHBACK FLIES, BEE FLIES**, AND **SOLDIER FLIES**. FLIES OF THE BRACHYCERA GROUP HAVE **SHORT ANTENNAE**.

BUG BITES

Flies are found all over the world, in every climate, except for the South Pole.

THERE ARE OVER **120,000 SPECIES** OF **FLIES** DISCOVERED SO FAR. IT IS BELIEVED THAT THIS NUMBER IS ONLY **HALF** OF THE **ACTUAL** NUMBER OF **SPECIES** OF FLIES IN THE **WORLD**.

WHILE SOME SPECIES OF FLIES ARE **BENEFICIAL** TO HUMANS, BECAUSE THEY EAT **PESTS** AND **PARASITES**, OTHERS ARE NOT. SOME SPECIES OF TRUE FLIES **SPREAD DEADLY DISEASES** TO ANIMALS AND **HUMANS**. THESE DISEASES INCLUDE **TYPHUS, YELLOW FEVER, DYSENTERY, AND MALARIA.**

HALTERES

BUG BITES

The first true flies evolved during the Triassic period, 230 million years ago.

MOSQUITOES

Endopterygota (insects with internal wing development)
Diptera (insects with two wings)

THE COMMON NAME **MOSQUITO** COMES FROM THE **SPANISH** AND MEANS **"LITTLE FLY."**

BOTH **MALE** AND **FEMALE** MOSQUITOES FEED ON **FLOWER NECTAR.** BUT **FEMALE** MOSQUITOES NEED **PROTEINS** TO PRODUCE **EGGS.** THEY GET THEIR PROTEINS BY **SUCKING** THE **BLOOD** OF **ANIMALS.**

ONLY FEMALE MOSQUITOES ARE **HEMATOPHAGOUS,** OR **BLOOD-EATERS.** MALE MOSQUITOES **DON'T NEED** TO SUCK **BLOOD** BECAUSE THEY DON'T PRODUCE EGGS.

MOSQUITOES **DON'T BITE,** BECAUSE THEY **DON'T** HAVE TEETH. THEY HAVE A **PROBOSCIS.** FEMALE MOSQUITOES USE THEIR **PROBOSCIS** TO **PIERCE** THROUGH THE **SKIN** OF ANIMALS TO SUCK IN THEIR **BLOOD.**

MOSQUITOES **FIND** THEIR **VICTIMS** BECAUSE THEY ARE **SENSITIVE** TO **CARBON DIOXIDE,** WHICH IS THE **GAS** PEOPLE AND ANIMALS **EXHALE** WHEN THEY **BREATHE.** MOSQUITOES ARE ALSO ATTRACTED TO **BODY WARMTH, SMELLS,** AND **SWEAT.**

WHEN THE MOSQUITO **INSERTS** ITS **PROBOSCIS** INTO AN ANIMAL, FIRST IT **INJECTS** A LITTLE OF ITS **SALIVA,** WHICH CONTAINS **ENZYMES** THAT **NUMB** THE **AREA** OF THE BITE. THE MOSQUITO'S **VICTIM** OFTEN **DOESN'T** EVEN **KNOW** THAT **IT'S BEING BITTEN.** THE SALIVA ALSO CONTAINS ENZYMES THAT **KEEP** THE **BLOOD** FROM **CLOSING** UP THE **WOUND,** LEAVING THE MOSQUITO **PLENTY** OF **TIME** TO **EAT.** THE **ITCHY BUMP** ON THE **SKIN** IS THE BODY'S **REACTION** TO THE **MOSQUITO'S SALIVA.**

MOSQUITOES CAN **SPREAD DISEASES.** THE MOSQUITO'S **SALIVA** MAY CONTAIN **BACTERIA, VIRUSES,** AND **PARASITES** THAT LIVE IN THE MOSQUITO AND CAN BE **TRANSMITTED** TO **PEOPLE** OR **ANIMALS.**

ALSO, THE MOSQUITO'S PROBOSCIS MAY **PICK UP** **BACTERIA** FROM A **PERSON** AND, THROUGH BITING, **TRANSMIT** THEM TO **ANOTHER PERSON.** BESIDES **MALARIA,** MOSQUITOES CAN **SPREAD WEST NILE** VIRUS, ELEPHANTIASIS, ENCEPHALITIS, AND MANY MORE DISEASES!

When a mosquito bites, the sheath (or labium) pulls back to uncover the stylet.

SHEATH (OR LABIUM)

STYLET

BUG BITES

The female proboscis is very strong. It can pierce through the skin of mammals, including humans, birds, and amphibians. Female mosquitoes can even pierce through the hard skin of reptiles.

MOSQUITOES

FEMALE MOSQUITOES **DEPOSIT** THEIR **EGGS** IN **STAGNANT WATER.** THIS COULD BE A **POND,** A **PUDDLE,** OR JUST **WATER COLLECTED** IN SOME **GARBAGE, PET DISH,** OR **GARBAGE CANS** LEFT **OUTSIDE.**

SOME MOSQUITOES **DEPOSIT** THEIR **EGGS** IN THE **SOIL,** ONE AT A TIME.

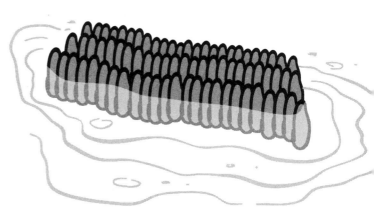

FEMALE MOSQUITOES DEPOSIT **100** OR MORE EGGS **EVERY THREE DAYS.** THEY CAN DEPOSIT OVER **2,000 EGGS** DURING THEIR **LIFETIME.** THE EGGS ARE **ATTACHED TOGETHER** AND **FLOAT** ON STAGNANT **WATER SURFACES.** THEY ARE **WHITE,** BUT **BECOME DARKER.**

THE **LARVA** OF THE MOSQUITO IS CALLED A **WRIGGLER.** IT EATS **WHATEVER** IT CAN **FIND** IN THE **WATER,** LIKE **OTHER LARVAE, EGGS, BACTERIA,** AND **ALGAE.** IN ORDER TO **BREATHE,** LARVAE **SUSPEND UPSIDE DOWN** UNDER THE **WATER SURFACE.** SOME SPECIES **LAY HORIZONTAL** UNDER THE SURFACE.

THE **PUPAE** OF THE MOSQUITOES ARE **VERY ACTIVE**, BUT **DON'T FEED**. THEY LIVE IN THE **WATER** AND COME TO THE **SURFACE** TO **BREATHE**. THEY HAVE **TWO TUBES**, CALLED **TRUMPETS**, ON THEIR **HEADS** AND BREATHE THROUGH THEM. THE PUPAL STAGE IS VERY SHORT, JUST A **DAY** OR **TWO**.

WHEN THE **PUPA MOLTS**, THE **ADULT EMERGES**. ADULTS **LIVE ON LAND** AND **DON'T NEED WATER** TO SURVIVE.

BUG BITES

Only female mosquitoes buzz. They make the noise by quickly flapping their wings. Each species flap their wings at a different speed. Male mosquitoes recognize females of their own species by the speed at which they flap their wings.

DANCE FLIES

Endopterygota (insects with internal wing development)
Diptera (insects with two wings)

THERE ARE OVER **3,500 SPECIES** OF **DANCE FLIES**. THEY ARE **MOSTLY CARNIVOROUS**, BUT SOME FEED ON **POLLEN**.

WHEN IT'S TIME FOR **MATING**, DANCE FLIES MEET NEAR **STREAMS** AND **PONDS**. THERE, DANCE FLIES FOLLOW **SPECIFIC MOTIONS**, AS IF THEY WERE **DANCING**.

TO LURE A DANCE FLY FEMALE, THE **MALE** OFFERS HER A **GIFT**, WHICH IS AN **INSECT** FOR THE **FEMALE** TO **EAT.** IN SOME SPECIES, THE MALE **WRAPS** THE **GIFT** UP IN **SILK.** MALES PRODUCE **SILK** FROM **GLANDS** IN THEIR **LEGS.** THE **WRAPPED GIFT** LOOKS LIKE A **BALLOON.** IN FACT, DANCE FLIES ARE ALSO CALLED **BALLOON FLIES.**

SOMETIMES THE MALE **TRICKS** THE **FEMALE** BY OFFERING HER A **DROP** OF **SALIVA** OR AN **EMPTY BALLOON** AS A GIFT.

ROBBER FLIES

Endopterygota (insects with internal wing development)
Diptera (insects with two wings)

ROBBER FLIES ARE **CARNIVOROUS** AND **VORACIOUS.** THEY ARE **NOT PICKY EATERS** AND **ATTACK INSECTS** LIKE OTHER **FLIES, GRASSHOPPERS, WASPS, BEES,** AND OFTEN THEY EVEN EAT **SPIDERS.**

SOME SPECIES OF ROBBER FLIES ARE **SKINNY** AND HAVE A **TAPERED ABDOMEN.** OTHERS ARE **CHUNKY, HAIRY,** AND LOOK LIKE **BUMBLE BEES.**

THE **ANTENNAE** ARE **SHORT.** SOMETIMES THERE'S A **LONG HAIR** STICKING OUT **FROM** THE **ANTENNAE.** THIS HAIR IS CALLED AN **ARISTA.**

SOMETIMES ROBBER FLIES **STALK** THEIR **PREY,** WAITING FOR IT TO **REST,** AND THEN **JUMP ON IT.** OTHER TIMES, ROBBER FLIES **GIVE CHASE** AND **ATTACK** THEIR PREY WHILE IT'S **FLYING.**

THE ROBBER FLY **CATCHES** ITS PREY BY **GRABBING** IT WITH ITS **LEGS, STABBING** IT IN THE **BACK** WITH ITS **PROBOSCIS,** AND **INJECTING SALIVA.** THE SALIVA CONTAINS **CHEMICALS** THAT **PARALYZE** THE VICTIM AND **LIQUEFY** ITS **INSIDES.**

THEN, THE ROBBER FLY FINDS A **RESTING PLACE** TO **EAT** ITS **MEAL.** SOMETIMES ROBBER FLIES EAT WHILE **HANGING** FROM A **TWIG** WITH **ONE** OR **TWO** OF THEIR **LEGS,** AND **HOLDING** ONTO THEIR **PREY** WITH THE **OTHERS.**

TO EAT ITS **MEAL,** THE ROBBER FLY **INSERTS** ITS **PROBOSCIS,** USING IT LIKE A **STRAW,** TO DRINK ITS PREY'S **LIQUEFIED INSIDES.**

THE ROBBER FLY'S **HEAD** IS **COVERED** BY **THICK HAIR**, LIKE A **BEARD**, CALLED **MYSTAX**. MYSTAX **PROTECTS** THE ROBBER FLY'S **FACE** FROM THE **STRUGGLES** OF ITS PREY.

SOME SPECIES OF ROBBER FLIES LOOK LIKE **BEES**, BUT THEY **DON'T HAVE** A **STINGER** AND **DON'T FEED** ON **POLLEN**. ROBBER FLIES ADOPTED THIS **DISGUISE** TO **PROTECT** THEMSELVES AGAINST **PREDATORS**. SOME **ANIMALS**, LIKE FROGS AND TOADS, **THINK TWICE** BEFORE **EATING** A **PREY** THAT MIGHT HAVE A **DANGEROUS STINGER** LIKE A BEE.

ROBBER FLIES HAVE **HUGE COMPOUND EYES** TO HELP THEM BE **SKILLFUL HUNTERS**.

THERE ARE ABOUT **7,000 SPECIES** OF **ROBBER FLIES** CLASSIFIED SO FAR.

A **FEMALE'S ABDOMEN** ENDS WITH A **LONG APPENDAGE** THAT LOOKS LIKE A **STINGER**. THIS IS THE **OVIPOSITOR**, THE ROBBER FLY'S **ORGAN** FOR **DEPOSITING EGGS**. THE **OVIPOSITOR** IS **NOT** A **STINGER**, BUT BEING SO THIN, **FEMALES** CAN **INSERT** IT INTO **HIDDEN** AND **SAFE PLACES** TO **DEPOSIT** THEIR **EGGS**.

ROBBER FLIES DEPOSIT THEIR **EGGS** IN THE **UNDERGROWTH**. THE **LARVAE** ARE **VORACIOUS** JUST LIKE THE ADULTS, AND **FEED** ON **EGGS**, OTHER **LARVAE**, **DEAD LEAVES**, AND **ROTTING BARK**. THE LARVAE TURN INTO **PUPAE** ALSO IN THE **UNDERGROWTH**.

FRUIT FLIES

Endopterygota (insects with internal wing development)
Diptera (insects with two wings)

FRUIT FLIES ARE SMALL INSECTS OFTEN FOUND FLYING AROUND RIPE AND ROTTING FRUIT. THEY FEED ON THE LIQUIDS PRODUCED BY THE FERMENTATION OF THE FRUIT.

THERE ARE **MANY SPECIES** OF FRUIT FLIES, BUT THE **MOST FAMOUS** IS THE ONE CALLED **DROSOPHILA MELANOGASTER** (WHICH MEANS "**MOIST-LOVING FLY** WITH A **DARK BELLY**"). THIS IS BECAUSE **SCIENTISTS** USE THE **DROSOPHILA** TO LEARN ABOUT **GENETICS** AND **DEVELOPMENTAL BIOLOGY** (HOW ANIMALS DEVELOP FROM A FERTILIZED EGG).

IT SEEMS THAT MANY OF THE **FRUIT FLY GENES**, OVER **70%**, ARE **SIMILAR** TO THOSE OF **PEOPLE**. BY STUDYING THESE GENES, SCIENTISTS CAN UNDERSTAND HOW CERTAIN **DISEASES** ARE **TRANSMITTED** FROM **GENERATION TO GENERATION**. THE STUDY OF FRUIT FLIES HAS TURNED OUT TO BE **IMPORTANT** IN **UNDERSTANDING** HEREDITARY HUMAN **ILLNESSES**, LIKE **PARKINSON'S** AND **ALZHEIMER'S**.

FRUIT FLIES ARE **VERY EASY TO BREED**. THE **LIFE CYCLE** OF A FRUIT FLY LASTS FOR **30 TO 40 DAYS**, SO IT'S EASY TO **SEE** HOW CERTAIN **HEREDITARY CHARACTERISTICS** GO FROM **PARENTS** TO **OFFSPRING**. THEY **DEPOSIT MANY EGGS**, SO SCIENTISTS DON'T RUN **OUT** OF **MATERIAL** FOR THEIR EXPERIMENTS.

BUG BITES

In 2004, fruit flies were sent to space. Scientists wanted to know how an environment without gravity, like space, affected the flies' genes.

BEE FLIES

Endopterygota (insects with internal wing development)
Diptera (insects with two wings)

ADULT BEE FLIES LOOK LIKE **BEES,** AND ALTHOUGH THEY **FEED ON POLLEN,** BEE FLIES **DON'T HAVE A STINGER.**

SOME SPECIES OF BEE FLIES GO THROUGH **HYPERMETAMORPHOSIS** TO BECOME ADULTS. HYPERMETAMORPHOSIS IS A **COMPLETE METAMORPHOSIS** WITH **TWO LARVAL STAGES.** SO THE HYPERMETAMORPHOSIS IS COMPOSED OF **FIVE STAGES** INSTEAD OF FOUR: **EGG, FIRST LARVA, SECOND LARVA, PUPA,** AND **ADULT.**

SOME SPECIES OF BEE FLY LARVAE EAT **GRASSHOPPER EGGS** AND **BEETLE GRUBS.**

BEE FLIES ARE **PARASITES** OF **SOLITARY BEES** AND **WASPS.** SOLITARY BEES AND WASPS DON'T LIVE IN **HIVES.** INSTEAD, THEY LIVE **ALONE.** SOLITARY BEES AND WASPS **BURROW** INTO THE **GROUND** TO CREATE A **NEST** FOR THEIR **EGGS** AND **LARVAE. BEE FLIES** SNEAK INSIDE THESE NESTS AND **DEPOSIT** THEIR **EGGS.**

FIRST, THE **BEE FLY LARVA** EATS THE SOLITARY BEE'S STORED **POLLEN** AND **NECTAR.** THEN, IT EATS THE SOLITARY BEE'S EGGS AND LARVAE. THE BEE FLY LARVA **PUPATES** IN THIS SAME **NEST** BEFORE EMERGING AS AN **ADULT.**

HUNCHBACK FLIES

Endopterygota (insects with internal wing development)
Diptera (insects with two wings)

HUNCHBACK FLIES HAVE A VERY SMALL HEAD, A BIG, HUNCHED THORAX, AND A HUGE ABDOMEN.

ADULT HUNCHBACK FLIES FEED ON POLLEN, BUT THEIR LARVAE ARE VORACIOUS PARASITES OF SPIDERS!

HUNCHBACK FLY FEMALES **DEPOSIT** THEIR **EGGS** ON **TREE TRUNKS** OR **PLANTS**. THEY CAN DEPOSIT OVER **3,500 EGGS** AT **ONE TIME!**

ONCE THE EGGS HATCH, THE **LARVAE** LOOK FOR A **SPIDER**. WHEN THEY FIND ONE, THEY **CREEP INTO** THE **SPIDER'S BODY, GNAWING A HOLE** IN ITS **LEG.** THEY SPEND MOST OF THEIR **LARVAL STAGE** INSIDE THE **SPIDER.**

DESPITE THE **INVASION,** THE **SPIDER DOESN'T** SEEM TO **NOTICE,** EVEN WHEN THE LARVAE **POKE HOLES** IN THE **SPIDER'S ABDOMEN** TO GET AIR.

BUT, WHEN THE **LARVAE** ARE READY TO **PUPATE,** THEY **EAT** THE **SPIDER'S INSIDES,** KILLING IT. ONCE THE LARVAE **EMERGE** FROM THE **DEAD SPIDER,** THEY PUPATE AND, LATER, BECOME ADULTS.

SOLDIER FLIES

Endopterygota (insects with internal wing development)
Diptera (insects with two wings)

SOLDIER FLY **ADULTS** FEED ON **POLLEN.** SOLDIER FLY **LARVAE** FEED ON **MANURE, CARCASSES, ROTTING GARBAGE,** AND **DECAYING PLANTS.**

SOLDIER FLY **LARVAE** AND **ADULTS** DON'T CARRY **DISEASE** AND ARE **NOT HARMFUL** TO **PEOPLE** OR **ANIMALS.** THE PRESENCE OF SOLDIER FLY LARVAE DETERS **HOUSEFLIES** FROM DEPOSITING THEIR **EGGS.** THIS IS A GOOD THING BECAUSE **HOUSEFLIES** CARRY **DISEASES.**

SOLDIER FLY LARVAE HAVE BEEN USED AS **CHICKEN FEED.** THE LARVAE ARE EASY TO **BREED** IN **MANURE** AND **CHICKEN FECES,** AND ARE **RICH** IN **PROTEINS.** BREEDING SOLDIER FLY LARVAE IS NOT ONLY VERY CHEAP, IT ALSO **REDUCES** THE AMOUNT OF **NATURAL DANGEROUS CHEMICALS** CONTAINED IN **MANURE.**

HUMPBACK FLIES

Endopterygota (insects with internal wing development)
Diptera (insects with two wings)

HUMPBACK FLIES ARE VERY SMALL INSECTS THAT EAT ALL KINDS OF DECOMPOSING MATTER, INCLUDING CARRION, ROTTING VEGETATION, FUNGI, AND FECES. HUMPBACK FLIES ARE ALSO CALLED SCUTTLE FLIES BECAUSE THEY OFTEN PREFER TO RUN AWAY THAN TO FLY.

SOME SPECIES OF HUMPBACK FLIES ARE CALLED DECAPITATING FLIES. EACH SPECIES HAS ITS PREFERRED VICTIM. ONE SPECIES DEPOSITS ITS EGGS INSIDE THE HEAD OF FIRE ANTS. WHEN THE EGGS HATCH, THE LARVAE FEED ON THE FIRE ANT'S BRAIN UNTIL THE HEAD FALLS OFF THE ANT'S BODY.

HOUSEFLIES

Endopterygota (insects with internal wing development)
Diptera (insects with two wings)

HOUSEFLIES LIVE IN THE SAME ENVIRONMENT WHERE PEOPLE LIVE, ESPECIALLY IF THERE'S MANURE OR GARBAGE NEARBY.

HOUSEFLIES CAN SEE VERY WELL AND ARE SENSITIVE TO SMALL CHANGES IN THE MOVEMENTS OF THE AIR, SO IT'S VERY HARD TO CATCH THEM.

HOUSEFLIES CAN'T EAT SOLID FOOD; THEY CAN ONLY SPONGE LIQUID FOODS WITH THEIR MOUTHS. IN ORDER TO EAT, HOUSEFLIES VOMIT DIGESTIVE FLUIDS ONTO FOOD. THE DIGESTIVE FLUIDS LIQUEFY THE FOOD. THEN, THE HOUSEFLY SPONGES IT UP WITH ITS MOUTH. SOMETIMES HOUSEFLIES VOMIT WHAT THEY HAVE JUST EATEN AND EAT IT UP AGAIN.

HOUSEFLIES CARRY MANY DISEASE-CAUSING PATHOGENS (BACTERIA, VIRUSES, AND WORMS). DISEASES ARE SPREAD WHEN HOUSEFLIES WALK ON OR EAT FECES AND GARBAGE, COLLECTING PATHOGENS ON THEIR FEET OR IN THEIR STOMACHS. THEN, THEY WALK, VOMIT, OR DEFECATE ON PEOPLE'S FOOD, DEPOSITING THESE PATHOGENS.

HOUSEFLIES CAN SPREAD TYPHOID, CHOLERA, SALMONELLA, DYSENTERY, TUBERCULOSIS, ANTHRAX, TAPEWORMS, ROUNDWORMS, AND MANY OTHER DISEASES.

THE HOUSEFLY HAS DARK RED COMPOUND EYES MADE UP OF MORE THAN 4,000 EYES.

THERE'S AN ARISTA (A HAIR-LIKE BRISTLE) ON EACH ANTENNA.

THE BODY OF THE HOUSEFLY IS COVERED WITH HAIR.

HOUSEFLIES TASTE WITH THEIR FEET AND MOUTH.

BUG BITES

Fossils of houseflies indicate that these animals evolved 63 million years ago in Asia.

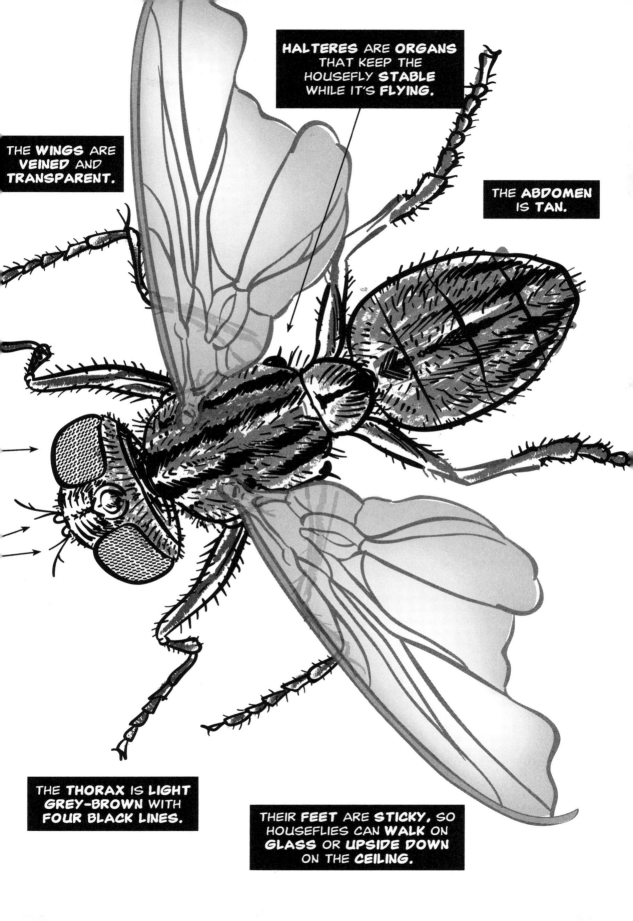

HOUSEFLIES

HOUSEFLIES ARE **VERY ACTIVE** DURING THE **SUMMER** AND BECOME **SLUGGISH** WHEN THE **TEMPERATURE DROPS.** AS **ADULTS,** HOUSEFLIES **CAN'T SURVIVE** THE **WINTER,** BUT AS **LARVAE** AND **PUPAE** THEY CAN IF THEY ARE IN **SHELTERED PLACES.**

HOUSEFLIES ARE **DIURNAL.** THIS MEANS THAT THEY ARE **ACTIVE** DURING THE **DAY** AND THEY **REST** AT **NIGHT.**

HOUSEFLIES GO THROUGH A **COMPLETE METAMORPHOSIS** TO
BECOME ADULTS. THE HOUSEFLY **FEMALE** DEPOSITS **THOUSANDS**
OF **EGGS** IN HER **LIFETIME**. SHE GENERALLY LAYS **PILES OF 100
EGGS** EVERY **THREE DAYS** DURING HER **ENTIRE ADULT LIFE**.

THE **EGGS** ARE **VERY SMALL**
AND **WHITE**. THEY LOOK LIKE
GRAINS OF **RICE**, BUT THEY ARE
SMALLER. THE **EGGS** ARE LAID IN
MOIST PLACES LIKE **MANURE,
FRESH CARCASSES,** OR
ROTTING GARBAGE. THESE
DECAYING MATERIALS WILL
FEED THE **LARVAE**.

Housefly egg

AFTER A **FEW DAYS** THE **EGGS
HATCH**. THE **LARVAE** OF THE HOUSEFLY
ARE CALLED **MAGGOTS**. THE **MAGGOTS**
ARE **LIGHT TAN** AND **SMALL**, BUT THEY
GROW UNTIL THEY ARE **ABOUT HALF** AN
INCH LONG. LARVAE EAT **WHATEVER
SURROUNDS** THEM, **IMMERSING** THEIR
HEADS INTO IT.

Housefly maggots

THEN, THE MAGGOTS
MOVE TO A **DRY PLACE**
AND **PUPATE**. THE
PUPAE ARE **DARK RED**.

A **FEW DAYS LATER**, THE
ADULT HOUSEFLIES **EMERGE** FROM
THE PUPAE. AS SOON AS THEY
BECOME ADULTS, THE FEMALES
MATE ONE TIME ONLY. THEY ARE
IMMEDIATELY **READY** TO **DEPOSIT
EGGS** RIGHT AFTER MATING.

Housefly pupa

THE **LIFESPAN** OF A HOUSEFLY
IS OF ABOUT **12** TO **25 DAYS** FOR
MALES AND UP TO **60 DAYS** FOR
FEMALES. **IN ONE YEAR** ALONE
HOUSEFLIES CAN SPAWN **TWELVE
GENERATIONS**.

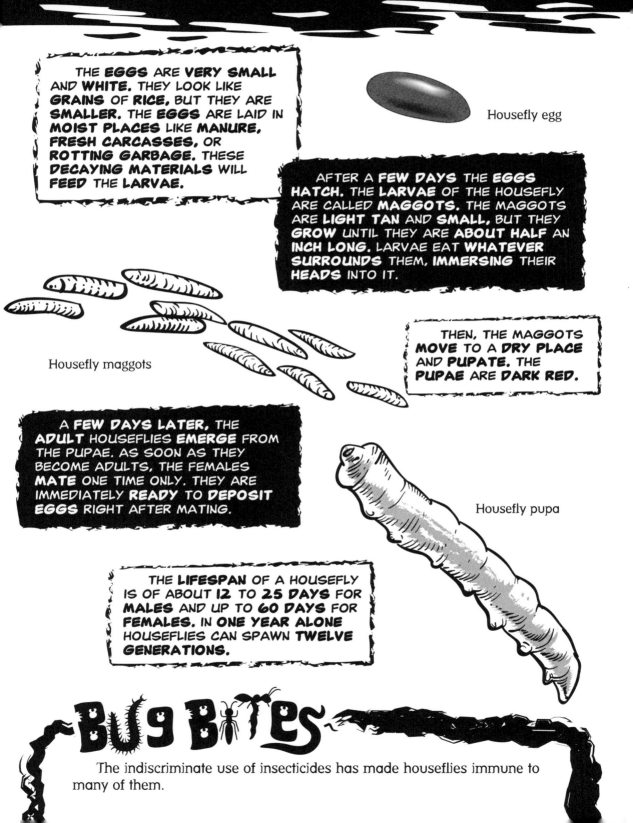

BUG BITES

The indiscriminate use of insecticides has made houseflies immune to
many of them.

HOUSEFLIES

DR. YAO AND DR. YUAN, TWO CHINESE ENTOMOLOGISTS, ASSERT THAT THE NUMBER OF PATHOGENS ON THE BODY OF A HOUSEFLY IS, ON AVERAGE, 1,941,000.

DR. DICKINSON FOUND OUT THAT HOUSEFLIES' EYES AND THEIR HALTERES ARE DIRECTLY CONNECTED. FOR THIS REASON, HOUSEFLIES CAN QUICKLY CHANGE DIRECTION WHILE FLYING, MAKING THEM REALLY HARD TO CATCH.

A HOUSEFLY CAN POOP EVERY 4 1/2 MINUTES.

FOR CENTURIES, **PHYSICIANS** HAVE BEEN APPLYING **CERTAIN SPECIES** OF **MAGGOTS** TO **PEOPLE'S WOUNDS**. THIS IS BECAUSE MAGGOTS ONLY **EAT DEAD FLESH**, PREVENTING **GANGRENE** AND **PROMOTING HEALING**.

ONCE THE **PUPAL STAGE ENDS**, THE **ADULT** HOUSEFLY **DOESN'T GROW** IN SIZE. IF THE HOUSEFLY IS **SMALL** IT IS BECAUSE IT DIDN'T HAVE ENOUGH TO **EAT** WHEN IT WAS A **LARVA**.

HOUSEFLIES' **SENSE OF TASTE**, LOCATED IN THEIR **FEET**, IS **10 MILLION TIMES** MORE **SENSITIVE** TO **SUGARS** THAN THE **HUMAN TONGUE**.

BUG BITES

Stable flies look like houseflies, but they can bite because they eat blood.

HORSEFLIES

Endopterygota (insects with internal wing development)
Diptera (insects with two wings)

THE **HORSEFLY** IS ONE OF THE **LARGEST FLIES,** SOME SPECIES MEASURING UP TO **ONE INCH** IN **LENGTH.** THERE ARE **OVER 3,000 SPECIES** DESCRIBED **WORLDWIDE.**

HORSEFLIES **FEED** ON **NECTAR,** BUT HORSEFLY **FEMALES** ALSO **NEED** THE **PROTEINS** CONTAINED IN **BLOOD** TO **DEVELOP** THEIR **EGGS.** MALES ONLY **HAVE** A **PROBOSCIS** TO **FEED** ON **NECTAR.** BUT FEMALES HAVE **MANDIBLES** THAT CAN **CUT** THROUGH **ANIMAL HIDE,** AND A **SPONGE-LIKE ORGAN** THAT **LICKS** THE GUSHING **BLOOD.**

MAXILLAE AND
MANDIBLES WORK LIKE
SCISSORS IN CUTTING
THROUGH THE SKIN OF
THE HORSEFLY'S VICTIM.
THE LABELLA SPONGES UP THE BLOOD
SPRINGING FROM THE WOUND.

HORSEFLIES CARRY PATHOGENS, LIKE
BACTERIA, VIRUSES, AND WORMS, AND CAN
EFFICIENTLY SPREAD DISEASES. THIS IS
BECAUSE THE BITE OF THE HORSEFLY IS VERY
PAINFUL AND THE VICTIM'S IMMEDIATE
RESPONSE IS TO CHASE THE HORSEFLY AWAY.
SO, THE HORSEFLY LOOKS FOR ANOTHER VICTIM
TO BITE. THE PATHOGENS THE HORSEFLY PICKS
UP ON THE FIRST VICTIM ARE THEN DEPOSITED
IN THE OPEN WOUND OF THE SECOND.
HORSEFLIES CAN SPREAD RABBIT FEVER
(TULAREMIA), LOA LOA (A WORM THAT INFESTS
SKIN AND EYES), AND ANTHRAX.

BLOWFLIES

Endopterygota (insects with internal wing development)
Diptera (insects with two wings)

BLOWFLIES ARE **METALLIC GREEN, BLUE,** OR **BLACK.** MANY SPECIES OF THIS GROUP FEED ON **CARRION, GARBAGE,** AND OTHER **ROTTING MATERIAL.** THE **MEAT** ON WHICH THEY **LAY** THEIR **EGGS** IS CALLED **BLOWN.**

SOME SPECIES OF BLOWFLIES ARE **PARASITES** OF **CATTLE.** FOR EXAMPLE, THE **SHEEP BLOWFLY** LAYS ITS **EGGS** UNDER THE **TAIL** OF **SHEEP** AND **GOATS.** THE **AMMONIA** IN THE **SHEEP'S URINE** ATTRACTS THESE **FLIES.** WHEN THE **EGGS** HATCH, THE **LARVAE BURROW** INTO THE **FLESH** OF THE **SHEEP.** THEIR PRESENCE CAUSES **INFECTION** AND, IF LEFT **UNTREATED,** THE **DEATH** OF THE **SHEEP.** THIS INFESTATION IS CALLED **MYIASIS.**

A **FORENSIC ENTOMOLOGIST** COLLECTS **INFORMATION** THAT CAN BE **CRUCIAL** DURING A **CRIME INVESTIGATION.** FOR EXAMPLE, SOME SPECIES OF **BLOWFLIES** ARE ABLE TO **REACH A CORPSE** WITHIN A **FEW HOURS AFTER DEATH.** THE **MAGGOTS** OF THESE FLIES **FEED ONLY** ON THE **ROTTING FLESH.** OTHER SPECIES OF BLOWFLIES REACH THE CORPSE **LATER ON.** THEIR **MAGGOTS** FEED ON THE **ROTTING FLESH** AND ON THE **OTHER FLIES' MAGGOTS.** BY **NOTICING** WHICH **INSECTS** ARE **PRESENT** AND AT WHAT **STAGE** OF THEIR **LIFE CYCLE** THEY ARE, **FORENSIC ENTOMOLOGISTS** CAN **DETERMINE** WITH **ACCURATE PRECISION** THE **TIME OF DEATH.**

THERE'S A KIND OF **BLOWFLY** THAT IS A **PARASITE** OF **PEOPLE,** THE **HUMAN BOTFLY.** THESE FLIES **DEPOSIT** THEIR **EGGS** ON **MOSQUITOES.** WHEN THE MOSQUITO **BITES** A **PERSON,** THE EGG **FALLS OFF** ITS BODY AND ON THE PERSON'S SKIN. AT CONTACT, THE EGG **HATCHES** AND THE **LARVA BURROWS** INTO THE **FLESH,** KEEPING ONLY ITS **AIR HOLE THROUGH** THE **SKIN.** THE BOTFLY LARVA ONLY CAUSES A **SMALL LOCAL INFECTION** AND SOME **SHARP PAIN** WHEN IT **FEEDS** ON THE **PERSON'S FLESH.** THE LARVA **GROWS** UNTIL IT'S **ABOUT 1/4** OF AN **INCH LONG.** THEN, IT **FALLS** TO THE **GROUND** TO PUPATE. **ADULT BOTFLIES** DON'T FEED ON **HUMAN FLESH.**

BECAUSE OF ITS **SPIKY BODY,** IT'S **NOT A GOOD IDEA** TO **PULL** THE **LARVA OUT,** BECAUSE IT MIGHT **BREAK INSIDE** THE **SKIN, CAUSING INFECTION.** IT'S BEST TO **SUFFOCATE** THE **AIR HOLE** WITH **PETROLEUM JELLY,** AND **REMOVE** THE **LARVA** WHEN IT **COMES OUT** TO **BREATHE.**

HYMENOPTERA

Endopterygota (insects with internal wing development)
Hymenoptera (insects with membranous wings)

THERE ARE **OVER 116,000 SPECIES** OF **HYMENOPTERA** IDENTIFIED BY SCIENTISTS SO FAR.

THE **HYMENOPTERA** IS SUCH A **VARIED GROUP** OF INSECTS THAT THERE'S **NO SINGLE, COMMON NAME** TO DESCRIBE THEM. **SAWFLIES, WASPS, BEES,** AND **ANTS** ARE ALL **HYMENOPTERA.**

THE **CHARACTERISTIC** THAT **DISTINGUISHES** THE **HYMENOPTERA** FROM OTHER GROUPS OF INSECTS IS THE **MEMBRANOUS WINGS.** THIS CHARACTERISTIC IS REFLECTED IN THE NAME **"MEMBRANOUS WINGS."**

THE **BIGGEST HYMENOPTERA** IS THE **TARANTULA HAWK,** WITH A **WINGSPAN** OF ABOUT **FOUR INCHES.**

TARANTULA HAWK LARVAE ARE **PARASITIC.** THAT MEANS THAT THEY **LIVE** AT THE **EXPENSE OF A HOST.** THE **FEMALE TARANTULA HAWK** USES ITS **STINGER** TO **STUN** A **TARANTULA SPIDER.** THEN, IT **DEPOSITS** ITS **EGGS INSIDE** THE **TARANTULA SPIDER'S ABDOMEN.** WHEN THE EGGS HATCH, THE **LARVAE EAT** THE **TARANTULA SPIDER** FROM THE **INSIDE** UNTIL IT **DIES.** AFTER THE **PUPAL STAGE,** THE **ADULT TARANTULA HAWK** EMERGES FROM THE **BODY** OF THE **TARANTULA SPIDER.** TARANTULA HAWK ADULTS ONLY **EAT POLLEN.**

MANY **FEMALE HYMENOPTERA** HAVE AN **OVIPOSITOR.** THIS IS AN **APPENDAGE** AT THE **END** OF THE **ABDOMEN** USED TO **DEPOSIT** THE **EGGS.** IN COLONIES OF **WASPS** AND **BEES,** THERE'S ONLY **ONE FEMALE,** THE **QUEEN,** THAT **DEPOSITS EGGS.** ALL THE **OTHER FEMALES** HAVE A **MODIFIED OVIPOSITOR,** CALLED A **STINGER.** WASPS AND BEES USE THEIR STINGER TO **DEFEND** THEIR **COLONY.**

SAWFLIES HAVE THE **OVIPOSITOR** IN THE **SHAPE** OF A **SAW.** SAWFLIES USE THEIR **OVIPOSITOR** TO **CUT PLANTS OPEN** AND TO **LAY** THEIR **EGGS INSIDE.**

HONEYBEES

Endopterygota (insects with internal wing development)
Hymenoptera (insects with membranous wings)

HONEYBEES LIVE IN **ORGANIZED COLONIES** WHERE EACH CASTE, THE **QUEEN**, THE **WORKERS**, AND THE **DRONES**, CARRIES OUT **SPECIFIC ACTIVITIES**. **WORKERS** REPRESENT **98%** OF THE **COLONY;** THE **QUEEN** AND THE **DRONES** REPRESENT THE REMAINING **2%.**

Workers have longer wings than the queen.

The queen bee is bigger than the workers and lighter in color.

Drones are the biggest bees.

THE DRONES

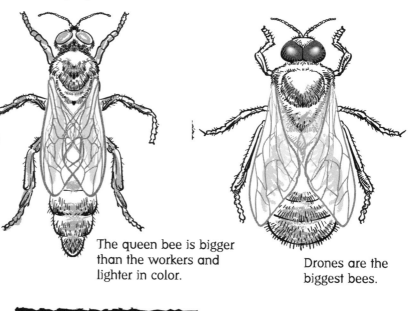

THE **DRONES** ARE BORN FROM THE QUEEN'S **UNFERTILIZED EGGS**. THEY ARE **MALE**, WHILE THE **QUEEN** AND THE **WORKERS** ARE ALL **FEMALES**.

DRONES MATE WITH THE **QUEEN** AND **DIE** IMMEDIATELY AFTER. THE **SURVIVING DRONES** LIVE IN THE **HIVE**, BUT CAN'T TAKE PART IN THE WORKERS' **DUTIES** BECAUSE THEY DON'T HAVE **POLLEN BASKETS** AND CAN'T PRODUCE **WAX**. SO, WHEN **FOOD** IS **SCARCE**, WORKERS **CHASE DRONES OUT** OF THE HIVE.

WORKERS AND **QUEEN LARVAE** HATCH FROM THE MOTHER QUEEN'S **FERTILIZED EGGS.**

QUEENS ARE **FED** WITH **ROYAL JELLY** THROUGHOUT THEIR LIVES.

THERE CAN ONLY BE **ONE QUEEN** IN THE HIVE AND A NEW QUEEN **STINGS** AND **KILLS** HER **RIVALS.** THE QUEEN'S **STINGER** IS **NOT BARBED** AND CAN BE **REUSED.**

A GROUP OF **YOUNG WORKERS** ALWAYS **SURROUNDS** THE **QUEEN**, **CLEANING HER** WITH THEIR **TONGUES** AND **REMOVING** HER **FECES.** WHEN THE QUEEN IS **HUNGRY,** SHE **TOUCHES** A WORKER AND SHE **REGURGITATES ROYAL JELLY** FOR THE QUEEN TO **EAT.**

AFTER **THREE YEARS,** THE QUEEN BECOMES **OLD** AND THE WORKERS **STARVE** HER TO **DEATH.** IN THE MEANWHILE, THEY **REAR** A FEW **QUEEN LARVAE** TO REPLACE THE OLD QUEEN.

THE **NEW QUEEN** LEAVES THE **HIVE** TO MATE WITH THE **DRONES.** THEN SHE COMES BACK AND STARTS **DEPOSITING** ABOUT **2,500 EGGS** PER **DAY,** OR ONE EGG EVERY **40 SECONDS!** THE QUEEN IS THE **ONLY BEE** IN THE COLONY THAT CAN **LAY EGGS.**

HONEYBEES

THE WORKERS

ALL **WORKERS** ARE **FEMALES**, BUT THEIR REPRODUCTIVE SYSTEM DOESN'T WORK.

WORKERS ARE BORN FROM THE QUEEN'S **FERTILIZED EGGS**. THEY LIVE FOR ABOUT **48 DAYS** IN THE **SUMMER**, WHEN THEY ARE VERY ACTIVE, AND **LONGER** DURING THE **WINTER**.

POLLEN BASKET

THE **DUTIES** OF A WORKER **DEPEND** ON HER **AGE** BECAUSE BEES NEED TO **DEVELOP CERTAIN GLANDS** TO PERFORM **SPECIFIC TASKS**.

FIRST TWO DAYS

AS SOON AS SHE **LEAVES** HER **CELL**, THE WORKER BEE **CLEANS** IT OUT. KEEPING THE HIVE CLEAN PREVENTS **DISEASES** AND **MOLD**.

EIGHT DAYS

WORKERS DEVELOP GLANDS TO PRODUCE **ROYAL JELLY** SO THEY CAN TAKE CARE OF THE **BROOD**. FEW WORKERS **TEND** TO THE **QUEEN**, WHICH ONLY EATS **ROYAL JELLY**.

AFTER TEN DAYS

WORKERS DEVELOP GLANDS TO SECRETE **WAX** SO THEY CAN **BUILD HONEYCOMBS**. THEY ALSO HELP **FORAGERS** UNLOADING **POLLEN**, MAKING **HONEY**, AND GUARDING THE **COLONY**. WORKERS PREPARE TO BECOME FORAGERS BY GOING ON **ORIENTATION FLIGHTS** TO LEARN WHERE THEIR **HIVE** IS **LOCATED** AND WHERE TO FIND FOOD.

AFTER 15 DAYS

WORKERS DEVELOP **VENOM GLANDS** FOR THEIR **STINGERS**. THEY CAN FINALLY **LEAVE** THE **HIVE** AND BECOME **FORAGERS**.

FORAGERS **COLLECT NECTAR** FROM **FLOWERS**. THE NECTAR IS AT THE **BOTTOM** OF THE **FLOWER**, AND, TO REACH IT, WORKERS GET **COVERED** IN **POLLEN**. WORKERS **GATHER** THE **POLLEN**, MOISTENING IT WITH **SALIVA**, AND **PACKING** IT IN THEIR **POLLEN BASKETS**. THESE ARE AREAS IN THE BEE'S **LEGS** THAT ARE **COVERED** WITH **HAIR**.

THE HIVE

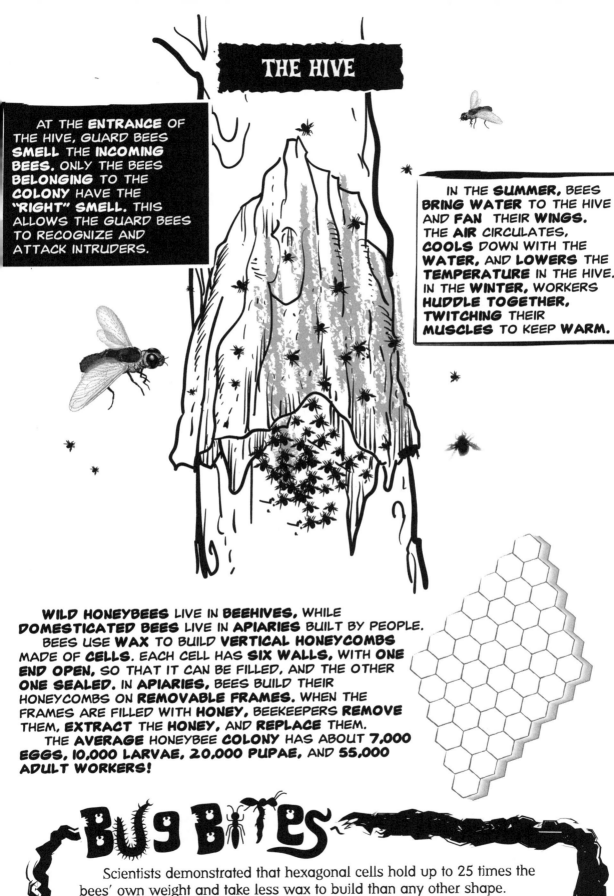

AT THE **ENTRANCE** OF THE HIVE, GUARD BEES **SMELL** THE **INCOMING BEES**. ONLY THE BEES **BELONGING** TO THE **COLONY** HAVE THE "RIGHT" **SMELL**. THIS ALLOWS THE GUARD BEES TO RECOGNIZE AND ATTACK INTRUDERS.

IN THE **SUMMER**, BEES **BRING WATER** TO THE HIVE AND **FAN** THEIR **WINGS**. THE **AIR CIRCULATES**, **COOLS** DOWN WITH THE **WATER**, AND **LOWERS** THE **TEMPERATURE** IN THE HIVE. IN THE **WINTER**, WORKERS **HUDDLE TOGETHER**, **TWITCHING** THEIR **MUSCLES** TO KEEP **WARM**.

WILD HONEYBEES LIVE IN **BEEHIVES**, WHILE **DOMESTICATED BEES** LIVE IN **APIARIES** BUILT BY PEOPLE. BEES USE **WAX** TO BUILD **VERTICAL HONEYCOMBS** MADE OF **CELLS**. EACH CELL HAS **SIX WALLS**, WITH **ONE END OPEN**, SO THAT IT CAN BE FILLED, AND THE OTHER **ONE SEALED**. IN **APIARIES**, BEES BUILD THEIR HONEYCOMBS ON **REMOVABLE FRAMES**. WHEN THE FRAMES ARE FILLED WITH **HONEY**, BEEKEEPERS **REMOVE** THEM, **EXTRACT** THE **HONEY**, AND **REPLACE** THEM. THE **AVERAGE** HONEYBEE **COLONY** HAS ABOUT **7,000 EGGS, 10,000 LARVAE, 20,000 PUPAE**, AND **55,000 ADULT WORKERS!**

BUG BITES

Scientists demonstrated that hexagonal cells hold up to 25 times the bees' own weight and take less wax to build than any other shape.

HONEYBEES

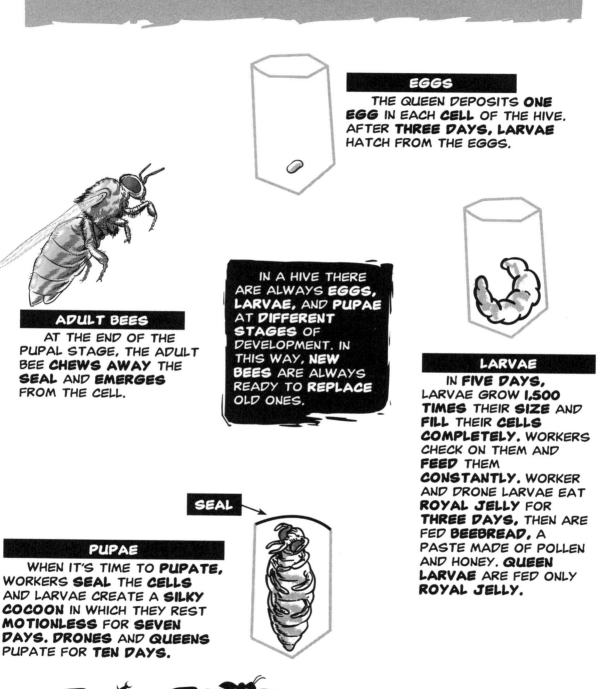

EGGS
THE QUEEN DEPOSITS **ONE EGG** IN EACH **CELL** OF THE HIVE. AFTER **THREE DAYS, LARVAE** HATCH FROM THE EGGS.

ADULT BEES
AT THE END OF THE PUPAL STAGE, THE ADULT BEE **CHEWS AWAY** THE **SEAL** AND **EMERGES** FROM THE CELL.

IN A HIVE THERE ARE ALWAYS **EGGS, LARVAE,** AND **PUPAE** AT **DIFFERENT STAGES** OF DEVELOPMENT. IN THIS WAY, **NEW BEES** ARE ALWAYS READY TO **REPLACE** OLD ONES.

LARVAE
IN **FIVE DAYS,** LARVAE GROW **1,500 TIMES** THEIR **SIZE** AND **FILL** THEIR **CELLS COMPLETELY.** WORKERS CHECK ON THEM AND **FEED** THEM **CONSTANTLY.** WORKER AND DRONE LARVAE EAT **ROYAL JELLY** FOR **THREE DAYS,** THEN ARE FED **BEEBREAD,** A PASTE MADE OF POLLEN AND HONEY. **QUEEN LARVAE** ARE FED ONLY **ROYAL JELLY.**

SEAL

PUPAE
WHEN IT'S TIME TO **PUPATE,** WORKERS **SEAL** THE **CELLS** AND LARVAE CREATE A **SILKY COCOON** IN WHICH THEY REST **MOTIONLESS** FOR **SEVEN DAYS.** DRONES AND QUEENS PUPATE FOR **TEN DAYS.**

BUG BITES
When a colony outgrows the hive, the old queen and many workers leave to nest somewhere else. This process is called swarming.

BEE DANCES

WORKERS THAT GO IN **SEARCH** OF **NEW FLOWER PATCHES** ARE CALLED **SCOUT BEES.** WHEN THEY FIND ONE, SCOUT BEES **COMMUNICATE** THE **LOCATION** OF THE **FLOWERS** TO THEIR **SISTERS** WITH A **DANCE.**

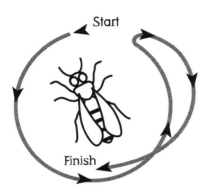

Start

Finish

THE ROUND DANCE
IF THE **FLOWERS** ARE **NEARBY,** THE SCOUT BEE DANCES IN **CIRCLES.**

THE SICKLE DANCE
IF THE **FLOWERS** ARE LOCATED BETWEEN **150** AND **500 FEET,** THE SCOUT BEE DANCES IN **HALF CIRCLES.**

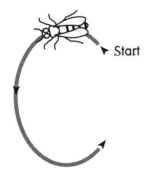

Start

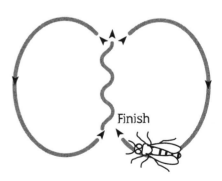

Finish

The scout bee dances following **half a circle.**

She dances following a **line** and **waggling** her **abdomen.** This **line** indicates the **direction** of the **flowers.**

The scout bee follows the **other half** of the **circle.**

THE WAGGLE DANCE
IF THE **FLOWERS** ARE MORE THAN **500 FEET AWAY,** THE SCOUT BEE DANCES THE **WAGGLE DANCE.** A **SLOW DANCE** INDICATES THAT THE **FLOWERS** ARE **VERY FAR AWAY.**

HONEYBEES

BEE STING

AT THE **END** OF THEIR **ABDOMEN,** WORKERS HAVE A **BARBED STINGER** THEY **USE** TO **ATTACK INTRUDERS.** THE STINGER RELEASES **VENOM,** WHICH CAUSES **INTENSE PAIN.** IT KEEPS RELEASING VENOM FOR **SIXTY SECONDS,** SO IT'S IMPORTANT TO **REMOVE** THE STINGER AS SOON AS POSSIBLE.

A STINGING BEE RELEASES AN **ALARM SMELL.** HER SISTERS **FOLLOW** THIS **SMELL** TO **LOCATE** AND **ATTACK** THE **INTRUDER.**

WHEN A BEE STINGS, THE STINGER **RIPS OFF** HER **GUTS** AND SHE **DIES.** BEES **SACRIFICE THEMSELVES** TO **PROTECT** THEIR **COLONY.**

BUG BITES

Some people are allergic to bees' venom and even just one sting can trigger an allergic reaction so severe that they can die.

HONEY

BEES DRINK **FLOWER NECTAR** WITH THEIR **STRAW-LIKE TONGUES.**
THEY **COLLECT** IT IN THEIR **HONEY-STOMACH,** A SPECIAL **SACK** IN
THEIR **STOMACHS** WHERE IT **DOESN'T** GET **DIGESTED.**

AT THE **HIVE,** BEES **REGURGITATE** THE **NECTAR** AND **DRINK** IT
AGAIN SEVERAL TIMES, THEN, THEY **STORE** IT IN THE **HONEYCOMBS.**

NECTAR IS ABOUT **80% WATER** AND **20% SUGAR,** WHILE **HONEY** IS
20% WATER AND **80% SUGAR.** SO, NECTAR TURNS INTO HONEY WHEN
ENOUGH **WATER EVAPORATES.**

BEES **EAT HONEY** IN
THE **WINTER MONTHS,** SO
BEEKEEPERS ARE CAREFUL
TO **LEAVE ENOUGH** FOR
THE **COLONY** TO **SURVIVE.**

ONE POUND OF
HONEY CONTAINS
THE **NECTAR** FROM
**TWO MILLION
FLOWERS.**

TEN BEES
PRODUCE **ONE
TABLESPOON**
OF **HONEY** IN
THEIR **LIFETIME.**

FORAGERS **VISIT**
UP TO ABOUT **100
FLOWERS** EVERY
DAY.

BEES **FLY 50,000
MILES** TO **COLLECT
NECTAR** ENOUGH FOR
ONE POUND OF **HONEY.**

HONEY **DOESN'T GET SPOILED
EASILY** BECAUSE IT CONTAINS **NATURAL
ANTIBACTERIAL PROPERTIES,
PRESERVATIVES, ANTIOXIDANTS,** AND
IS **SLIGHTLY ACID.** BECAUSE OF ITS
ANTISEPTIC PROPERTIES, HONEY HAS
BEEN USED TO **CURE WOUNDS, BURNS,**
AND **SORE THROAT** FOR **CENTURIES.**

HONEYBEES

ROYAL JELLY

ROYAL JELLY IS A **LIQUID** THAT WORKERS **SECRETE** FROM THEIR **MOUTHS.** IT LOOKS LIKE A **WHITE CREAM** AND IT'S ALSO CALLED **BEE MILK.** ROYAL JELLY CONTAINS **VITAMINS, PROTEINS,** AND **SUGARS,** AND GETS **SPOILED** VERY **EASILY.** BEES PRODUCE IT TO **EAT** IT **IMMEDIATELY.**

PROPOLIS

PROPOLIS IS A **STRONG ANTIBACTERIAL SUBSTANCE** THAT BEES PRODUCE MIXING **TREE RESINS** AND **SALIVA.** BEES USE PROPOLIS TO **PREVENT** THE SPREADING OF **GERMS.** IF A **DEAD ANIMAL** ENDS UP IN THE HIVE AND BEES **CAN'T CARRY** IT OUT, THEY **SEAL** IT WITH **PROPOLIS,** WHICH PREVENTS IT FROM **DECOMPOSING** AND **BREEDING DISEASE.**

WAX

BEES HAVE **EIGHT GLANDS** IN THEIR **ABDOMEN** THAT SECRETE **WAX.** BEES USE THEIR WAX TO **BUILD** AND **REPAIR HONEYCOMBS,** AND TO **SEAL CELLS** AFTER THEY HAVE BEEN **FILLED** WITH **HONEY.**

BUMBLEBEES

Endopterygota (insects with internal wing development)
Hymenoptera (insects with membranous wings)

THE **SCIENTIFIC NAME** OF THE **BUMBLEBEE** IS BOMBUS, WHICH MEANS **"BOOMING,"** DUE TO ITS **BUZZING SOUND.**

BUMBLEBEES **DIE** AT THE **END** OF THE **SUMMER.** ONLY THE **QUEEN SURVIVES,** AND SHE **REPOPULATES** HER **COLONY** EVERY YEAR.

THE **DISPROPORTION** BETWEEN THE BUMBLEBEE'S **BIG BODY** AND **SMALL WINGS** LED SCIENTISTS TO WONDER **HOW** THEY COULD **FLY.** THEY NOTICED THAT BUMBLEBEES **MOVE** THEIR **WINGS** IN **CIRCLES,** WHICH CREATE **TINY AIR VORTEXES** SUPPORTING THE BUMBLEBEE. SO, ALTHOUGH BUMBLEBEES HAVE BEEN **FLYING** FOR **THOUSANDS** OF **YEARS,** SCIENTISTS HAVE ONLY JUST **FIGURED OUT** HOW THEY ARE ABLE TO.

BUMBLEBEES ARE THE **ONLY BEES** ABLE TO **BUZZ-POLLINATE,** A **FAST** WAY TO GET **A LOT** OF **POLLEN.** THEY **HOLD** ONTO A FLOWER, **QUICKLY FLICKERING** THEIR **WINGS.** THE VIBRATION **DETACHES** THE **POLLEN,** WHICH **FALLS** AND GETS STUCK ON THE BUMBLEBEE.

AFRICANIZED HONEYBEES

Killer Bees

Endopterygota (insects with internal wing development)
Hymenoptera (insects with membranous wings)

WARWICK E. KERR, A BRAZILIAN ENTOMOLOGIST, BRED AN **AFRICAN SPECIES** WITH THE **ITALIAN HONEYBEE** TO CREATE THE **AFRICANIZED HONEYBEE,** WHICH PRODUCES **MORE HONEY.** UNFORTUNATELY, AFRICANIZED HONEYBEES TURNED OUT TO BE **VERY AGGRESSIVE** AND, IN **1957** A FEW **ESCAPED** KERR'S **LAB.** AFRICANIZED BEES **SPREAD** THROUGHOUT **SOUTH** AND **CENTRAL AMERICA,** AND, SINCE **1990,** THE **SOUTHERN STATES** OF THE **U.S.**

AFRICANIZED BEES **ATTACK** IN **LARGE NUMBERS** AND **CHASE** THEIR **VICTIM** FOR A **QUARTER** OF A **MILE.** THEY EVEN **AWAIT** HIM IF HE TRIES TO **HIDE UNDERWATER.** THEY ARE SO **AGGRESSIVE** THEY ARE NICKNAMED **KILLER BEES.**

THE **THREAT** THESE BEES POSE WILL **SOON END.** AFRICANIZED QUEENS **MATE** WITH **COMMON HONEYBEES** AND THEIR **OFFSPRING** ARE **LESS AGGRESSIVE** BEES.

CUCKOO BEES

Endopterygota (insects with internal wing development)
Hymenoptera (insects with membranous wings)

CUCKOO BEES ARE **PARASITES** OF **BEE COLONIES**. THE **BEHAVIOR** OF THIS BEE **RESEMBLES** THAT OF **CUCKOO BIRDS**, WHICH **DEPOSIT** THEIR **EGGS** IN **OTHER BIRDS' NESTS**. THE OTHER BIRD **DOESN'T NOTICE** THE **DIFFERENCE**, AND **REARS** THE **CUCKOO CHICKS** AS IF THEY WERE ITS **OWN**. IN A **SIMILAR WAY**, A **CUCKOO BEE QUEEN** ENTERS THE **HIVE** UNNOTICED, **KILLS** THE **QUEEN**, AND **DEPOSITS** HER **EGGS**. THE WORKERS **DON'T NOTICE** THE **SWITCH**, AND **REAR** THE **CUCKOO BEE'S BROOD**.

SOLITARY BEES

Endopterygota (insects with internal wing development)
Hymenoptera (insects with membranous wings)

SOLITARY BEES DON'T FORM COLONIES, DON'T PRODUCE HONEY, AND ONLY A FEW SPECIES PRODUCE WAX. SOME SPECIES DIG UNDERGROUND BURROWS, OTHERS NEST IN HOLLOW TREE TRUNKS.

FEMALES BUILD CELLS THEY FILL WITH EGGS AND SOME POLLEN FOR THE LARVAE, AND THEN SEAL THEM. WHEN THE EGGS HATCH, THE LARVAE EAT THE POLLEN, TURN INTO PUPAE, AND THEN BECOME ADULTS.

FEMALE BEES HATCH FROM THE EGGS DEPOSITED DEEPER IN THE HIVE, WHILE MALES HATCH FROM THE EGGS CLOSER TO THE EXIT. IN THIS WAY, THE MALE BEES ARE THE FIRST TO LEAVE THE CELL. THEY WAIT FOR THE FEMALES EXITING THE NEST TO MATE.

BUG BITES

There are many more species of solitary bees (over 18,000) than there are of communal bees (six species).

VELVET WASPS

Endopterygota (insects with internal wing development)
Hymenoptera (insects with membranous wings)

A **VELVET WASP'S BLACK BODY** IS COVERED BY **FUZZY, RED,** OR **ORANGE HAIR.** THEY **DON'T FLY** AND **LIVE** ON THE **GROUND,** SO PEOPLE OFTEN **CONFUSE** THEM WITH **ANTS.** IN FACT, THEY ARE SOMETIMES MISTAKENLY CALLED **VELVET ANTS.**

VELVET WASPS ARE **PARASITES** OF OTHER INSECTS, LIKE **WASPS, BEES,** AND **BEETLES.** VELVET WASPS **INFILTRATE WASPS'** OR **BEES' COLONIES.** THEY **DEPOSIT** THEIR **EGGS** IN THE SAME **CELLS** WHERE THERE ARE **WASP** OR **BEE LARVAE.** WHEN THE EGGS HATCH, THE **VELVET WASP LARVAE** EAT THE **WASPS' LARVAE.**

THE VELVET WASP'S **STINGER** IS **VERY LONG** AND **CURVED,** AND CAN INFLICT AN **EXTREMELY PAINFUL STING.** FOR THIS REASON, VELVET WASPS ARE ALSO CALLED **COW KILLERS** (BUT THEY CAN'T REALLY KILL A COW). VELVET WASP **MALES CAN'T STING.**

FEMALE VELVET WASPS **DON'T HAVE WINGS,** WHILE **MALES DO.**

WASPS

Endopterygota (insects with internal wing development)
Hymenoptera (insects with membranous wings)

JUST LIKE BEES, THERE ARE SPECIES OF **SOLITARY WASPS** AND SPECIES OF **WASPS** THAT LIVE IN **COLONIES.** MOST WASP SPECIES ARE **NOT HAIRY** LIKE HONEYBEES.

WASPS **DON'T PRODUCE HONEY** OR **WAX.**

YELLOW JACKETS AND **HORNETS LIVE** IN **COLONIES,** WHICH HAVE **THREE CASTES:** THE **QUEEN,** THE **DRONES,** AND THE **WORKERS.** EACH **CASTE** PERFORMS A **SPECIFIC TASK.** THE QUEEN LAYS **EGGS,** THE **DRONES** MATE WITH THE QUEEN, AND **WORKERS** CARE FOR THE **HIVE.**

THE **HIVE** IS MADE OF A **PAPER-LIKE FOIL** WASPS **PRODUCE** BY **CHEWING WOOD.** THE **COLONY DIES** OUT DURING THE **WINTER,** AND IS **REPOPULATED** BY THE **SURVIVING QUEEN** IN THE **SPRING.**

INSIDE THE HIVE, LARVAE ARE **FED CHEWED INSECTS** THAT WASPS **REGURGITATE.**

YELLOW JACKETS HAVE A **KEEN SENSE** OF **SMELL** AND **ARRIVE PROMPTLY** WHEN **PEOPLE** ARE HAVING A **PICNIC.** PEOPLE NEED TO **GENTLY GUIDE** THEM **AWAY** FROM FOOD BECAUSE YELLOW JACKETS ARE **AGGRESSIVE WASPS.** ALSO, IF DISTURBED, YELLOW JACKETS CAN **STING MANY TIMES.** THIS IS BECAUSE THE STINGER **DOESN'T EASILY** GET **RIPPED** FROM THE **WASP'S BODY** AS HAPPENS WITH THE STINGER OF THE BEE.

IN MANY SPECIES, **ADULT WASPS** EAT **POLLEN** AND **NECTAR,** WHILE THEIR **LARVAE** ARE **PARASITES** OF OTHER **INSECTS** OR **SPIDERS.** SOME WASPS EAT **FRUITS** AND **DEAD ANIMALS,** AND SOME ARE PREDATORS.

BUG BITES

W.A.S.P. is the acronym for Women Airforce Service Pilots. The W.A.S.P. were the first women in U.S. history to fly military airplanes during World War II.

POLLINATION

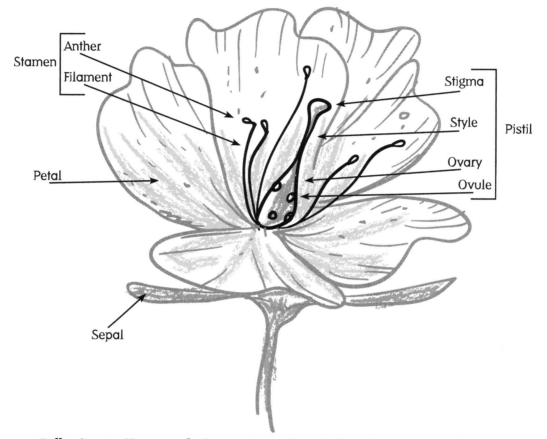

Stamen
Anther
Filament
Stigma
Style
Pistil
Petal
Ovary
Ovule
Sepal

Pollination is the way plants create seeds, which, in turn, create other plants. Many plants reproduce through pollination. To create a seed, the pollen is carried from one flower to another.

Many plants rely on insects to carry their pollen to other plants, or to receive pollen from other plants. These insects are called pollinators.

To attract pollinating insects, plants offer them food. This food is called nectar. Nectar is a sweet liquid made mainly of water and sugar. Plants secrete nectar from the bottom of their flowers, where it collects.

Insects are attracted to the nectar, but to reach the bottom of the flower they often brush against the anthers, which are covered in pollen. The pollen sticks on the insect. When the insect moves to another flower, some of the pollen from the previous flower ends up on the pistil of the second one. The pollen fertilizes the flower, which then produces a seed.

Plants and pollinating insects have a mutualistic relationship. This means that both the plant and the insect benefit from each other. The plant gets pollinated; the insect gets fed.

There are many pollinating insects, like bees, wasps, flies, and butterflies. But, there are other animals that pollinate plants, like bats and humming birds.

The pollen from a flower can only pollinate a flower of the same species. For example, pollen from a rose can only pollinate a rose of the same species.

STAMEN

THE **STAMEN** IS THE **MALE ORGAN** OF THE **FLOWER.** IT'S MADE UP OF THE **FILAMENT,** THE **ANTHER,** AND THE **POLLEN.**

POLLEN

POLLEN LOOK LIKE **POWDER** AND IS LOCATED ON THE **ANTHER.**

This bumblebee eats the nectar from the flower. Pollen sticks to her body.

FILAMENT

THE **FILAMENT** SUPPORTS THE **ANTHER.**

ANTHER

THE **ANTHER** PRODUCES **POLLEN.**

THE **PISTIL** IS THE **FEMALE ORGAN** OF THE **FLOWER.** IT'S MADE UP OF THE **STIGMA, STYLE,** AND **OVARY.**

STIGMA

THE **STIGMA** IS THE **TOP** OF THE **PISTIL.**

STYLE

THE **STYLE** IS A **TUBE** THAT CONNECTS THE **STIGMA** WITH THE **OVARY.**

When the bumblebee visits another flower, some of the pollen collected on her body ends on the pistil. Now this flower is fertilized and can create a seed.

OVARY

THE **OVARY** CONTAINS THE **OVULES.**

OVULES

THE **OVULES** AND THE **POLLEN** TOGETHER CREATE **SEEDS.**

ANTS

Endopterygota (insects with internal wing development)
Hymenoptera (insects with membranous wings)

ANTS LIVE IN **HIGHLY ORGANIZED COLONIES.** ANTS ARE DIVIDED INTO **THREE CASTES,** THE **QUEEN,** THE **WORKERS,** AND THE **MALE ANTS,** EACH PERFORMING **VERY DIFFERENT TASKS.**

THE QUEEN

WHEN A QUEEN STARTS A **NEW COLONY** AND THE **FOOD** IS **SCARCE,** THE **FIRST ANTS** ARE **SMALLER.** SOMETIMES THE **QUEEN** HAS TO **EAT** HER OWN **EGGS** IN ORDER TO **KEEP ALIVE** AND **CARE** FOR HER **BROOD.**

BUG BITES

Wasps first appeared during the late Jurassic period, about 150 million years ago. Ants descended from wasps and appeared in fossils that are about 120 million years old.

MALE ANTS

MALE ANTS HAVE **WINGS** BECAUSE THEY MATE WHILE **FLYING. THEY DIE** RIGHT AFTER MATING. MALE ANTS THAT DON'T MATE ARE UNABLE TO TAKE PART IN ANY **ACTIVITY** BENEFITING THE **COLONY.**

THE WORKERS

THE **WORKERS** ARE ALL **STERILE,** WHICH MEANS THAT THEY **CANNOT REPRODUCE,** AND THEY ARE **ALL FEMALES.**

EXCEPT FOR LAYING EGGS, THE **WORKERS PERFORM** ALL THE **ACTIVITIES** NEEDED TO KEEP THE **COLONY** RUNNING. THEY **FORAGE** FOR **FOOD, CHASE** AWAY **INTRUDERS, BUILD** AND **CLEAN** THE **NEST,** AND **CARE** FOR THE **BROOD.**

Ants should not be confused with termites. Ants are hymenoptera and descended from wasps, while termites are isoptera and descended from cockroaches.

ANTS

ANTS SEEM TO **KNOW** WHAT **JOB** NEEDS TO BE DONE AT ANY GIVEN TIME. FOR EXAMPLE, IF **FOOD** IS **NEEDED,** WORKERS START **FORAGING.** IF THEY ARE **UNDER ATTACK,** WORKERS RUN TO **DEFEND** THEIR **COLONY.** HOW CAN ANT COLONIES BE SO **EFFICIENT** WHEN THERE IS **NO ONE IN CHARGE?** THE QUEEN, IN FACT, **DOES NOT SUPERVISE** THE WORKERS OR **GIVE** ANY **ORDERS.**

SCIENTISTS HAVE DISCOVERED THAT ANTS **COORDINATE** THE **WORK** BY **COMMUNICATING** WITH EACH OTHER WITH **CHEMICALS.** FOR EXAMPLE, **FORAGING ANTS** SECRETE A **SPECIFIC CHEMICAL.** THE **SMELL** OF THIS CHEMICAL IS VERY **DIFFERENT** FROM THAT SECRETED BY **ANTS CARING** FOR THE **BROOD.** IF THERE ARE **TOO MANY ANTS FORAGING** AND **NOT ENOUGH ANTS CARING** FOR THE **BROOD,** THERE WILL ALSO BE **A LOT** OF **"FORAGING"** CHEMICALS, AND FEW **"CARING FOR THE BROOD"** CHEMICALS. ANTS PERCEIVE THIS **IMBALANCE** AND SOME ANTS WILL **SWITCH TASKS,** BRINGING THE **BALANCE BACK.**

BUG BITES

There are over 9,000 species of ants described so far, but scientists predict that there are over 10,000 to be discovered yet.

THE SAME HAPPENS WHEN ANTS **LOOK** FOR **FOOD**. WHEN AN **ANT** FINDS SOME **FOOD**, SHE BRINGS IT BACK TO THE **NEST**. ON HER WAY BACK, THE ANT **LEAVES** A **TRAIL** OF **CHEMICALS**. OTHER ANTS **PICK UP** THE **SCENT**. THEY TOO WILL **LEAVE** A **TRAIL** OF **CHEMICALS**, MAKING THE **SMELL** OF THE ORIGINAL TRAIL EVEN **STRONGER**.

WHEN THE FOOD IS ALL **PICKED OUT**, THE ANTS **STOP LEAVING** CHEMICALS ALONG THE **TRAIL**. THE SMELL GETS WEAKER, AND THIS WILL **DISCOURAGE** OTHER ANTS FROM **FOLLOWING** THAT **PARTICULAR TRAIL**.

ANTS EAT **SEEDS**, FRUIT, **INSECT EGGS**, INSECTS, AND **CARCASSES**.

CHEMICALS TELL WORKERS WHICH **ANTS** BELONG TO THEIR **COLONY** AND WHICH DO NOT. IF AN ANT DOESN'T HAVE THE **CORRECT** **"SMELL"** IT WILL BE CONSIDERED AN **INTRUDER**, AND IN MOST CASES **CHASED AWAY** OR **KILLED**.

AN ANT COLONY CAN HAVE **MORE THAN ONE QUEEN**. SOMETIMES, **SEVERAL** COLONIES CAN **AGGREGATE** AND BECOME A **SUPER-COLONY**. THE BIGGEST SUPER-COLONY KNOWN SO FAR STRETCHES FOR **4,000 MILES**, FROM THE **COAST** OF **PORTUGAL** TO THE **MEDITERRANEAN COAST** OF **SPAIN, SOUTHERN FRANCE**, AND **NORTHERN ITALY**. THIS SUPER-COLONY IS MADE UP OF **BILLIONS** OF **ANTS**.

ANTS

SOME SPECIES OF ANTS **HERD** PLANT PARASITES CALLED **APHIDS,** WHICH FEED ON **PLANT SAP!** THE APHIDS OOZE A SUGARY FLUID CALLED **HONEYDEW** FROM THEIR **ANUS.** ANTS **DRINK** THIS FLUID AND, IN EXCHANGE, **PROTECT** THE APHIDS FROM **PREDATORS** AND OFTEN **MOVE** THEM TO PLANTS **RICHER** IN **SAP.** APHIDS ARE **PROMPTED** TO OOZE HONEYDEW WHEN ANTS **MASSAGE** THEM WITH THEIR LEGS OR ANTENNAE.

HONEY POT ANTS USE THEIR **BODIES** TO STORE **FOOD.** THEY **DRINK** AND **COLLECT** NECTAR IN THEIR **ABDOMEN,** WHICH BECOMES **SO BIG** THAT THE ANTS CANNOT MOVE. THESE ANTS **HANG** FROM THE **CEILING** OF THEIR NEST **STORAGE ROOMS.** WHEN FOOD IS SCARCE, THE HONEY POT ANTS **REGURGITATE** THE **NECTAR** FOR THEIR SISTERS TO **DRINK.** SOMETIMES **ANTS** FROM A DIFFERENT COLONY **STEAL** THE **HONEY POT ANTS** FOR THEIR **JUICE,** AND EVEN **PEOPLE** LIKE TO **SQUEEZE** THEM TO DRINK THE **NECTAR.**

LEAFCUTTER ANTS EAT A **FUNGUS** THAT THEY **GROW** IN THEIR **NEST.** THESE ANTS **CUT** THE **LEAVES** OF **TREES** TO PRODUCE A **FERTILIZER** FOR THE **FUNGUS.** WHEN A **NEW QUEEN** LEAVES THE **COLONY** TO START HER OWN, SHE **BRINGS** WITH

RED FIRE ANTS ARE THE **MOST VENOMOUS** SPECIES OF ANTS. THEY WERE ACCIDENTALLY IMPORTED FROM **SOUTH AMERICA** TO **MOBILE, ALABAMA,** IN 1930, BY A CARGO SHIP. RED FIRE ANTS ARE FOUND IN THE **SOUTHERN STATES** OF THE **U.S.**

FIRE ANTS GET THEIR **NAME** FROM THEIR **VENOM,** WHICH GIVES A **BURNING SENSATION,** LIKE **FIRE,** WHEN INJECTED. EACH STING PRODUCES A **VERY ITCHING PUSTULE,** WHICH MIGHT BECOME **INFECTED** AND **LEAVE A SCAR** IF **SCRATCHED.**

RED FIRE ANTS NEST IN **SUNNY AREAS,** ESPECIALLY ON **GRASSLAND, OPEN FIELDS,** OR **PLAYGROUNDS.** THEY BUILD A **NEST** AND **COVER** ITS **ENTRANCE** WITH A **DOME** MADE OF **DIRT GRANULES.** THIS DOME CAN BE **20 INCHES HIGH.** UNDER THE GROUND, FIRE ANTS DIG A **NEST** THAT CAN BE **5 FEET DEEP.**

FIRE ANTS ARE **VERY AGGRESSIVE.** A FIRE ANT IN **DANGER** SECRETES A **CHEMICAL** THAT **ATTRACTS** HER **SISTERS.** THEY WILL **ATTACK** THE **INTRUDER** UNTIL IT **RUNS AWAY** OR **DIES.**

ONCE SHE FINDS THE INTRUDER, THE FIRE ANT FIRST **BITES** IT WITH HER **JAWS.** WHEN SHE HAS A **GOOD HOLD** OF HER **VICTIM'S SKIN,** THE FIRE ANT **STINGS** IT WITH THE STINGER AT THE **TIP** OF HER **ABDOMEN.** THE STINGER **INJECTS** HER **POWERFUL VENOM** INTO THE **VICTIM.** SWINGING AROUND, AND STILL HOLDING ON WITH HER JAWS, THE FIRE ANT CAN **STING REPEATEDLY,** EVEN WHEN SHE **RUNS OUT** OF VENOM.

BUTTERFLIES

Endopterygota (insects with internal wing development)
Lepidoptera (insects with scales on their wings)

THE SCIENTIFIC NAME **LEPIDOPTERA** MEANS "**INSECTS WITH SCALES ON THEIR WINGS.**" IN FACT, THESE INSECTS' WINGS ARE **COVERED** BY **TINY** AND **OVERLAPPING SCALES,** ARRANGED LIKE **SHINGLES** ON A **ROOF.** THE SCALES ARE **COLORFUL, IRIDESCENT,** AND OFTEN **FORM PATTERNS** AND **INTRICATE DESIGNS.**

The pipeline swallowtail is a poisonous butterfly and some predators avoid eating it.

The black swallowtail is not poisonous, but mimics the pipeline swallowtail's wing design in order to avoid being eaten.

IN SOME SPECIES, THE **WING DESIGNS** ARE A **WARNING** THAT THE **BUTTERFLY** IS **POISONOUS. PREDATORS,** LIKE BIRDS, LEARN TO **RECOGNIZE** THESE **DESIGNS** AND **AVOID EATING** THAT SPECIES OF BUTTERFLIES.

OTHER SPECIES ARE **NOT POISONOUS,** BUT THEIR WINGS **MIMIC** THE **DESIGNS** OF THE **POISONOUS BUTTERFLIES.** WITH THIS TRICK THEY **KEEP PREDATORS AWAY.** THIS BEHAVIOR IS CALLED **MIMICRY.**

OTHER **BUTTERFLIES**, ESPECIALLY **MOTHS**, CAMOUFLAGE THEMSELVES IN THE **ENVIRONMENT** WITH **WINGS** THAT **LOOK LIKE BARK** OR **LEAVES**.

MANY BUTTERFLIES HAVE **SPOTS** THAT **LOOK LIKE EYES** ON THEIR **HIND WINGS**. MANY PREDATORS **ATTACK** FROM **BEHIND**, USING THE **ELEMENT** OF **SURPRISE** TO **OVERCOME** THEIR **VICTIM**. BUT, WHEN THEY **SEE THE "EYES"** THEY THINK THAT THAT'S THE **FRONT** OF THE **BUTTERFLY**, AND THEY TRY TO **ATTACK FROM** THE **OTHER SIDE**. HAVING **FOOLED** ITS **POTENTIAL PREDATOR**, THE **BUTTERFLY SEES** IT AND **FLIES** SAFELY **AWAY!**

BUTTERFLIES	MOTHS
MOST SPECIES ARE **DIURNAL**.	MOST SPECIES ARE **NOCTURNAL**.
THE **ANTENNAE** ARE GENERALLY **THIN** WITH A **KNOB** AT THE **TIP**.	THE **ANTENNAE** ARE **FEATHERY**.
WHEN AT **REST**, THEY KEEP THEIR WINGS **CLOSE TOGETHER** AND **UPRIGHT**.	THEY KEEP THEIR WINGS **FOLDED BACK** LIKE A **TENT**, OR **SPREAD OPEN**.
BUTTERFLY **PUPAE** ARE **ENCASED** IN A **SHELL**.	MOTH **LARVAE** SPIN A **SILKY COCOON** IN WHICH THEY **PUPATE**.
THE **BODY** OF A BUTTERFLY IS **THINNER** AND COVERED BY TINY HAIR.	THE **BODY** OF A MOTH IS **STOUTER** AND COVERED BY THICKER HAIR.
BUTTERFLIES ARE MORE **COLORFUL**.	MOTHS ARE **DULLER**.

BUTTERFLIES

BUTTERFLIES **TASTE** PLANT **LEAVES** WITH THEIR **FEET** AND **DEPOSIT** THEIR **EGGS** ON THE **PLANTS** THAT THE **CATERPILLARS** WILL **EAT.** THIS IS BECAUSE SOME CATERPILLARS ONLY EAT **ONE KIND** OF **PLANT,** WHILE OTHERS HAVE A MORE **VARIED DIET.**

ONCE IT HATCHES, THE **CATERPILLAR** STARTS **EATING IMMEDIATELY. CATERPILLARS** NEED TO **GROW** ABOUT **25,000 TIMES** THEIR **SIZE** AND **STORE ENERGY.** THIS IS BECAUSE WHEN THEY **PUPATE,** THEY **CAN'T EAT.**

MOST CATERPILLARS EAT **PLANTS,** BUT SOME SPECIES ARE **CARNIVOROUS** AND EAT **SMALL INSECTS.**

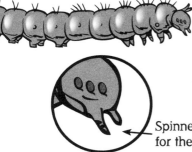

Caterpillars have six ocelli on the lower part of their head, but they can't see well.

Spinnerets produce silk for the cocoon.

WHEN THEY **PUPATE,** CATERPILLARS FORM A **CHRYSALIS (OR SHELL)** FROM THEIR **LAST MOLT'S EXOSKELETON.** THE CHRYSALIS IS **ATTACHED** TO A **TWIG** WITH A **SILK PAD,** SPUN BY THE CATERPILLAR'S **SPINNERETS,** WHICH ARE **ORGANS** IN ITS MOUTH, AND THE **CREMASTER,** A **HOOK-LIKE APPENDAGE** AT THE END OF THE CATERPILLAR'S **ABDOMEN.** OTHERS CREATE **GIRDLE-LIKE BANDS** TO **SUPPORT** THE **PUPA.** IT'S DURING THIS TIME THAT THE **CATERPILLAR** TURNS INTO A **BUTTERFLY.**

Silk pad
Cremaster

Silk band

AS SOON AS THEY **EMERGE** FROM THE CHRYSALIS, **BUTTERFLIES** NEED TO HANG **UPSIDE DOWN** FROM PLANTS. THIS IS BECAUSE THEY NEED TO **FILL** THE **VEINS** IN THEIR **WINGS** WITH **HEMOLYMPH,** OR **BLOOD,** OTHERWISE THEY **WON'T** BE ABLE TO **FLY.**

BUG BITES

The term **chrysalis** means "golden" in Greek. This is because many caterpillars form a golden-colored pupa.

CATERPILLARS NEED TO **PROTECT THEMSELVES** BECAUSE THEY ARE **VERY NUTRITIOUS** FOR MANY **PREDATORS**, LIKE BIRDS, WASPS, AND SPIDERS. SOME CATERPILLARS HAVE **STINGING SPINES** ON THEIR BACKS. OTHERS ARE **TOXIC** BECAUSE THEY **FEED** ON **POISONOUS PLANTS**. OTHERS **SECRETE A NOXIOUS CHEMICAL** FROM AN **ORGAN** CALLED THE **OSMETERIUM**. SOME CATERPILLARS **HIDE** IN THE VEGETATION, WHILE OTHERS **LOOK LIKE BIRD POOP**. SOME **SCARE** THEIR **PREDATORS** AWAY WITH THE **EYESPOTS** (SPOTS THAT LOOK LIKE EYES) ON THEIR **BACKS**, WHICH MAKE THEM LOOK LIKE **BIGGER** AND **INTIMIDATING ANIMALS**.

Black swallowtail caterpillars are poisonous.

Zebra butterfly caterpillars and saddlebacks have stinging spines.

Eyespot

Tiger swallowtail caterpillars have eyespots.

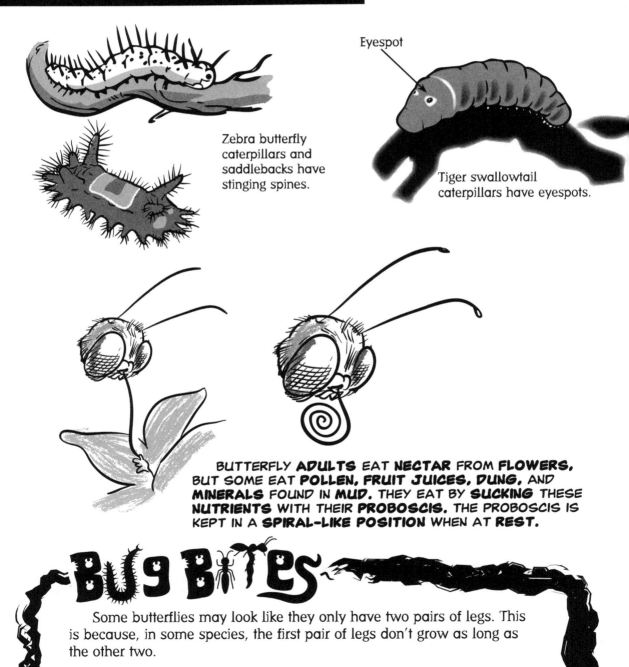

BUTTERFLY **ADULTS** EAT **NECTAR** FROM **FLOWERS**, BUT SOME EAT **POLLEN, FRUIT JUICES, DUNG,** AND **MINERALS** FOUND IN **MUD**. THEY EAT BY **SUCKING** THESE **NUTRIENTS** WITH THEIR **PROBOSCIS**. THE PROBOSCIS IS KEPT IN A **SPIRAL-LIKE POSITION** WHEN AT **REST**.

BUG BITES

Some butterflies may look like they only have two pairs of legs. This is because, in some species, the first pair of legs don't grow as long as the other two.

BUTTERFLIES

BUTTERFLIES HAVE **COMPOUND EYES** AND ARE ABLE TO **SEE ULTRAVIOLET LIGHT.** MANY SPECIES HAVE **DESIGNS** ON THEIR **WINGS VISIBLE** IN THIS KIND OF LIGHT.

BUTTERFLIES **TASTE** WITH THEIR **FEET** AND THEIR **PALPS,** **HAIR-LIKE ORGANS** ON THE **SIDES** OF THEIR **MOUTHS,** WHICH ARE **SENSITIVE TO SUGARS** AND OTHER **CHEMICALS.** THEY **SMELL** WITH THEIR **ANTENNAE.**

This is how big these butterflies really are when compared to a person's hand.

The Queen Alexandra birdwing butterfly

BIRDWINGS ARE **BUTTERFLIES** WITH **HUGE WINGS.** THEY GET THEIR NAME BECAUSE THEY **FLY** IN A **BIRD-LIKE WAY.** SOME OF THE **BIGGEST BUTTERFLIES** BELONG TO THIS GROUP. ONE IS THE **QUEEN ALEXANDRA,** WITH A **WINGSPAN OF 15 INCHES;** ANOTHER IS THE **GOLIATH BIRDWING,** WITH A **WINGSPAN OF 12 INCHES.**

The Goliath birdwing

Skippers are a group of small butterflies. They are named skippers because they are much faster than the other butterflies.

SILK

THE **SILKWORM**, THE **CATERPILLAR** OF A SPECIES OF **MOTH**, PRODUCES **SILK**, A MATERIAL USED TO MAKE **FABRIC** FOR **CLOTHING**, **FURNISHING**, AND **CARPETS**. THESE MOTHS ARE **DOMESTICATED**, **CANNOT FLY**, AND **CANNOT SURVIVE** IN THE **WILD**.

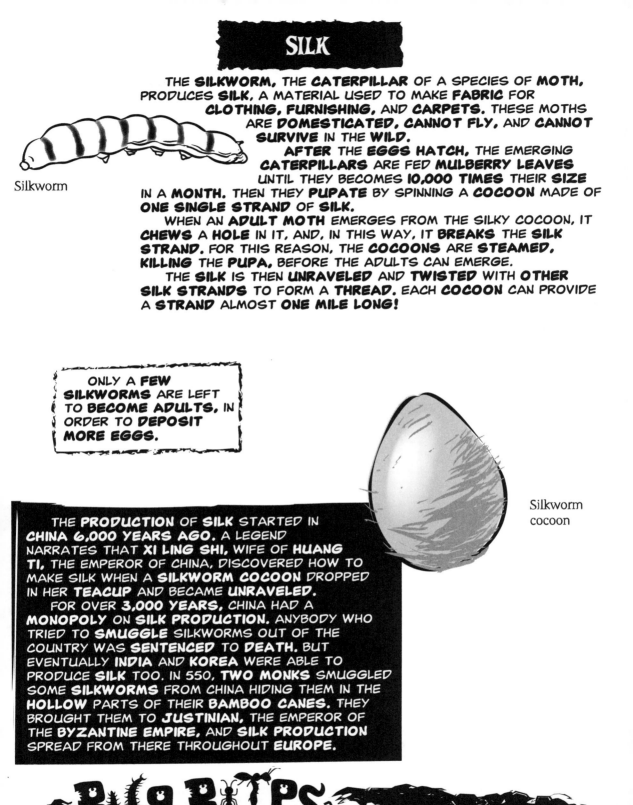

Silkworm

AFTER THE **EGGS HATCH**, THE EMERGING **CATERPILLARS** ARE FED **MULBERRY LEAVES** UNTIL THEY BECOMES **10,000 TIMES** THEIR **SIZE** IN A **MONTH**. THEN THEY **PUPATE** BY SPINNING A **COCOON** MADE OF **ONE SINGLE STRAND** OF **SILK**.

WHEN AN **ADULT MOTH** EMERGES FROM THE SILKY COCOON, IT **CHEWS** A **HOLE** IN IT, AND, IN THIS WAY, IT **BREAKS** THE **SILK STRAND**. FOR THIS REASON, THE **COCOONS** ARE **STEAMED**, **KILLING** THE **PUPA**, BEFORE THE ADULTS CAN EMERGE.

THE **SILK** IS THEN **UNRAVELED** AND **TWISTED** WITH **OTHER SILK STRANDS** TO FORM A **THREAD**. EACH **COCOON** CAN PROVIDE A **STRAND** ALMOST **ONE MILE LONG!**

ONLY A **FEW SILKWORMS** ARE LEFT TO **BECOME ADULTS**, IN ORDER TO **DEPOSIT MORE EGGS**.

Silkworm cocoon

THE **PRODUCTION** OF **SILK** STARTED IN **CHINA 6,000 YEARS AGO**. A LEGEND NARRATES THAT **XI LING SHI**, WIFE OF **HUANG TI**, THE EMPEROR OF CHINA, DISCOVERED HOW TO MAKE SILK WHEN A **SILKWORM COCOON** DROPPED IN HER **TEACUP** AND BECAME **UNRAVELED**.

FOR OVER **3,000 YEARS**, CHINA HAD A **MONOPOLY** ON **SILK PRODUCTION**. ANYBODY WHO TRIED TO **SMUGGLE** SILKWORMS OUT OF THE COUNTRY WAS **SENTENCED** TO **DEATH**. BUT EVENTUALLY **INDIA** AND **KOREA** WERE ABLE TO PRODUCE **SILK** TOO. IN 550, **TWO MONKS** SMUGGLED SOME **SILKWORMS** FROM CHINA HIDING THEM IN THE **HOLLOW** PARTS OF THEIR **BAMBOO CANES**. THEY BROUGHT THEM TO **JUSTINIAN**, THE EMPEROR OF THE **BYZANTINE EMPIRE**, AND **SILK PRODUCTION** SPREAD FROM THERE THROUGHOUT **EUROPE**.

BUG BITES

The larvae of a species of moths feed on clothes made of natural fibers, like wool. Mothballs are often used to keep these moths away. The adults don't feed and die right after mating.

SCORPIONFLIES

Exopterygota (insects with external wing development)
Mecoptera (insects with long wings)

HANGINGFLIES, A SPECIES OF SCORPIONFLIES, HANG FROM PLANTS WITH THEIR FRONT LEGS AND CATCH INSECTS THAT FLY BY.

THESE INSECTS EVOLVED IN THE PERMIAN PERIOD, 300 MILLION YEARS AGO. FLIES, BUTTERFLIES, AND FLEAS DESCENDED FROM THEM.

SCORPIONFLIES EAT INSECTS DEAD OR ALIVE, AND ROTTING PLANTS. SOME SPECIES ARE ABLE TO STEAL PREY FROM SPIDER WEBS.

TO **ATTRACT** A **MATE**, THE **MALE** SCORPIONFLY OFFERS THE **FEMALE** A BIT OF **FOOD** AS A GIFT. SOME MALES ATTRACT FEMALES BY **REGURGITATING FOOD** FOR THEM TO **EAT**. OFTEN MALES **STEAL** FOOD FROM ONE ANOTHER, EITHER BY **FORCE** OR POSING AS **FEMALES**.

THE **SCORPIONFLY'S CURVED** AND **POINTY ABDOMEN** RESEMBLES A **SCORPION'S STINGER**, BUT SCORPIONFLIES **CAN'T STING**.

MECOPTERA MEANS "INSECTS WITH **LONG WINGS**." IN SOME SPECIES, THE **ADULTS** DON'T HAVE **WINGS** AND **CAN'T FLY**.

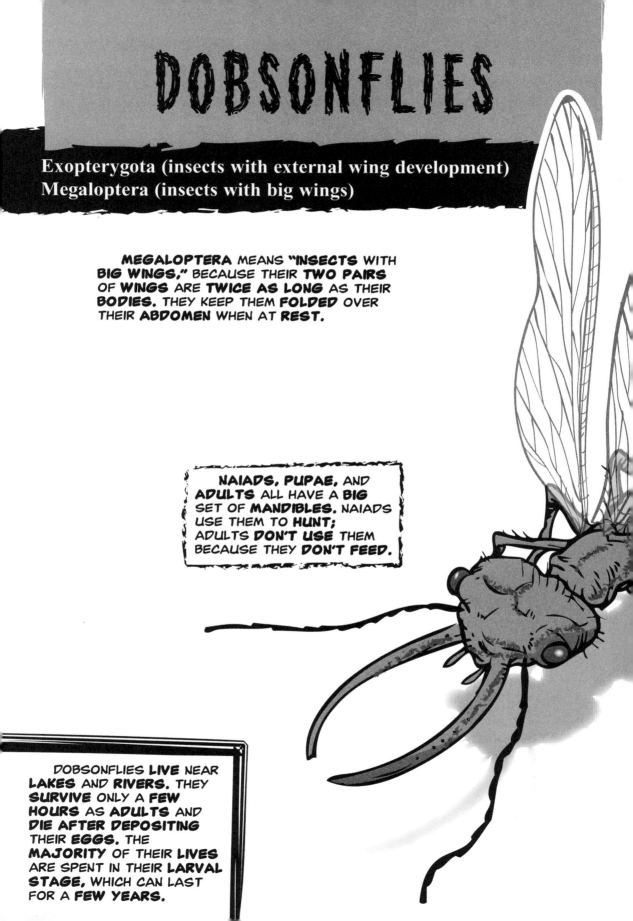

DOBSONFLIES

Exopterygota (insects with external wing development)
Megaloptera (insects with big wings)

MEGALOPTERA MEANS **"INSECTS** WITH **BIG WINGS,"** BECAUSE THEIR **TWO PAIRS** OF **WINGS** ARE **TWICE AS LONG** AS THEIR **BODIES.** THEY KEEP THEM **FOLDED** OVER THEIR **ABDOMEN** WHEN AT **REST.**

NAIADS, PUPAE, AND **ADULTS** ALL HAVE A **BIG** SET OF **MANDIBLES.** NAIADS USE THEM TO **HUNT;** ADULTS **DON'T USE** THEM BECAUSE THEY **DON'T FEED.**

DOBSONFLIES **LIVE NEAR LAKES** AND **RIVERS.** THEY **SURVIVE** ONLY A **FEW HOURS** AS **ADULTS** AND **DIE AFTER DEPOSITING** THEIR **EGGS.** THE **MAJORITY** OF THEIR **LIVES** ARE SPENT IN THEIR **LARVAL STAGE,** WHICH CAN LAST FOR A **FEW YEARS.**

DOBSONFLY **NAIADS** ARE CALLED **HELLGRAMMITES**. **FISHERMEN** CATCH THEM TO USE THEM AS **BAIT**. DOBSONFLY **NAIADS** EAT **INSECTS, LARVAE,** AND **SMALL INVERTEBRATES** THEY **HUNT** IN THE **WATER.** NAIADS **CRAWL OUT** OF THE **WATER** TO **PUPATE.** THE **PUPA** IS **ACTIVE, FEEDS,** AND EVEN **BITES** IN **SELF-DEFENSE.**

WHEN THEY **FEEL THREATENED,** DOBSONFLIES SPRAY A **STINKING CHEMICAL** FROM THEIR **ANUS.**

BUG BITES

Dobsonfly females can deposit up to 3,000 eggs!

FLEAS

Endopterygota (insects with internal wing development)
Siphonaptera (wingless insects with a pipe-like mouth)

FLEAS ARE **PARASITES** OF MAMMALS AND **BIRDS** AND **FEED** ON **BLOOD.** ALTHOUGH FLEAS ARE NOT PICKY EATERS, THEY HAVE A **PREFERRED HOST.** SO, **CAT FLEAS** MIGHT BITE THE **CAT'S OWNER,** BUT PREFER TO **LIVE** ON THE **CAT.**

THE TERM **SIPHONAPTERA** IS COMPOSED OF THREE WORDS: **"SIPHON"** OR "PIPE," **"A"** OR "WITHOUT," AND **"PTERA"** OR "WINGS." FLEAS ARE **WINGLESS INSECTS** WITH A **PIPE-LIKE MOUTH** FOR SUCKING **BLOOD.**

FLEAS ARE **SMALL INSECTS,** ONLY UP TO **1/8** OF AN **INCH LONG.** THE **EXOSKELETON** IS **TOUGH** AND CAN ENDURE PRESSURE. IN FACT, IT'S **VERY HARD** TO **KILL** A FLEA SIMPLY **SQUEEZING** IT BETWEEN TWO FINGERS. THIS IS BECAUSE FLEAS HAVE TO **SURVIVE** BEING **SCRATCHED.**

THE **BODY** OF THE FLEA IS **FLATTENED** AND COVERED WITH **SPINES POINTING BACK.** THESE TWO **FEATURES** MAKE IT **EASY** FOR THE FLEAS TO **SCUTTLE AROUND** THICK **FUR** OR **FEATHERS.** ALSO, THE **SPINES** HELP THE FLEA TO **STAY** PUT WHEN THE **HOST GROOMS** OR **SCRATCHES** ITSELF.

FLEAS HAVE VERY **LONG HIND LEGS** AND CAN **JUMP** OVER **100 TIMES** THEIR **BODY LENGTH** AND **50 TIMES** THEIR **BODY HEIGHT!** A FLEA'S **JUMP** CAN BE **13-INCH LONG** AND **7-INCH HIGH.**

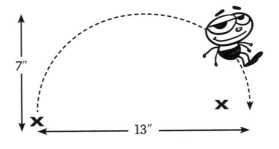

7"

13"

FLEAS

FLEAS HAVE A **COMPLETE METAMORPHOSIS**. FEMALES **DEPOSIT** THE **EGGS** ON THEIR **HOST**. EACH FEMALE CAN LAY **700 EGGS** IN HER LIFE! **ALMOST 75%** OF THE EGGS **FALL OFF** THE **HOST**. **EGGS** AND **LARVAE** ARE OFTEN FOUND WHERE **PETS SPEND** MOST OF THEIR **TIME**, LIKE THEIR **BEDS**.

THE **LARVAE** ARE VERY **DIFFERENT** FROM THE **ADULT FLEAS**, AND LOOK LIKE **WORMS**. THEY ARE **WHITE** AND **BLIND**. THEY **SCAVENGE** ON BITS OF **SKIN** OR **FEATHERS** SHED BY THEIR **HOSTS**, OR **ADULT FLEAS'** **FECES**, WHICH **CONTAIN BLOOD**.

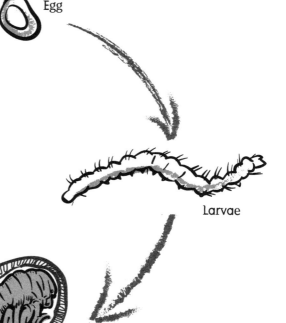
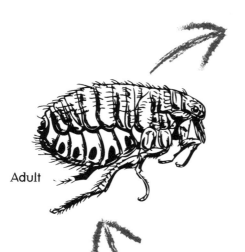

Egg

Larvae

Pupa

Adult

LARVAE SPIN A **SILKY COCOON**, **CAMOUFLAGING** THEM WITH BITS OF **DEBRIS**. THE **PUPAL STAGE** CAN LAST FOR **SIX MONTHS**, AND **ADULTS** EMERGE ONLY WHEN THEY **FEEL THE PRESENCE** OF A **HOST**. FLEAS SENSE **BODY HEAT**, **SWEAT**, AND **SMELL**. FOR THIS REASON, A **HOST** RETURNING TO ITS **NEST** AFTER A PERIOD OF **ABSENCE** OFTEN TRIGGERS **INFESTATIONS**.

THE NEWLY EMERGED **ADULT FLEAS** CAN GO FOR **ONE YEAR WITHOUT EATING**, BUT FEEDING ON **BLOOD** IS **NECESSARY** FOR FLEAS. **FEMALES** THAT DON'T FEED ON BLOOD **CANNOT DEPOSIT EGGS**.

FLEAS CARRY THE **BUBONIC PLAGUE**, OR **BLACK DEATH**, A FATAL DISEASE.
BUBONIC PLAGUE IS CAUSED BY A **BACTERIUM**. IF UNTREATED, INFECTED
PEOPLE DEVELOP **BUBOES** (SWELLING IN THE ARMPITS AND THIGHS), **HIGH
FEVER**, AND **DIE**.

FLEAS BECOME **INFECTED** WHEN THEY **BITE INFECTED RATS**. THE BACTERIA
MAKE **FLEAS UNABLE TO DIGEST**, AND THE **STARVING FLEAS** START **BITING
OTHER ANIMALS**, INCLUDING **PEOPLE**, TRYING TO SATISFY THEIR HUNGER. WHEN
FLEAS BITE, THEY OFTEN **VOMIT** IN THE **WOUND, SPREADING BACTERIA**.

IT WAS ESTIMATED THAT, IN THE **PAST**, THE THREE BUBONIC PLAGUE
PANDEMICS **KILLED OVER 125 MILLION PEOPLE. TODAY**, THIS DISEASE IS
EASILY TREATED WITH ANTIBIOTICS.

BUG BITES

Flea circuses were a popular attraction at the end of the 1800s. Fleas
appeared to be performing actions, like pulling a chariot, or walking on a
suspended wire while holding objects. In reality the shows were a mix of
optical illusions and tricks, with mostly dead fleas glued to props.

TWISTED-WINGED PARASITES

Endopterygota (insects with internal wing development)
Strepsiptera (insects with twisted wings)

A **TWISTED-WINGED PARASITE** IS AN **INSECT** THAT LIVES AT THE **EXPENSE** OF **ANOTHER INSECT,** CALLED A **HOST.** INSECTS THAT HOST TWISTED-WINGED PARASITES ARE **WASPS, BEES,** AND **SILVERFISH.**

TWISTED-WINGED PARASITE **FEMALES** LIVE THEIR ENTIRE LIVES **WEDGED** BETWEEN THE **SEGMENTS** OF THE **ABDOMEN** OF THEIR **HOSTS,** WITH ONLY THE **HEADS VISIBLE.** THE PARASITES **FEED** ON THE **BLOOD** OF THEIR **HOSTS,** WITHOUT KILLING THEM.

Female twisted-winged parasites wedged inside a wasp's abdomen.

ADULT MALES ONLY **LIVE** FOR A **FEW HOURS.** DURING THIS TIME, THEY NEED TO **FIND** A **FEMALE** AND **MATE. ADULT MALES DON'T EAT.**

Head

Twisted-winged parasite female

FEMALE PARASITE ADULTS HAVE **NO LEGS, EYES,** OR **WINGS. ADULT MALES,** ON THE OTHER HAND, **FLY AWAY** FROM THEIR HOST AT THE END OF THE **PUPAL STAGE.**

Male twisted-winged parasite

TWISTED-WINGED PARASITE **FEMALES** DON'T DEPOSIT THEIR **EGGS. EGGS** HATCH **INSIDE** THE **FEMALE BODY.** A FEMALE PRODUCES **THOUSANDS** OF **EGGS.**

LARVAE JUMP FROM THEIR MOTHER'S **HOST** AND LAND ON **ANOTHER.** THEY SECRETE **DIGESTIVE FLUIDS** THAT **SOFTEN** THE **EXOSKELETON** OF THE NEW HOST, ALLOWING THE LARVAE TO **WEDGE THEMSELVES INSIDE** ITS **BODY.**

AFTER EMERGING FROM THE **PUPAL STAGE,** TWISTED-WINGED PARASITE **MALES** WILL **FLY AWAY.** TWISTED-WINGED PARASITE **FEMALES** WILL **REMAIN WEDGED INSIDE** THEIR **HOST.**

CADDISFLIES

Endopterygota (insects with internal wing development)
Trichoptera (insects with hairy wings)

TRICHOPTERA MEANS **"HAIRY WINGS"** BECAUSE **CADDISFLIES' WINGS** ARE **COVERED** WITH **TINY HAIR.**

IN SOME SPECIES, NAIADS **SPIN SILK** FROM **ORGANS** IN THEIR **MOUTH** TO BUILD A **SMALL CASE,** OR CONTAINER. OTHERS MAKE THEIR CASE WITH **SILT.** NAIADS **DRAG** THEIR CASE AROUND AND USE IT FOR **PROTECTION,** TO AMBUSH **PREY,** AND TO **PUPATE.**

EACH **SPECIES** OF CADDISFLY NAIAD BUILDS A **SPECIFIC CASE.** SOME LOOK LIKE **TUBES** AND THE NAIADS **ENLARGE** THEM AS THEY **GROW.** SOME LOOK LIKE **SMALL DOMES.** NAIADS HAVE TO BUILD **NEW ONES** WHEN THEY **OUTGROW** THEM. A FEW SPECIES ONLY BUILD A CASE TO **PUPATE.**

CADDISFLY NAIADS **LIVE** IN **FRESH WATERS.** THEY DON'T HAVE WINGS LIKE THE ADULT CADDISFLIES, AND **BREATHE** THROUGH **GILLS.** NAIADS HAVE **BIG MANDIBLES** TO PREY ON WATER **INVERTEBRATES** OR TO EAT **ALGAE,** DEPENDING ON THE SPECIES.

IT HAS BEEN SUGGESTED THAT THE COMMON NAME **CADDISFLY** COMES FROM THE TERM **"CADDICE MEN."** THESE PEOPLE WERE **STREET VENDORS** OF **RIBBONS** AND **FABRICS** IN THE **1600S.** CADDICE MEN USED TO **SHOWCASE** THEIR **WARES** BY **PINNING** THEM TO THEIR **CLOTHES.** SIMILARLY, CADDISFLY **NAIADS** ATTACH **BITS** OF **DEBRIS,** LIKE ALGAE AND **SAND,** TO THEIR CASE TO **CAMOUFLAGE** IT.

AT THE **END** OF THE **PUPAL STAGE,** THE PUPA EMERGES FROM THE COCOON AND **SWIMS** TO THE **SHORE.** AFTER CRAWLING **OUT** OF THE **WATER,** THE **ADULT** CADDISFLY **EMERGES** FROM THE **EXOSKELETON** OF THE **PUPA.**

ADULTS ONLY **LIVE** FOR A **SHORT TIME** AND **DON'T FEED.** IN SOME SPECIES THE **ANTENNAE** ARE **MUCH LONGER** THAN THE **BODY.**

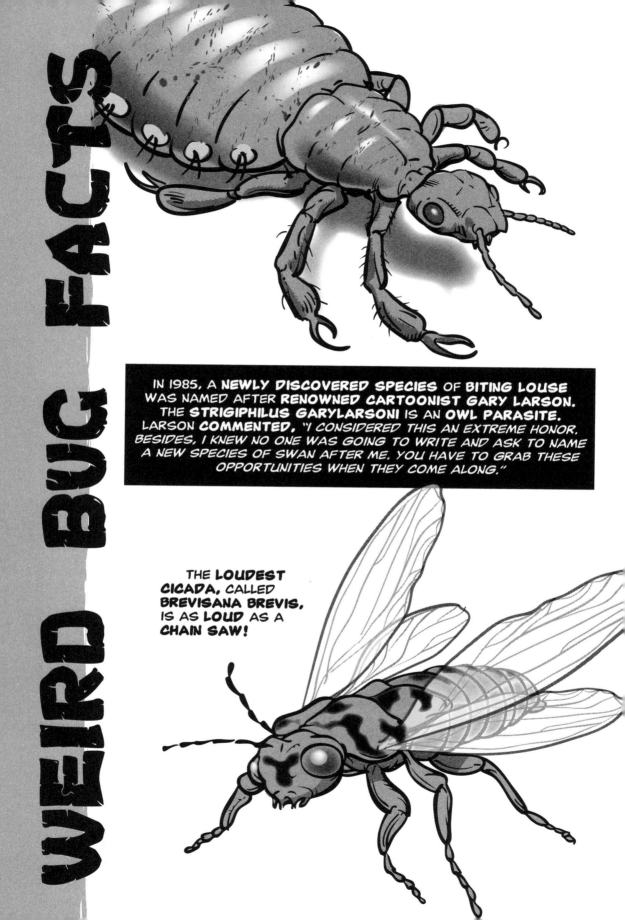

WEIRD BUG FACTS

IN 1985, A **NEWLY DISCOVERED SPECIES** OF BITING LOUSE WAS NAMED AFTER **RENOWNED CARTOONIST GARY LARSON.** THE **STRIGIPHILUS GARYLARSONI** IS AN **OWL PARASITE.** LARSON **COMMENTED,** "I CONSIDERED THIS AN EXTREME HONOR. BESIDES, I KNEW NO ONE WAS GOING TO WRITE AND ASK TO NAME A NEW SPECIES OF SWAN AFTER ME. YOU HAVE TO GRAB THESE OPPORTUNITIES WHEN THEY COME ALONG."

THE **LOUDEST CICADA,** CALLED **BREVISANA BREVIS,** IS AS **LOUD** AS A **CHAIN SAW!**

IN JUST **ONE SEASON**, **ONE APHID** CAN PRODUCE **12 GENERATIONS**, OR **1,560 HEPTILLION OFFSPRING** IF NONE OF THEM DIED. THAT'S **1,560** FOLLOWED BY **21 ZEROS**.

THE **TASMANIAN PARASITIC WASP** HAS THE **SHORTEST WINGSPAN**, ONLY **0.0078 INCHES!**

THE **MEGARACHNE** WAS A **20 INCH LONG SPIDER** THAT LIVED IN THE **PERMIAN PERIOD**. IT'S NOW EXTINCT.

WEIRD BUG FACTS

LICE

Exopterygota (insects with external wing development)
Anoplura (insects without a stinging tail)

LICE ARE **SMALL PARASITES** THAT HAVE EVOLVED TO **LIVE** ON A **SPECIFIC HOST.** FOR EXAMPLE, **LICE** THAT LIVE ON **HUMANS** AREN'T ABLE TO SURVIVE ON ANY **OTHER ANIMAL.**

THERE ARE **ABOUT 500 SPECIES** OF **LICE,** SOME LIVE ON **BIRDS,** SOME LIVE ON **MAMMALS,** LIKE **GORILLAS** OR **ELEPHANTS,** AND OTHERS LIVE ON **PEOPLE.**

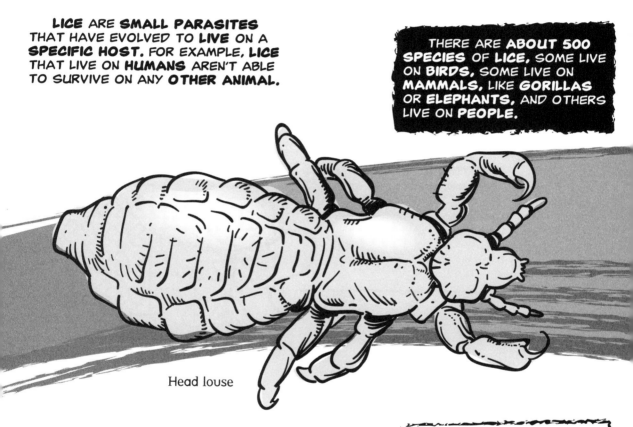

Head louse

LICE **CANNOT FLY** OR **JUMP.** THEY SURVIVE BY **SUCKING** THE **BLOOD** OF THEIR **HOSTS.** IF THEY **FALL OFF** THEIR HOSTS, LICE **DIE** WITHIN A **FEW DAYS.**

LICE DEPOSIT **EGGS** CALLED **NITS.** THE **LOUSE** ATTACHES ITS **EGGS** TO **HAIR STRANDS** USING ITS **STICKY SALIVA.** THE EGGS TAKE ABOUT **EIGHT DAYS** TO **HATCH.** THE EMERGING **NYMPH** CLOSELY RESEMBLES AN **ADULT LOUSE,** EXCEPT FOR ITS SIZE. **NYMPHS** FEED ON THEIR **HOST'S BLOOD,** JUST LIKE THE **ADULTS.**

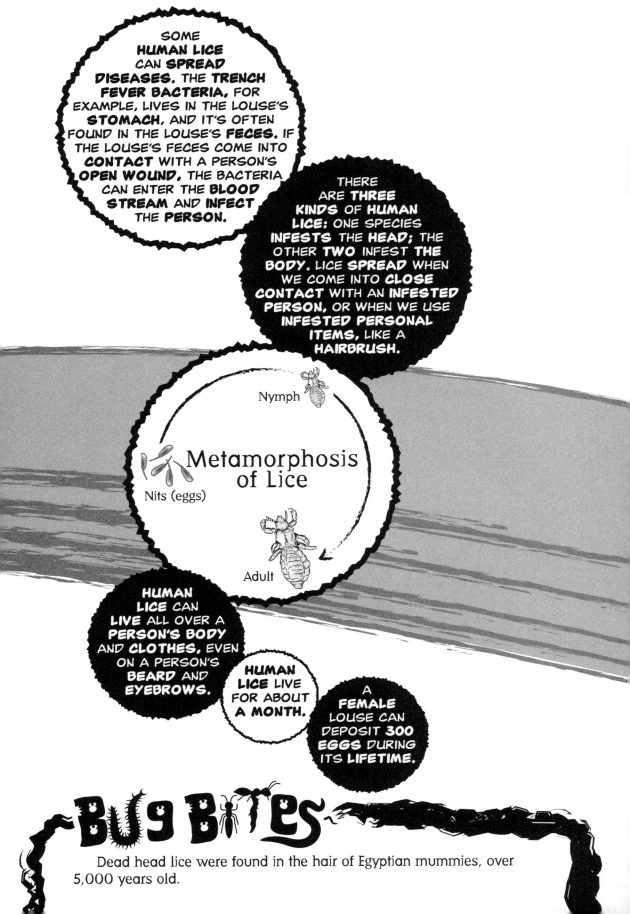

SOME **HUMAN LICE** CAN **SPREAD DISEASES.** THE **TRENCH FEVER BACTERIA,** FOR EXAMPLE, LIVES IN THE LOUSE'S **STOMACH,** AND IT'S OFTEN FOUND IN THE LOUSE'S **FECES.** IF THE LOUSE'S FECES COME INTO **CONTACT** WITH A PERSON'S **OPEN WOUND,** THE BACTERIA CAN ENTER THE **BLOOD STREAM** AND **INFECT** THE **PERSON.**

THERE ARE **THREE KINDS OF HUMAN LICE:** ONE SPECIES INFESTS THE **HEAD;** THE OTHER **TWO** INFEST **THE BODY.** LICE **SPREAD** WHEN WE COME INTO **CLOSE CONTACT** WITH AN **INFESTED PERSON,** OR WHEN WE USE **INFESTED PERSONAL ITEMS,** LIKE A **HAIRBRUSH.**

Nymph

Metamorphosis of Lice

Nits (eggs)

Adult

HUMAN LICE CAN **LIVE** ALL OVER A **PERSON'S BODY** AND **CLOTHES,** EVEN ON A PERSON'S **BEARD** AND **EYEBROWS.**

HUMAN LICE LIVE FOR ABOUT **A MONTH.**

A **FEMALE** LOUSE CAN DEPOSIT **300 EGGS** DURING ITS **LIFETIME.**

BUG BITES

Dead head lice were found in the hair of Egyptian mummies, over 5,000 years old.

EARWIGS

Exopterygota (insects with external wing development)
Dermaptera (insects with skin-like wings)

EARWIGS ARE **FLAT** AND **LONG INSECTS** WITH A PAIR OF **PINCER-LIKE CERCI** AT THE **END** OF THEIR **ABDOMEN.** THEY ARE COMMONLY KNOWN AS **PINCER BUGS.** ALTHOUGH EARWIGS **CAN PINCH** WITH THEIR POWERFUL CERCI, THEY ARE **NOT VENOMOUS.**

THE SCIENTIFIC TERM **DERMAPTERA** MEANS **"SKIN-LIKE WINGS"** AND REFERS TO THE **TWO FOREWINGS.** THEY'RE **HARDENED** TO **PROTECT** THE **HIND WINGS,** LIKE THE **SKIN PROTECTS** THE DELICATE **ORGANS INSIDE.**

BUG BITES

In ancient times, people believed that, while they were sleeping, earwigs crawled into their ears to eat their brains!

EARWIGS ARE **OMNIVOROUS.**
THEY EAT **FRUITS, VEGETABLES,
INSECTS,** AND **CATERPILLARS.**
SOMETIMES THEY EAT MEMBERS
OF THEIR **OWN SPECIES!**

THE HIND WINGS ARE **THIN**
AND **TRANSPARENT.**

AFTER MATING, THE EARWIG FEMALE
DEPOSITS HER **EGGS** IN A **HOLE** SHE DIGS IN
THE **SOIL.** EARWIG FEMALES **CARE** FOR THEIR EGGS,
CLEANING AND **PROTECTING** THEM FROM
PREDATORS, PARASITES, AND **MOLD.** THEY OFTEN
BRING FOOD TO THEIR NEST FOR THE **NYMPHS** ONCE
THEY HATCH.

BUG BITES

The word "earwigging" means to whisper secrets into someone's ears
or to eavesdrop.

COCKROACHES

Exopterygota (insects with external wing development)
Dictyoptera (insects with net-like wings)

COCKROACHES AND **PRAYING MANTIDS** BELONG TO THE SAME GROUP CALLED **DICTYOPTERA**. THIS IS BECAUSE THESE INSECTS **EVOLVED** FROM A **COMMON ANCESTOR**.

COCKROACHES HAVE **TWO SETS** OF **WINGS**. THE **FOREWINGS** ARE **HARDENED** AND **FLAT** TO **PROTECT** THE SECOND SET OF SOFTER **WINGS**.

THE **LEGS** ARE **LONG** AND **THIN**.

COCKROACHES EVOLVED **350 MILLION YEARS AGO**, DURING THE **DEVONIAN PERIOD** OF THE PALEOZOIC ERA, **150 MILLION YEARS** BEFORE THE AGE OF **DINOSAURS**.

COCKROACHES **DEPOSIT** THEIR **EGGS** IN **SMALL OOTHECAE.** AN OOTHECA IS AN **EGG CONTAINER.** THE **FEMALE** CARRIES THE OOTHECA **UNDER** HER **BELLY** UNTIL IT'S TIME FOR THE **EGGS** TO **HATCH.**

THE **ANTENNAE** ARE **LONG.**

COCKROACHES ARE MAINLY **NOCTURNAL** (THEY STAY AWAKE AT NIGHT). THEY **SCAVENGE** ON ANYTHING THEY FIND, ESPECIALLY **GARBAGE** AND **ROTTING** OR **DECAYING MATTER.**

COCKROACHES CAN WITHSTAND ABOUT **15 TIMES** THE AMOUNT OF **NUCLEAR RADIATION** NEEDED TO KILL A **PERSON.** BUT THIS IS NOT MUCH IF COMPARED TO THE **FRUIT FLIES,** WHICH CAN WITHSTAND **160 TIMES** MORE RADIATION THAN PEOPLE.

BUG BITES

It's true that a cockroach can live for four weeks without its head. This is because cockroaches have several nerve centers, called ganglia, along their body. Ganglia coordinate movements, so even without its head, a cockroach can move around. But eventually, not being able to feed, it will die.

PRAYING MANTIDS

Exopterygota (insects with external wing development)
Dictyoptera (insects with net-like wings)

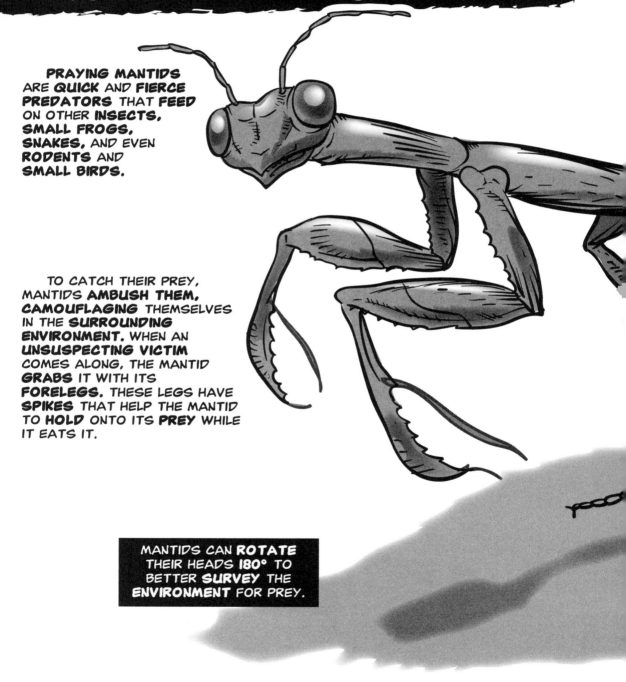

PRAYING MANTIDS ARE **QUICK** AND **FIERCE** **PREDATORS** THAT **FEED** ON OTHER **INSECTS,** **SMALL FROGS,** **SNAKES,** AND EVEN **RODENTS** AND **SMALL BIRDS.**

TO CATCH THEIR PREY, MANTIDS **AMBUSH THEM,** **CAMOUFLAGING** THEMSELVES IN THE **SURROUNDING** **ENVIRONMENT.** WHEN AN **UNSUSPECTING VICTIM** COMES ALONG, THE MANTID **GRABS** IT WITH ITS **FORELEGS.** THESE LEGS HAVE **SPIKES** THAT HELP THE MANTID TO **HOLD** ONTO ITS **PREY** WHILE IT EATS IT.

MANTIDS CAN **ROTATE** THEIR HEADS **180°** TO BETTER **SURVEY** THE **ENVIRONMENT** FOR PREY.

SOME SPECIES OF PRAYING MANTIDS ARE **CANNIBALISTIC** (THEY EAT INSECTS OF THEIR SAME SPECIES). DURING MATING, **FERTILIZATION** OCCURS ONLY IF THE **FEMALE EATS** THE **BRAIN** OF THE **MALE.** WHEN **FOOD** IS **SCARCE,** MANTID **NYMPHS** EAT THEIR **SIBLINGS.**

MANTID IS A GREEK WORD THAT MEANS **"PROPHET"** OR "SPIRITUAL PERSON." THEY WERE NAMED THIS WAY BECAUSE, WHEN AT REST, MANTIDS KEEP THEIR **FORELEGS FOLDED** AS IF THEY WERE **PRAYING.** FOR THIS REASON THESE INSECTS SHOULD NOT BE CALLED **PREYING** MANTIDS, ALTHOUGH THEY ARE EXCELLENT PREDATORS, BUT **PRAYING** MANTIDS.

BUG BITES

Praying mantids can be kept as pets or raised to control pests.

WEB SPINNERS

Exopterygota (insects with external wing development)
Embioptera (insects with lively wings)

WEB SPINNERS ARE SMALL INSECTS THAT CAN SPIN A SILKY WEB FROM GLANDS IN THEIR FORELEGS. WEB SPINNERS BUILD THEIR NESTS WITH THE SILK.

THEY BELONG TO A GROUP OF INSECTS CALLED EMBIOPTERA, WHICH MEANS "LIVELY WINGS." IT REFERS TO THE RAPID MOVEMENTS OF THESE INSECTS' WINGS.

ONLY MALE WEB SPINNERS HAVE WINGS.

WEB SPINNER FEMALES EAT ALL SORTS OF VEGETABLE MATTER, LIKE DEAD LEAVES, BARK, LICHENS, AND MOSSES.
WHEN WEB SPINNER MALES EMERGE AS ADULTS THEY DON'T WASTE ANY TIME TO EAT. THEY LIVE A VERY SHORT LIFE, ONLY A FEW HOURS, DURING WHICH THEY HAVE TO FIND A FEMALE AND MATE.

ROCK CRAWLERS

Exopterygota (insects with external wing development)
Grylloblattodea (cricket and cockroach-like insects)

ROCK CRAWLERS BELONG TO A GROUP OF INSECTS CALLED GRYLLOBLATTODEA. THIS WORD MEANS "LOOKING LIKE A CRICKET AND A COCKROACH." THESE INSECTS SEEM TO HAVE A MIX OF CRICKET AND COCKROACH FEATURES.

ROCK CRAWLERS ARE NOCTURNAL. THEY HIDE DURING THE DAY UNDER ROCKS OR IN CAVES. AT NIGHT THEY EAT ROTTING LEAVES AND DEAD INSECTS.

ROCK CRAWLERS LIVE IN VERY COLD PLACES ON MOUNTAINS IN CANADA, RUSSIA, NORTH KOREA, AND JAPAN.

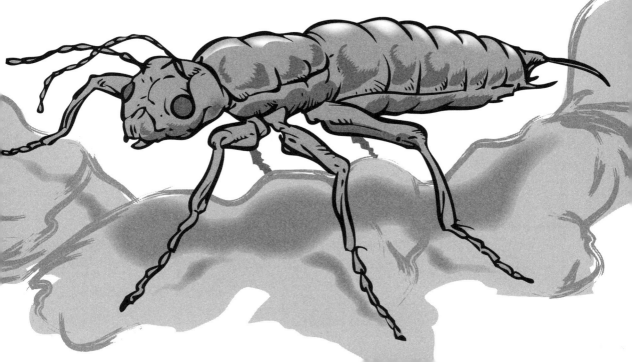

MAYFLIES

Exopterygota (insects with external wing development)
Ephemeroptera (short-lived insects)

EPHEMEROPTERA MEANS **"SHORT-LIVED INSECTS WITH WINGS."** IT INDICATES A GROUP OF **SMALL INSECTS** THAT HAVE A **VERY SHORT LIFESPAN.** SOME MAYFLIES, IN FACT, **LIVE** ONLY FOR A **FEW HOURS** OR A **FEW DAYS** AS **ADULTS.**

MAYFLIES ARE **NOT FLIES.** FLIES HAVE ONLY TWO WINGS, WHILE **MAYFLIES** HAVE **FOUR.** THE **TRIANGULAR FOREWINGS** OF THE MAYFLY ARE **MUCH BIGGER** THAN ITS **HIND WINGS.**

AT THE **TIP** OF THEIR **ABDOMEN,** MAYFLIES HAVE **TWO** OR **THREE LONG CAUDAL FILAMENTS.**

ADULTS DON'T EAT, SPENDING THEIR SHORT LIVES ONLY TO **MATE.**

MAYFLIES ARE **VERY SENSITIVE** TO **POLLUTION**. FOR THIS REASON, THE PRESENCE OF MAYFLIES IN A **BODY** OF **WATER** INDICATES THE **GOOD QUALITY** OF THAT **WATER**.

SWARMING **ADULTS** MATE NEAR THE **WATER**.

FEMALES **DEPOSIT** THEIR **EGGS** ON THE **SURFACE** OF **FRESHWATER LAKES** OR **STREAMS**. THEN, BOTH MALES AND FEMALES **DIE**.

THE MAYFLY **MOLTS AGAIN** INTO THE **FINAL STAGE**, THE **ADULT** (OR IMAGO).

NAIADS **RISE TO** THE **SURFACE** OF THE WATER. WHILE STILL IN THE WATER THEY **MOLT** INTO A **SUBIMAGO**. A SUBIMAGO IS AN **ADULT MAYFLY** THAT IS **NOT READY** TO **MATE**. THIS STAGE ONLY LASTS FOR A **FEW HOURS**.

WHEN THE EGGS HATCH, THE **NEWBORNS** ARE CALLED **NAIADS**. THIS IS BECAUSE THE MAYFLY LARVAE LIVE **UNDERWATER**. THE NAIADS BREATHE THROUGH **GILLS**, OR **SMALL OPENINGS** ALONGSIDE THEIR **ABDOMEN**. DEPENDING ON THE SPECIES, MAYFLY NAIADS EAT **WEEDS** OR **PREY** ON **INSECTS**. MAYFLY NAIADS DON'T HAVE **WINGS**. **MAYFLIES** REMAIN IN THEIR **LARVAL STAGE** FOR **TWO MONTHS** TO **TWO YEARS**.

TRUE BUGS

Exopterygota (insects with external wing development)
Hemiptera (insects with half-hard and half-soft wings)

THE **INSECTS** IN THIS GROUP HAVE **TWO PAIRS** OF WINGS. THE **FIRST PAIR,** OR THE **FOREWINGS,** HAVE **TWO AREAS.** THE **FIRST HALF** OF THE **FOREWINGS** IS **THICKER** AND **TOUGHER** IN THE **BASAL REGION,** OR THE PART **CLOSER** TO THE **BODY.** THE FOREWINGS BECOME **SOFTER** AND **THINNER** TOWARD THE **TIPS.**

THE **SECOND PAIR,** OR THE **HIND WINGS,** IS **SOFT** ALL OVER.

THE **SCIENTIFIC NAME** REFLECTS THE CHARACTERISTIC OF THE **HALF-HARD** AND **HALF-SOFT FOREWINGS.** THE WORD **HEMI** MEANS "**HALF,**" AND THE WORD **PTERA** MEANS "**WINGS.**" BUT SOME SPECIES ARE **WINGLESS.**

MANY TRUE BUGS SECRETE **WAX-LIKE RESINS;** SOME, LIKE THE **STINK BUGS,** OOZE A **REPELLING FLUID** THAT **SMELLS BAD;** OTHERS **HIDE** IN A **WHITE FOAM,** LIKE THE **SPITTLE BUGS.**

THE TRUE BUGS' **MOUTH** CAN **STAB** AND **SUCK.** MANY SPECIES OF TRUE BUGS ARE **PARASITES** OF **PLANTS,** LIKE THE **PLANTHOPPERS;** OTHERS ARE **PARASITES** OF **ANIMALS,** LIKE THE **ASSASSIN BUGS;** MANY EAT **INSECTS.**

THE WORD **BUG** WAS **FIRST USED** TO INDICATE THE **TRUE BUGS.** FOR THIS REASON, THE **HEMIPTERA** ARE KNOWN AS **TRUE BUGS.**

ASSASSIN BUGS

Exopterygota (insects with external wing development)
Hemiptera (insects with half-hard and half-soft wings)

ASSASSIN BUGS ARE **QUICK** AND **EFFICIENT HUNTERS.** MANY SPECIES EAT OTHER **INSECTS,** BUT OTHERS FEED ON THE **BLOOD** OF **MAMMALS.**

ASSASSIN BUGS HAVE A **FORMIDABLE ROSTRUM,** OR BEAK, THAT THEY USE TO **STAB** THEIR **PREY** AND **INJECT** IT WITH **VENOM.** THIS QUICKLY **LIQUEFIES** THE VICTIM'S **INTERNAL ORGANS** THAT THE ASSASSIN BUG **SUCKS** OUT WITH ITS **ROSTRUM.**

ASSASSIN BUGS USE THEIR **ROSTRUM** FOR **DEFENSE.** THEY CAN EITHER INFLICT AN **EXCRUCIATING BITE** OR **SPRAY** THEIR **VENOM,** WHICH CAUSES **IRRITATION** AND, IF DIRECTED TO THE EYES, **TEMPORARY BLINDNESS.**

BLOOD-FEEDING ASSASSIN BUGS MIGHT SOMETIMES **ATTACK PEOPLE.** SOME SPECIES ARE CALLED **KISSING BUGS** BECAUSE THEY **BITE PEOPLE** ON THEIR **LIPS** WHILE THEY **SLEEP.** LIPS ARE **SOFTER** AND **EASIER** TO **PIERCE.** WHILE **SUCKING** THEIR **BLOOD,** THESE BUGS MIGHT ACTUALLY **INFECT PEOPLE** WITH A **PARASITE** THAT CAUSES **CHAGAS DISEASE,** A POTENTIALLY **FATAL ILLNESS.**

BUG BITES

Despite their alarming name, many species of assassin bugs are beneficial because they feed on pests and parasites.

WATER SCORPIONS

Exopterygota (insects with external wing development)
Hemiptera (insects with half-hard and half-soft wings)

WATER SCORPIONS GOT THEIR NAME BECAUSE THEY VAGUELY RESEMBLE SCORPIONS. THEY HAVE TWO PREDATORY FORELIMBS AND A LONG TUBE AT THE END OF THEIR ABDOMEN. BUT, WATER SCORPIONS ARE INSECTS, WHILE SCORPIONS ARE ARACHNIDS.

WATER SCORPIONS LIVE IN PONDS AND LAKES, EATING INSECTS, WORMS, AND LARVAE THEY AMBUSH IN THE WATER. THEY GRAB THEIR UNAWARE PREY WITH THEIR FORELEGS AND SUCK ITS INSIDES WITH THEIR ROSTRUM.

WATER SCORPIONS LIVE UNDERWATER AND BREATHE THROUGH THEIR TAILS, WHICH THEY USE LIKE A SNORKEL.

BUG BITES

Some water scorpions are so thin they are called needle bugs or water sticks.

BED BUGS

Exopterygota (insects with external wing development)
Hemiptera (insects with half-hard and half-soft wings)

BED BUGS ARE BLOOD-SUCKING PARASITES OF BIRDS, MAMMALS, AND HUMANS.

BEDBUGS FIND THEIR PREY BECAUSE THEY ARE ATTRACTED TO BODY WARMTH.

WHEN THEY SUCK BLOOD, BEDBUGS INJECT THEIR VICTIM WITH A MILD ANESTHETIC AND AN ANTICOAGULANT. THE ANESTHETIC PREVENTS THE VICTIM FROM FEELING PAIN, AND THE ANTICOAGULANT KEEPS THE BLOOD FLUID.

WHEN THEY FIND A VICTIM, BEDBUGS NEST NEARBY AND COME OUT AT NIGHT TO FEED. THEY ARE OFTEN FOUND IN MATTRESSES OR BED FRAMES. THE RHYME "SLEEP TIGHT, DON'T LET THE BEDBUGS BITE" WAS WRITTEN IN HONOR OF THIS BUG.

WATER STRIDERS

Exopterygota (insects with external wing development)
Hemiptera (insects with half-hard and half-soft wings)

WATER STRIDERS ARE INSECTS CAPABLE OF SKATING ON THE SURFACE OF WATER. THEY CAN DO SO BECAUSE THEIR RAPID MOVEMENTS CAUSE SMALL VORTEXES IN THE WATER. THESE VORTEXES ALLOW THE INSECT TO PROPEL ITSELF FORWARD. ALSO, WATER STRIDERS' LEGS ARE COVERED WITH TINY HAIRS, WHICH ENTRAP AIR BUBBLES. THE WATER-REPELLING LEGS KEEP THESE INSECTS FROM SINKING AND ACTUALLY ALLOW THEM TO REST ON THE WATER SURFACE.

THE LEGS OF THIS INSECT ARE EXTREMELY SENSITIVE TO WATER VIBRATION. VIBRATIONS WARN THE WATER STRIDER OF A PREDATOR GETTING NEAR. VIBRATIONS ALSO REVEAL THE PRESENCE OF PREY.

WATER STRIDERS USE THEIR FIRST PAIR OF LEGS TO GRAB THEIR PREY. THEY USE THEIR SECOND PAIR LIKE OARS, TO PROPEL THEMSELVES ON WATER, AND THE LAST PAIR OF LEGS TO CHANGE DIRECTION.

APHIDS

Exopterygota (insects with external wing development)
Homoptera (insects with wings of the same size)

APHIDS ARE PEST PARASITES OF PLANTS. THEY PIERCE THE STEMS WITH THEIR BEAKS AND INJECT THEIR SALIVA. THE SALIVA MAKES THE SAP MORE FLUID AND EASIER FOR THE APHID TO DRINK.

NEAR THE END OF THEIR ABDOMEN, APHIDS HAVE TWO CORNICLES, OR TUBES. AS A DEFENSE MECHANISM, THE CORNICLES SECRETE A WAX-LIKE FLUID THAT HARDENS, ENTRAPPING THE PREDATOR.

IN THE FALL, APHIDS MATE AND FEMALES DEPOSIT THEIR EGGS.
IN THE SPRING, THE NYMPHS HATCHING FROM THESE EGGS ARE ALL FEMALES.
DURING THE SUMMER, FEMALES DON'T MATE, BUT PRODUCE EGGS. THE APHIDS BORN FROM THESE EGGS ARE ALL FEMALES.
AT THE END OF THE SUMMER, APHID MALES APPEAR.
DURING JUST ONE SEASON A SINGLE APHID CAN SPAWN TWELVE GENERATIONS.

APHIDS CAN HAVE TELESCOPIC GENERATIONS. THIS MEANS THAT A FEMALE APHID CAN CARRY EGGS THAT HATCH WITHIN HER BODY, AND HER DAUGHTERS ARE ALREADY CARRYING EGGS BEFORE BEING BORN.

SCALES

Exopterygota (insects with external wing development)
Homoptera (insects with wings of the same size)

SCALES ARE **PEST PARASITES** OF **PLANTS.** THEY ARE GENERALLY **STUCK** ON A **STEM,** AND **DON'T MOVE.**

DEPENDING ON THE SPECIES, **SCALES** SECRETE **WAX-LIKE** RESINS OR **COTTON-LIKE FUZZ.** THEY **COVER** THEMSELVES **UP** WITH THESE **SECRETIONS** FOR **PROTECTION.**

MALE SCALES LIVE ONLY FOR A **FEW HOURS** TO MATE. THEY **DON'T** EVEN **EAT.** MALES HAVE **TWO SETS** OF **WINGS,** BUT SOME SPECIES **LACK** THE **SECOND SET.**

FEMALE SCALES DON'T HAVE **WINGS.** AFTER THEY **HATCH** FROM THE EGGS, FEMALE **NYMPHS HAVE LEGS** AND ARE ABLE TO **CRAWL.** BUT WHEN THEY BECOME **ADULTS,** FEMALE SCALES **DON'T HAVE** ANY **LEGS,** **ANTENNAE,** OR **EYES.**

CICADAS

Exopterygota (insects with external wing development)
Homoptera (insects with wings of the same size)

MALE CICADAS MAKE A SOUND WITH ABDOMINAL ORGANS CALLED TIMBALS. THEY PLAY THEIR "SONG" TO ATTRACT FEMALES. EACH CICADA SPECIES EMITS A SPECIFIC SONG.

CICADAS HAVE TWO PAIRS OF TRANSPARENT WINGS. WHEN AT REST, THEY ARE KEPT IN A ROOF-LIKE POSITION.

Cicada

Old exoskeleton

THE MAGICICADAS ARE SPECIES OF CICADAS WITH A VERY LONG LIFE CYCLE. DEPENDING ON THE SPECIES, NYMPHS SPEND EITHER 13 OR 17 YEARS UNDERGROUND BEFORE EMERGING AS ADULTS.

WHEN THE EGG HATCHES, THE NYMPH FALLS TO THE GROUND AND NESTS.
WHEN IT'S TIME TO MOLT, THE NYMPH CRAWLS OUT FROM THE NEST.
THE EXOSKELETON CRACKS ALONG THE BACK, AND THE ADULT CICADA EMERGES.

TERMITES

Exopterygota (insects with external wing development
Isoptera (insects with same size wings)

TERMITES ARE INSECTS THAT LIVE IN **HIGHLY ORGANIZED COLONIES** WHERE THE POPULATION IS DIVIDED INTO **THREE CASTES: WORKERS, SOLDIERS,** AND **REPRODUCTIVE TERMITES.**

REPRODUCTIVE TERMITES

REPRODUCTIVE TERMITES ARE **MALE** AND **FEMALE TERMITES** THAT CAN **REPRODUCE.** THEY HAVE **WINGS** AND THEY **SWARM, LOOKING** FOR A **MATE.** THE **NEW COUPLE** REMOVES ITS **WINGS,** BECOMING THE **KING** AND **QUEEN** OF A **NEW COLONY.** THE QUEEN MATES WITH THE KING AND STARTS DEPOSITING **EGGS.** WHEN THE EGGS HATCH, THE NEWLY BORN TERMITES ARE **NON-FERTILE WORKERS.**

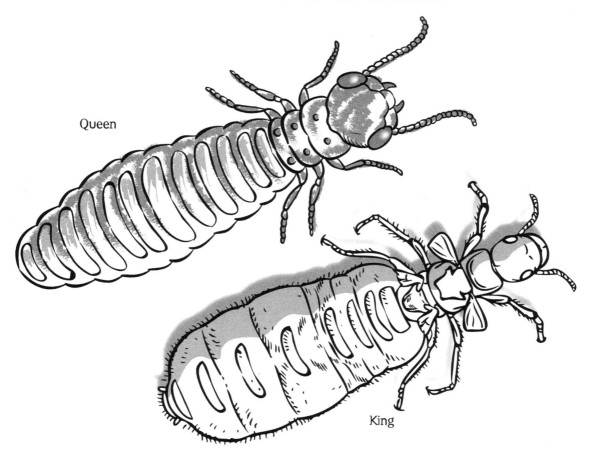

Queen

King

WORKERS CARE FOR EVERY ASPECT OF THE COLONY, FROM BUILDING TUNNELS AND CLEANING, TO CARING FOR THE BROOD AND THE QUEEN. ONE VERY IMPORTANT JOB THE WORKERS PERFORM IS FEEDING THOSE MEMBERS OF THE COLONY THAT CAN'T FEED THEMSELVES. THESE ARE THE QUEEN, WHICH IS TOO BIG TO BE ABLE TO MOVE AROUND, AND THE LARVAE. IN SOME SPECIES, THE WORKERS FEED THE SOLDIERS, TOO. THIS IS BECAUSE THE SOLDIERS' JAWS ARE SO BIG THAT THEY CAN'T FEED THEMSELVES.

BUG BITES

Termites feed their sisters through **trophallaxis.** This means that termites regurgitate from their mouth or expel from their anus nutrients for their sisters to eat.

TERMITES

SOLDIERS

SOLDIERS ARE TERMITES WITH A **BIGGER HEAD.** IN SOME SPECIES, SOLDIERS HAVE **HUGE JAWS;** IN OTHERS THEY HAVE A **BIG SNOUT.** THE SOLDIERS' JOB IS TO **PROTECT** THE **COLONY** FROM **INTRUSION,** OFTEN AIDED BY THE WORKERS.

TERMITES FEED ON **CELLULOSE,** A SUBSTANCE FOUND IN **WOOD, PAPER, GRASSES,** AND **COTTON.** CELLULOSE IS VERY **HARD** TO **DIGEST.** TERMITES ARE ABLE TO ACCOMPLISH THIS BECAUSE THEY HAVE **SPECIAL BACTERIA** IN THEIR **GUTS.** TERMITE **NYMPHS** ARE BORN **WITHOUT** THESE **BACTERIA.** FOR THIS REASON THEY ARE OFTEN FED **FECES** BY THE **WORKERS.** IN THIS WAY, THE **BACTERIA ESTABLISH** THEMSELVES IN THE **YOUNG TERMITES' GUTS.**

TERMITES ARE CONSIDERED **PESTS** BECAUSE THEY **EAT** THE **WOOD STRUCTURE** OF **BUILDINGS.** BUT THESE INSECTS ARE VERY **IMPORTANT** FOR THE **ENVIRONMENT** BECAUSE THEY RECYCLE **DECOMPOSING MATERIALS** LIKE **DEAD WOOD** AND **LEAF LITTER.**

DRAGONFLIES VS. DAMSELFLIES

WHILE AT FIRST **ANTS** AND **TERMITES** MIGHT **LOOK SIMILAR,** THEY ARE **VERY DIFFERENT.**

ANTS

A **WINGED QUEEN** ANT HAS **TWO PAIRS** OF WINGS. THE **FIRST PAIR** IS MUCH **BIGGER** THAN THE **SECOND.**

ANTS' ANTENNAE ARE **V-SHAPED.**

ANTS HAVE A **NARROW WAIST.**

TERMITES

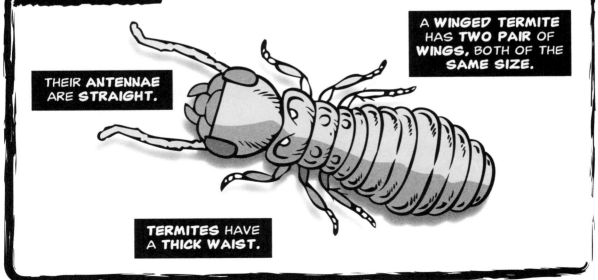

A **WINGED TERMITE** HAS **TWO PAIR** OF **WINGS,** BOTH OF THE **SAME SIZE.**

THEIR **ANTENNAE** ARE **STRAIGHT.**

TERMITES HAVE A **THICK WAIST.**

DRAGONFLIES & DAMSELFLIES

Exopterygota (insects with external wing development)
Odonata (insects with teeth)

DRAGONFLIES' **HUGE COMPOUND EYES** ARE MADE OF **THOUSANDS** OF **SMALLER EYES** AND TAKE UP A **LARGE PORTION** OF THEIR **HEADS.** THE EYES ARE **VERY SENSITIVE** TO **MOVEMENT,** MAKING THESE INSECTS AWARE OF ANY **POSSIBLE PREY** CLOSE BY.

THEIR **MANDIBLES** ARE **DENTED** TO BETTER **CHEW** THEIR **PREY.**

THE **LEGS** ARE **PUSHED FORWARD** AND **VERY CLOSE TOGETHER,** IN A **BASKET-LIKE POSTURE.** LEGS IN THIS POSITION CAN **EFFICIENTLY CATCH** AND **HOLD** ONTO **PREY** WHILE THE INSECT IS **FLYING.**

THE **FOUR WINGS** ARE **VERY LONG** AND **MOVE INDEPENDENTLY** FROM ONE ANOTHER. THEY ALLOW THESE INSECTS TO MAKE **SWIFT CHANGES** IN **DIRECTION** AND **SUDDEN NOSE-DIVES** WHEN **FLYING**, TO BETTER CATCH **FAST-MOVING PREY.**

THE GROUP **ODONATA** INCLUDES **DRAGONFLIES** AND **DAMSELFLIES.** THE WORD ODONATA MEANS "INSECTS WITH **TOOTH-LIKE DENTS.**"

DRAGONFLIES AND DAMSELFLIES ARE **PERFECTLY EQUIPPED** TO BE **FIERCE PREDATORS.**

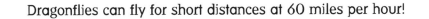

BUG BITES

Dragonflies can fly for short distances at 60 miles per hour!

DRAGONFLIES & DAMSELFLIES

BOTH DRAGONFLIES AND DAMSELFLIES MATE **NEAR** THE **STILL WATERS** OF **LAKES** AND **PONDS.** FEMALES DEPOSIT THEIR **EGGS** DIRECTLY INTO THE **WATER.**

WHEN THE EGGS HATCH, THE **NAIADS** LIVE THEIR ENTIRE **LARVAL STAGE UNDER WATER.** THEY'RE EQUIPPED WITH **GILL-LIKE ORGANS** TO BE ABLE TO BREATHE, BUT **DON'T HAVE WINGS,** LIKE THE ADULTS.

NAIADS CAN BE **FIERCE PREDATORS** JUST LIKE THE ADULT INSECTS. THEY FEED ON **WORMS, OTHER LARVAE, TADPOLES,** AND EVEN **SMALL FISH.**

NAIADS HAVE A **RETRACTABLE** AND **CLAWED LIP.** IT'S CALLED THE **MASK,** BECAUSE, WHEN AT **REST,** IT **FOLDS UNDER** THE **NAIAD'S HEAD,** PARTLY **HIDING** ITS **FACE.** WHEN A **PREY SWIMS BY,** THE NAIAD **QUICKLY EXTENDS** ITS **LIP FORWARD, GRABBING** IT WITH THE **LIP'S CLAWS.** THEN, THEY RETRACT THEIR **LIP,** BRINGING THE PREY CLOSE TO THE NAIAD'S **MOUTH** TO BE EATEN.

SOME SPECIES SPEND AS LONG AS **FIVE YEARS** IN THE **LARVAL STAGE.** WHEN IT'S TIME TO MOLT INTO THE ADULT STAGE, THE NAIADS **CRAWL OUT** OF THE **WATER.** THERE, THE ADULT INSECT **BREAKS FREE** FROM THE NAIAD'S **EXOSKELETON** THROUGH A **CRACK** ALONG THE **BACK.**

THE NEWLY EMERGED ADULTS MUST **WAIT** FOR THEIR **WINGS** TO **DRY BEFORE** THEY CAN **FLY.**

DRAGONFLIES VS. DAMSELFLIES

DRAGONFLIES' EYES ARE SO **BIG** THAT THEY **TOUCH.**

DRAGONFLIES' BODIES ARE **BULKY.**

WHEN AT **REST, DRAGONFLIES' WINGS** REMAIN **SPREAD OUT.**

DURING THE **LARVAL STAGE,** THE **DRAGONFLY NAIADS' GILLS** ARE LOCATED **INSIDE** ITS **ANUS.**

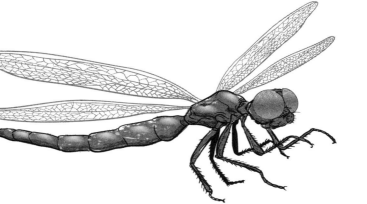

DAMSELFLIES' EYES ARE **VERY BIG,** BUT **DO NOT TOUCH.**

DAMSELFLIES' BODIES ARE **SLENDER.**

WHEN AT REST, THE **DAMSELFLY'S WINGS** ARE **FOLDED VERTICALLY** OVER THE **BODY.**

DURING THE LARVAL STAGE, THE **DAMSELFLY NAIADS' GILLS** LOOK LIKE **THREE FEATHER-LIKE TAILS** AT THE **TIP** OF THE **ABDOMEN.**

CRICKETS

Exopterygota (insects with external wing development)
Orthoptera (insects with straight wings)

INSECTS IN THIS GROUP INCLUDE OVER 20,000 SPECIES OF CRICKETS AND GRASSHOPPERS. THE NAME ORTHOPTERA MEANS "STRAIGHT WINGS" AND REFERS TO THE FOREWINGS, ALSO CALLED TEGMINA. THEY ARE HARD AND PROTECT A PAIR OF SOFTER HIND WINGS, FOLDED LIKE A FAN.

IN ASIA IT'S QUITE COMMON TO KEEP CRICKETS AS PETS TO ENJOY THEIR CHIRPING.

CRICKETS HAVE THEIR HEARING ORGANS ON THEIR FIRST PAIR OF LEGS.

MOLE CRICKETS LIVE UNDERGROUND AND, LIKE MOLES, THEY DIG WITH THEIR FIRST PAIR OF LEGS.

CRICKETS STRIDULATE, OR CHIRP, USING THEIR FOREWINGS. THE TEGMINA HAVE RIDGES AND ONE OF THESE HAS DENTS. CRICKETS CHIRP WHEN THEY STROKE ONE WING AGAINST THE DENTED RIDGE OF THE OTHER.
EACH SPECIES CHIRPS IN ITS OWN WAY. IT'S MOSTLY MALES THAT CHIRP TO ATTRACT A MATE AND AS A WARNING SOUND AGAINST OTHER MALES. BUT, IN SOME SPECIES, FEMALES CHIRP, TOO.

KATYDIDS GET THEIR NAME FROM THE WAY THEY CHIRP, WHICH SOUNDS LIKE, "KATY DID! KATY DID!" THEY LOOK LIKE GRASSHOPPERS, BUT THEIR ANTENNAE ARE MUCH LONGER, OFTEN LONGER THAN THEIR OWN BODY.

BUG BITES

Count how many chirps a snowy tree cricket makes in 15 seconds then add 40. The sum will give you the outside temperature. Many cricket species have their own chirping/temperature rate.

GRASSHOPPERS

Exopterygota (insects with external wing development)
Orthoptera (insects with straight wings)

SOME **GRASSHOPPERS CHIRP** WHEN THEY **STROKE** THEIR **DENTED LEGS AGAINST** THEIR **WINGS.** OTHER SPECIES **SNAP** THEIR **WINGS TOGETHER.**

GRASSHOPPERS **HEAR** WITH **ORGANS,** CALLED **TYMPANA,** LOCATED ALONG THE **SIDES** OF THEIR **ABDOMEN.**

GRASSHOPPERS AND CRICKETS **DEPOSIT** THEIR **EGGS** INTO THE **SOIL.** WHEN THE EGGS HATCH, THE EMERGING **NYMPHS LOOK LIKE** THE **ADULTS,** WITH A FEW DIFFERENCES. NYMPHS ARE **SMALLER, CAN'T MATE,** AND **DON'T HAVE WINGS.**

ALL THE ORTHOPTERA ARE **SKILLED JUMPERS.** THEIR **LAST PAIR** OF **LEGS,** IN FACT, IS QUITE **BIGGER** THAN THE **OTHERS.**

LOCUSTS ARE A KIND OF **GRASSHOPPER** THAT, UNDER THE RIGHT CONDITIONS, **CONGREGATE** AND **MIGRATE.** AS **NASA** REPORTS, A **SWARM** CAN CONTAIN **56 BILLION LOCUSTS,** COVER OVER **700 SQUARE MILES,** AND EAT **423 MILLION POUNDS** OF **VEGETATION** AND **CROPS EVERY DAY.** THIS CAN BRING **FAMINE** TO **ONE TENTH** OF THE **WORLD'S POPULATION.**

IN THE LAST CENTURY, **LOCUSTS** HAVE **SWARMED SEVEN TIMES,** AND ONE SWARM LASTED **13 YEARS.**

THE **FOOD** AND **AGRICULTURE ORGANIZATION** OF THE **UNITED NATIONS (FAO)** STARTED A **PROGRAM** TO **CONTROL LOCUST MIGRATIONS.** WITH THE AID OF **JIM TUCKER,** FROM **NASA'S GODDARD SPACE FLIGHT CENTER,** FAO IS ABLE TO **PREDICT CONGREGATIONS** OF **LOCUSTS.** SWARMS ARE TRIGGERED BY **RAIN** AND SUDDEN **GROWTH** OF **VEGETATION,** WHICH ARE **VISIBLE** FROM A **SATELLITE.** THESE AREAS CAN BE **TREATED** WITH **INSECTICIDES** TO PREVENT AN **EXPLOSION** OF THE **LOCUSTS' POPULATION.**

WALKING STICK & LEAF INSECTS

Exopterygota (insects with external wing development)
Phasmatodae (phantom-like insects)

THE SCIENTIFIC NAME **PHASMATODAE** MEANS **"LOOKING LIKE A PHANTOM,"** BECAUSE THESE INSECTS ARE **HARD TO SEE.** SOME LOOK LIKE **TWIGS, LEAVES,** OR **LICHENS,** AND THEY **BLEND PERFECTLY** WITH THEIR **SURROUNDING ENVIRONMENT.**

WALKING STICKS SHOULD BE **HANDLED WITH CARE.** WHEN **THREATENED,** SOME SPECIES **SPRAY CHEMICALS,** WHICH CAN CAUSE **SUPERFICIAL IRRITATION** AND **TEMPORARY BLINDNESS** IN SOME **PEOPLE.**

MOST WALKING STICKS **MOVE SLOWLY** THROUGH **VEGETATION,** TRYING **NOT TO ATTRACT ATTENTION.** IF A **PREDATOR DISCOVERS** THEM, SOME **FAKE** THEIR OWN **DEATH,** HOPING TO **LOOK** EVEN **MORE LIKE** A **LEAF** OR A **TWIG.** OTHER SPECIES HAVE A **SPUR** ON THEIR **LEGS,** WHICH THEY USE FOR **SELF-DEFENSE.**

SOME SPECIES **DROP** THEIR **EGGS** TO THE **GROUND** WHERE THEY'RE **COLLECTED** BY **ANTS**. THE ANTS ONLY **EAT** A **SMALL PART** OF THE **EGG CASE**, WHICH **HELPS** THE **NYMPHS** TO **HATCH**. IN THIS WAY, THE **EGGS** AND THE **YOUNG NYMPHS** ARE **PROTECTED** FROM **PREDATORS**, LIKE BIRDS, IN THE ANTS' NEST.

IN A FEW SPECIES, THE **MALES** HAVE **WINGS**. IN GENERAL, **FEMALES** ARE **BIGGER** THAN **MALES**.

THESE INSECTS OFTEN **EAT** THEIR OWN EXOSKELETON AFTER A **MOLT**.

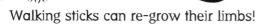

BUG BITES

Walking sticks can re-grow their limbs!

STONEFLIES

Exopterygota (insects with external wing development)
Plecoptera (insects with folded wings)

STONEFLIES ARE GROUPED IN **PLECOPTERA**, WHICH MEANS "**INSECTS WITH FOLDED WINGS.**" THIS IS BECAUSE THESE INSECTS KEEP THEIR **TWO PAIRS** OF **WINGS FOLDED** ON **TOP** OF **EACH OTHER** WHEN AT **REST.**

STONEFLIES **LIVE NEAR FRESH WATERS.** SOME SPECIES LIKE THE **FAST-MOVING WATERS** OF **RIVERS,** OTHERS PREFER **LAKES.** THEY LIVE ON THE **BANKS,** ON **ROCKS** OR **SAND.**

STONEFLIES' **PREDATORS** ARE **TROUT, SALMON,** OTHER **FRESHWATER FISH,** AND **BIRDS.**

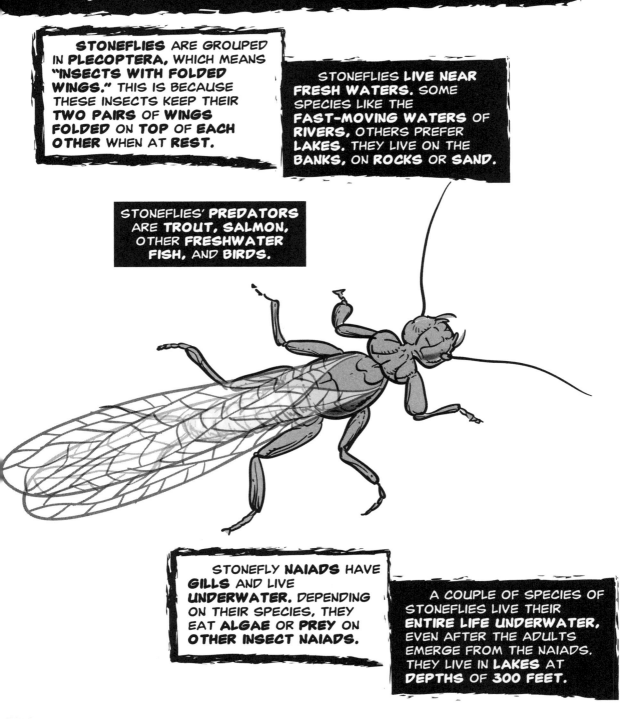

STONEFLY **NAIADS** HAVE **GILLS** AND LIVE **UNDERWATER.** DEPENDING ON THEIR SPECIES, THEY EAT **ALGAE** OR **PREY** ON **OTHER INSECT NAIADS.**

A COUPLE OF SPECIES OF STONEFLIES LIVE THEIR **ENTIRE LIFE UNDERWATER,** EVEN AFTER THE ADULTS EMERGE FROM THE NAIADS. THEY LIVE IN **LAKES** AT **DEPTHS** OF **300 FEET.**

BITING LICE

Exopterygota (insects with external wing development)
Mallophaga (eaters of locks of wool)

INSECTS BELONGING TO THIS GROUP ARE **SMALL PARASITES** OF **BIRDS** AND **MAMMALS.** THE SCIENTIFIC WORD **MALLOPHAGA** MEANS "EATERS OF **LOCKS** OF **WOOL.**" THIS IS BECAUSE **MANY SPECIES** OF **BITING LICE** EAT BITS OF THEIR **HOST'S FEATHERS, SKIN,** AND **DANDRUFF.** SOME SPECIES EAT **BLOOD.**

DIFFERENT **SPECIES** OF **BITING LICE** HAVE EVOLVED TO THRIVE ON A **SPECIFIC HOST** AND WON'T SURVIVE IF MOVED TO ANOTHER.

SOME BITING LICE ARE **PESTS** OF **CHICKENS.** CHICKENS DON'T SEEM **BOTHERED** BY A FEW BITING LICE, BUT SOMETIMES **INFESTATION** OCCURS. THIS MAY CAUSE **MANGE, LOSS** OF **WEIGHT,** AND **LESS EGG PRODUCTIVITY.**

WHEN THE **HOST DIES,** THE **BITING LICE DIE** TOO UNLESS THEY ARE ABLE TO QUICKLY **MOVE** TO A **NEW HOST.**

BUG BITES

To avoid infestation of lice, birds often take dust baths.

BOOKLICE & BARKLICE

Exopterygota (insects with external wing development)
Psocoptera (gnawing insects with wings)

PSOCOPTERA ARE SMALL LOUSE-LIKE INSECTS THAT LIVE IN DAMP AND DARK PLACES, LIKE BASEMENTS, UNDER TREE BARK OR DEAD LEAVES.

THE SCIENTIFIC NAME MEANS "GNAWING INSECT WITH WINGS," AND REFERS TO THE FACT THAT THEY CHEW ON BARK, BOOK PASTE, FUNGI, AND LICHENS.

BOOK AND BARKLICE ARE NOT PARASITES. SOME SPECIES LIVE IN BIRD NESTS, FEEDING ON BITS OF SHED FEATHERS, WITHOUT ENDANGERING THEIR HOSTS. BUT SCIENTISTS THINK THAT PARASITES LIKE LICE EVOLVED FROM THIS GROUP OF INSECTS.

THRIPS

Exopterygota (insects with external wing development)
Thysanoptera (insects with fringed wings)

IF **ROUGHLY HANDLED,** THRIPS CAN **BITE,** BUT THEY'RE **NOT VENOMOUS** AND THE **VIRUSES** THEY TRANSMIT ARE **NOT DANGEROUS** TO **PEOPLE.**

THYSANOPTERA MEANS **"INSECTS WITH FRINGED WINGS,"** AND REFER TO THESE INSECTS' **TWO PAIRS** OF **THIN WINGS** WITH **FUR-LIKE EDGES.** NOT ALL ADULT THRIPS HAVE WINGS.

THRIPS LIVE ON **PLANTS, FLOWERS,** AND **FRUITS,** FEEDING ON THE **SAP,** WHICH THEY **SUCK** WITH THEIR **POINTY MOUTHS.** FOR THIS REASON, AND FOR THE FACT THAT **MANY SPECIES** SPREAD **PLANT VIRUSES,** THRIPS ARE CONSIDERED **PESTS.** BUT OTHER SPECIES ARE **CONSIDERED BENEFICIAL** BECAUSE THEY EAT **MITES** AND **FUNGI.**

ANGEL INSECTS

Exopterygota (insects with external wing development)
Zoraptera (insects purely without wings)

WHILE SOME INSECTS GET THEIR **WINGS** WHEN THEY BECOME **ADULTS**, SCIENTISTS THOUGHT THAT THE **INSECTS** IN THIS GROUP WERE **WINGLESS THROUGHOUT THEIR LIVES**. THE **SCIENTIFIC TERM**, IN FACT, IS COMPOSED OF THREE WORDS, WHICH MEAN **"PURELY WITHOUT WINGS."** IT TURNED OUT THAT THESE INSECTS CAN **PRODUCE** A **NEW GENERATION** OF **WINGED INDIVIDUALS**. THEY **FLY AWAY** IN **SEARCH** OF A **BETTER PLACE** WHERE TO **NEST**.

IT HAS BEEN SAID THAT THE COMMON NAME **ANGEL INSECTS** WAS INSPIRED BY A **RELIGION** CALLED **ZOROASTRIANISM**. FOLLOWERS OF THIS RELIGION BELIEVE THAT **THOSE** WHO **LEAD** A **WHOLESOME**, OR PURE, **LIFE** BECOME **ANGELS** WHEN THEY **DIE**. BECAUSE THESE **INSECTS** ARE **PURELY WINGLESS**, THEY MIGHT BECOME **WINGED ANGELS** IN THE **AFTERLIFE**.

THESE INSECTS ARE **VERY SMALL**, LESS THAN **1/8** OF AN **INCH**.

WINGLESS ANGEL INSECTS ARE **BLIND**, WHILE **WINGED** CAN SEE.

ANGEL INSECTS RESEMBLE **TERMITES** BECAUSE THEY LIVE IN **GROUPS,** BUT THEY ARE **NOT** AS **ORGANIZED.** ALSO, LIKE TERMITES, ANGEL INSECTS ARE ABLE TO **REMOVE** THEIR **WINGS.**

ANGEL INSECTS **EAT FUNGI, MOSSES,** AND **MITES.** THEY **NEST** UNDER **DEAD LEAVES** OR **ROTTING WOOD.**

ANGEL INSECT **MALES** BRING A **DROP** OF **LIQUID** THEY **OOZE** FROM THEIR **HEADS** TO THE **FEMALES** AS A **COURTSHIP GIFT.** MATING TAKES PLACE AFTER THE FEMALES HAVE **EXAMINED** AND **ACCEPTED** THIS **GIFT.**

16. WHAT DOES AN **INEXPERIENCED BUTTERFLY** DO?

-HE JUST **WINGS** IT!

17. WHAT DO YOU CALL A **BUG** WITH **LARYNGITIS?**

-A **HOARSE**-FLY!

18. WHAT DID THE **BEE** PLAY IN THE SCHOOL **BAND?**

-THE **HORN**-ET!

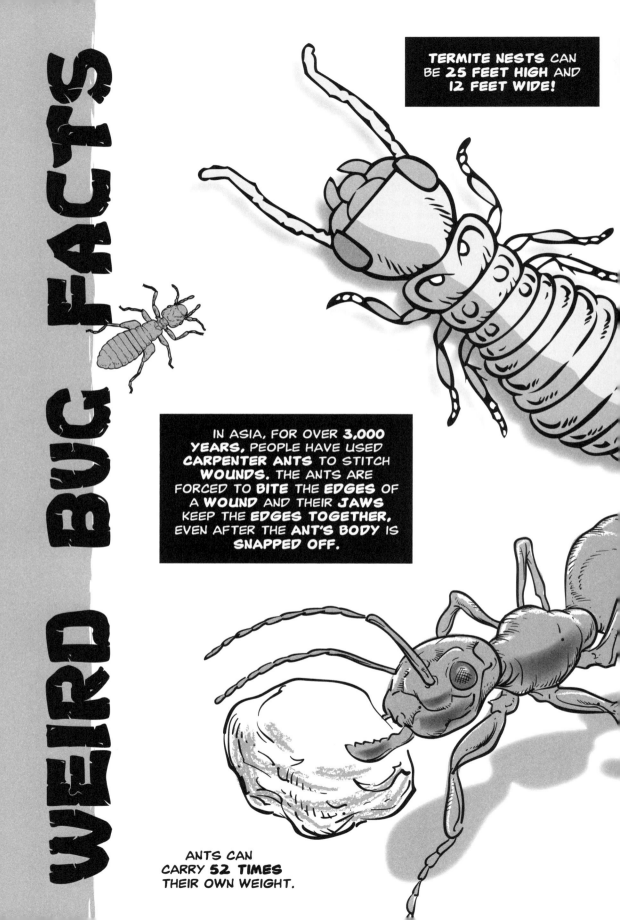

WEIRD BUG FACTS

TERMITE NESTS CAN BE **25 FEET HIGH** AND **12 FEET WIDE!**

IN ASIA, FOR OVER **3,000 YEARS,** PEOPLE HAVE USED **CARPENTER ANTS** TO STITCH **WOUNDS.** THE ANTS ARE FORCED TO **BITE** THE **EDGES** OF A **WOUND** AND THEIR **JAWS** KEEP THE **EDGES TOGETHER,** EVEN AFTER THE **ANT'S BODY** IS **SNAPPED OFF.**

ANTS CAN CARRY **52 TIMES** THEIR OWN WEIGHT.

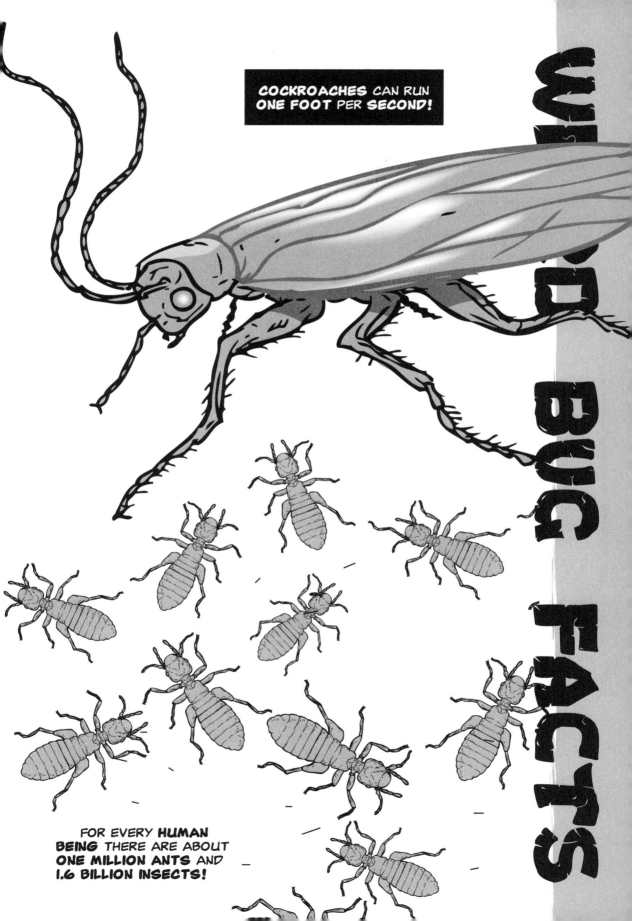

COCKROACHES CAN RUN ONE FOOT PER SECOND!

WEIRD BUG FACTS

FOR EVERY **HUMAN BEING** THERE ARE ABOUT **ONE MILLION ANTS** AND **1.6 BILLION INSECTS!**

Alabama

THE CITY OF **SELMA** IS THE **BUTTERFLY CAPITAL** OF ALABAMA, AND THE **EASTERN TIGER SWALLOWTAIL** IS ITS **MASCOT.**
THE EASTERN TIGER SWALLOWTAIL ALSO BECAME THE **STATE OF ALABAMA'S OFFICIAL BUTTERFLY** IN 1989.

THE OFFICIAL **INSECT** OF **ALABAMA** IS ALSO A BUTTERFLY. THE **MONARCH BUTTERFLY** WAS DESIGNATED **STATE INSECT** ON MAY 19, 1989.

Alaska

KIDS IN **ALASKA** WERE ASKED TO **VOTE** FOR THEIR **FAVORITE INSECT.** THE CHOICES WERE: THE **FOUR-SPOTTED SKIMMER DRAGONFLY, UNMARKED SLENDER MOSQUITO, MOURNING CLOAK BUTTERFLY,** AND **BUMBLEBEE.** THE **FOUR-SPOTTED SKIMMER DRAGONFLY** WON WITH ALMOST **4,000 VOTES** AND BECAME THE **STATE INSECT** ON AUGUST 24, 1995.

Arizona

THE **ARIZONA STATE BUTTERFLY** HAS BEEN THE **TWO-TAILED SWALLOWTAIL** SINCE MAY 9, 2001. THIS BUTTERFLY IS **NATIVE** OF **NORTH AMERICA**. IT'S **YELLOW**, WITH **BLACK LINES**, AND **BLUE SPOTS**.

Arkansas

THE **OFFICIAL INSECT** OF THE STATE OF **ARKANSAS** IS THE **HONEYBEE** AS OF FEBRUARY 1, 1973. THE ACT STATES THAT THIS **"DILIGENT** AND **WILLING WORKER** TYPIFIES THE **OUTSTANDING CITIZENS** OF THE STATE OF **ARKANSAS."**

California

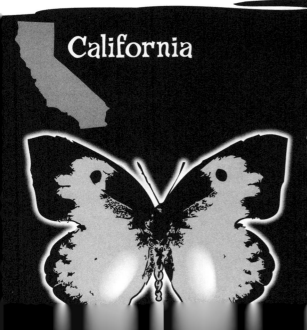

THE **DOGFACE BUTTERFLY** BECAME THE OFFICIAL **STATE INSECT** IN 1972 BECAUSE IT'S FOUND **ONLY** IN **CALIFORNIA.**
IT WAS NAMED **DOGFACE** BECAUSE THE **SPOTS** ON THE **WINGS** OF THE **MALES** RESEMBLE THE **PROFILE** OF A **DOG.** THE DOGFACE BUTTERFLY **FEMALES** HAVE **TWO BLACK DOTS.**
THE DOGFACE BUTTERFLY WAS **DEPICTED** ON A **U.S. POSTAL STAMP** IN 1977, WITH **THREE** OTHER **BUTTERFLIES.** THEY WERE THE **BALTIMORE CHECKERSPOT** (SEE MARYLAND), THE **OREGON SWALLOWTAIL** (SEE OREGON), AND THE **FALCATE ORANGE-TIPS.**
ANOTHER **U.S. POSTAL STAMP** DEPICTING THE **DOGFACE BUTTERFLY** WAS ISSUED IN 2007.

STATE INSECTS

Colorado

THE **INSECT** OF THIS STATE WAS NAMED THE **COLORADO HAIRSTREAK BUTTERFLY** ON APRIL 27, 1996.

THE COLORADO HAIRSTREAK BUTTERFLY DOESN'T FEED ON **NECTAR,** BUT RATHER ON THE **SAP** OF THE **GAMBEL OAK.**

Connecticut

ON OCTOBER 1, 1977, THE STATE OF **CONNECTICUT** DESIGNATED THE **EUROPEAN PRAYING MANTIS** AS **STATE INSECT.**

AS THE NAME REVEALS, THIS PRAYING MANTIS IS A **NATIVE** OF **EUROPE.** IT WAS **INTRODUCED** IN THE **UNITED STATES** ABOUT **80 YEARS AGO** AS A **NATURAL PEST CONTROL.** THIS IS BECAUSE THE EUROPEAN PRAYING MANTIS EATS **INSECTS** THAT DAMAGE **CROPS.**

Delaware

THE **LADYBUG** BECAME THIS **STATE'S INSECT** AFTER **MRS. MOLLIE BROWN-RUST** AND HER **SECOND GRADERS** FROM THE LULU ROSS ELEMENTARY SCHOOL, MILFORD, DELAWARE, **LOBBIED** THE **STATE**. THE KIDS CHOSE THE **LADYBUG** OVER THE **CRICKET** AND THE **MOSQUITO**. THEY REASONED THAT THE LADYBUG PREYS ON **PESTS**, LIKE **APHIDS** AND **SCALES**, AND KEEPS THE **PEACH BLOSSOM** (THE **STATE FLOWER**) SAFE. THE STATE LEGISLATORS **AGREED** AND ELECTED THE LADYBUG **STATE INSECT** ON APRIL 25, 1974.

THE **TIGER SWALLOWTAIL** WA ELECTED **OFFICIAL BUTTERFLY** OI **STATE** OF **DELAWARE** ON JUNE IC THIS WAS POSSIBLE THANKS TO TI EFFORTS OF A TEACHER, **MS. CYN** **POCHOMIS,** AND THE **KIDS** AT RICHARDSON PARK LEARNING CENTE NEWARK, DELAWARE.

DELAWARE IS THE **FIRST** AND **ONLY** STATE TO HAVE AN **OFFICIAL MACROINVERTEBRATE.**
A **MACROINVERTEBRATE** IS AN ANIMAL THAT **LACKS A BACKBONE** AND IS **BIG ENOUGH** TO BE SEEN **WITHOUT** A MAGNIFYING LENS.
THE **MACROINVERTEBRATE** OF THE STATE OF **DELAWARE** IS THE **STONEFLY.** STONEFLIES ARE **INSECTS** THAT LIVE NEAR THE **WATER** AND **CAN'T SURVIVE** IF THE WATER IS **POLLUTED.** THE STATE OF DELAWARE CHOSE THE STONEFLY TO CALL ATTENTION TO THE **SUPERIOR QUALITY** OF THE **WATERS** OF THIS STATE.

STATE INSECTS

Florida

IN 1996, GOVERNOR LAWTON CHILES DECLARED THE **ZEBRA LONGWING BUTTERFLY** THE OFFICIAL **INSECT** OF THE STATE OF **FLORIDA**.

UNLIKE MOST BUTTERFLIES, THE ZEBRA LONGWING FEEDS BOTH ON **NECTAR** AND **POLLEN**. FOR THIS REASON, IT LIVES FOR UP TO **THREE MONTHS**, QUITE A **LONG TIME** FOR A BUTTERFLY.

ZEBRA LONGWING **CATERPILLARS** EAT **PASSION FLOWER LEAVES**. THE PASSION FLOWER'S **NATURAL CHEMICALS** MAKE THE **CATERPILLAR** QUITE **DISGUSTING** TO ITS **PREDATORS**.

EVERY EVENING DURING THE **SUMMER**, GROUPS OF **60** OR **MORE** ZEBRA LONGWING BUTTERFLIES RETURN TO THE **SAME PLACES** TO **SLEEP**.

Georgia

THE **HONEYBEE** BECAME **STATE INSECT** IN 1975 BECAUSE OF THIS INSECT'S **CONTRIBUTION** TO **AGRICULTURE**, WHICH IS WORTH **$15 BILLION** ANNUALLY.

THE **TIGER SWALLOWTAIL** WAS DESIGNATED **STATE BUTTERFLY** OF GEORGIA IN 1988.

Idaho

THE **MONARCH BUTTERFLY** HAS BEEN THE **IDAHO STATE INSECT** SINCE 1992.

MONARCH BUTTERFLIES **MIGRATE** TO **WARMER STATES** DURING THE **WINTER** AND COME BACK **NORTH** FOR THE **SUMMER.** SINCE THE **LIFESPAN** OF A MONARCH IS **SHORTER** THAN ONE **YEAR,** IT'S STILL **UNCLEAR** HOW THE **NEWER GENERATIONS** ARE ABLE TO **COME BACK** TO THE **SAME PLACES** THE **OLDER GENERATIONS** CAME FROM.

Illinois

IN 1974, THE **THIRD GRADE STUDENTS** OF DENNIS SCHOOL, IN DECATUR, ILLINOIS, LOBBIED THE **LEGISLATORS** TO DESIGNATE THE **MONARCH BUTTERFLY** AS **STATE INSECT.** IN 1975, GOVERNOR DANIEL WALKER GRANTED THEIR REQUEST.

MONARCH BUTTERFLIES ARE **ORANGE** WITH **BLACK LINES** AND **WHITE DOTS.**

Kansas

THE **HONEYBEE** HAS BEEN THE OFFICIAL **INSECT** OF THE STATE OF **KANSAS** SINCE **1976.**

THE HONEYBEE IS THE OFFICIAL INSECT OF **MANY STATES** DUE TO ITS **IMPORTANCE** AS A **POLLINATOR,** AND BECAUSE IT PRODUCES **HONEY** AND **WAX.**

Kentucky

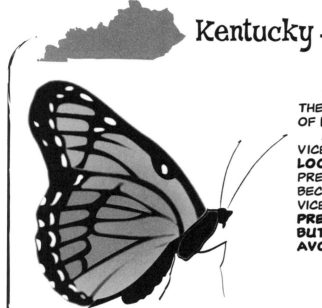

THE GENERAL ASSEMBLY DECLARED THE **VICEROY** THE **OFFICIAL BUTTERFLY** OF **KENTUCKY** IN 1990.

AS A **DEFENSE MECHANISM**, THE VICEROY BUTTERFLY HAS EVOLVED TO **LOOK JUST LIKE** A **MONARCH**. PREDATORS **AVOID** EATING **MONARCHS** BECAUSE THEY'RE **POISONOUS**. VICEROYS ARE **NOT POISONOUS**, BUT **PREDATORS CAN'T TELL** THESE **TWO BUTTERFLIES APART**, AND END UP **AVOIDING BOTH**.

TO **DISTINGUISH** A VICEROY FROM A MONARCH, LOOK AT THE **HIND WINGS**. IF THERE'S A **CURVED BLACK LINE** ACROSS THEM IT'S A **VICEROY**. IF THERE'S NOT, IT'S A **MONARCH**.

Monarch butterfly   Viceroy butterfly

Louisiana

THE **HONEYBEE** BECAME THE **LOUISIANA STATE INSECT** IN 1977.

THE **COMMON NAME** HAS THE **SAME MEANING** AS THE SCIENTIFIC NAME **APIS MELLIFERA. APIS** MEANS "BEE," AND **MELLIFERA** MEANS "CARRYING HONEY."

Maine

THE **MAINE STATE INSECT** HAS BEEN THE **HONEYBEE** SINCE 1975.

IN **ANCIENT TIMES**, HONEYBEES FIRST APPEARED IN **AFRICA**, AND THEN **MIGRATED** TO **EUROPE**. HONEYBEES WERE IMPORTED TO **NORTH AMERICA** FOR THE FIRST TIME IN **1622.**

Maryland

THE **BALTIMORE CHECKERSPOT BUTTERFLY** HAS BEEN THE **STATE INSECT** OF **MARYLAND** SINCE 1973.

THE BALTIMORE CHECKERSPOT IS **NATIVE** TO **NORTH AMERICA. THE WINGS** ARE **BLACK** WITH **BROWN, ORANGE,** AND **TAN SPOTS,** AND **TWO ORANGE CRESCENTS** ALONG THE **WINGS' BORDERS.**

THE **FIRST U.S. POSTAL STAMP** TO DEPICT **INSECTS** FEATURED **FOUR BUTTERFLIES.** ONE WAS THE **BALTIMORE CHECKERSPOT,** THE OTHERS WERE THE **DOGFACE** (SEE CALIFORNIA), THE **SWALLOWTAIL** (SEE OREGON), AND THE FALCATE ORANGE-TIP BUTTERFLY.

STATE INSECTS

Massachusetts

SECOND GRADE STUDENTS OF THE KENNEDY SCHOOL, IN FRANKLIN, MASSACHUSETTS, AND THEIR TEACHER, MS. PAMELA JOHNSON, LOBBIED THEIR **STATE LEGISLATOR.** THEY WANTED TO DESIGNATE THE **LADYBUG** AS THE **OFFICIAL STATE INSECT.** THE **BILL** PASSED IN **1975.**

Minnesota

THE **FOURTH GRADE STUDENTS** OF O. H. ANDERSON ELEMENTARY SCHOOL, MAHTOMEDI, MINNESOTA, CHOSE THE **MONARCH** AS THEIR **STATE BUTTERFLY.** THE **BILL** BECAME **LAW** ON MARCH 31, 2000.

Mississippi

THE **HONEYBEE** BECAME THE **OFFICIAL INSECT** OF **MISSISSIPPI** IN 1980.

IN **GREEK MYTHOLOGY**, WHEN **ZEUS** (THE **KING** OF THE **GODS**) WAS A **BABY**, TWO **NYMPHS** CARED FOR HIM. ONE WAS **AMALTHEA**, WHO BROUGHT HIM **MILK**, AND THE OTHER WAS **MELISSA**, WHO BROUGHT HIM **HON**EY. MELISSA MEANS **HONEYBEE**.

THE **SPICEBUSH SWALLOWTAIL** IS THIS STATE'S **OFFICIAL BUTTERFLY**. THE SPICEBUSH SWALLOWTAIL IS **BLACK** WITH **CREAMY SPOTS** ALONG THE **OUTER BORDERS** OF ITS **WINGS**. THE **FEMALE** HAS **BLUE SPOTS** ON THE **HIND WINGS**. ON THE **UNDERSIDE** OF THE **WINGS**, BOTH **MALES** AND **FEMALES** HAVE **TWO ROWS** OF **BRIGHT ORANGE MARKS**.

THE MOST **POPULAR STATE INSECTS** ARE THE **HONEYBEE** (SEVENTEEN STATES), THE **MONARCH BUTTERFLY** (SEVEN STATES), AND THE **LADYBUG** (SIX STATES).

STATE INSECTS

Missouri

GOVERNOR JOHN ASHCROFT OF **MISSOURI** DESIGNATED THE **HONEYBEE** AS **STATE INSECT** ON JULY 3, 1985.

THE **HONEY** OF THE HONEYBEE IS THE **OLDEST SWEETENER** KNOWN TO PEOPLE. IT'S A **GREAT SOURCE** OF NATURAL **CARBOHYDRATES,** WHICH ARE **ESSENTIAL NUTRIENTS.**

Montana

FIFTH GRADERS FROM GREAT FALLS, MONTANA, PETITIONED THEIR **STATE.** THEY WANTED TO DECLARE THE **MOURNING CLOAK** MONTANA'S **OFFICIAL BUTTERFLY.** DURING THE **SENATE HEARING,** LEGISLATOR JAMES WHITAKER **SPONSORED** THE **BILL.** HE STATED THAT THE MOURNING CLOAK "IS A **TRUE MONTANAN,** SPENDING BOTH **SUMMER** AND **WINTER** IN THE **STATE.** IT IS OFTEN THE **LAST BUTTERFLY** SEEN IN THE **FALL** AND IT IS THE **FIRST** TO APPEAR ON **EARLY SPRING DAYS."** THE MOURNING CLOAK HAS BEEN THE **STATE BUTTERFLY** SINCE 2001.

THIS BUTTERFLY'S **SHAPE** AND **COLOR** RESEMBLE A **MOURNING CLOAK,** A GARMENT PEOPLE IN **MOURNING** USED TO WEAR. THE BUTTERFLY IS **BLACK,** WITH A WIDE **CREAMY OUTER BORDER,** AND AN **INNER BORDER** OF **BRIGHT BLUE SPOTS** ALONG THE **WINGS.**

Nebraska

ON MARCH 14, 1975, GOVERNOR J. JAMES EXON DECLARED THE **HONEYBEE** THE **OFFICIAL INSECT** OF THE STATE OF **NEBRASKA.** THIS FOLLOWED A **PETITION** FROM THE **GRADE SCHOOL STUDENTS** OF AUBURN, NEBRASKA.

New Hampshire

FIFTH GRADERS FROM THE BROKEN GROUND GRAMMAR SCHOOL OF CONCORD, NEW HAMPSHIRE, AND THEIR TEACHER, **MRS. MARILYN FRASER,** LOBBIED THEIR **LEGISLATORS** TO DESIGNATE THE **LADYBUG** AS **OFFICIAL INSECT.** GOVERNOR MELDRIM THOMSON JR. SIGNED THE **LAW,** AND THE LADYBUG BECAME **STATE INSECT** ON **FLAG DAY,** JUNE 14, 1977. ALL THE **MEMBERS** OF THE **SENATE** SIGNED A COPY OF THE **BILL** AND DONATED IT TO THE **BROKEN GROUND SCHOOL STUDENTS** IN RECOGNITION OF THEIR **EFFORTS.**

New Jersey

GOVERNOR BRENDAN T. BYRNE DECLARED THE **HONEYBEE** NEW JERSEY **INSECT** ON JUNE 20, 1974.

HONEYBEES ADD **NATURAL ANTIBACTERIAL PROPERTIES** TO THEIR **HONEY.** ANTIBACTERIALS, HIGH ACIDITY, AND LOW AMOUNT OF WATER KEEP THE HONEY **CLEAN** OF **PATHOGENS** AND PREVENT IT FROM **ROTTING.**

STATE INSECTS

New Mexico

MRS. **RUTH BRADFORD** AND HER **SIXTH GRADERS** OF THE EDGEWOOD ELEMENTARY SCHOOL CHOSE **THREE INSECTS** AS POSSIBLE CANDIDATES FOR STATE INSECT. **STUDENTS** ACROSS NEW MEXICO VOTED IN FAVOR OF THE **TARANTULA HAWK WASP**. THEIR **PETITION** WAS SIGNED INTO **LAW** IN **1989.**

ON APRIL 6, 2003, GOVERNOR BILL RICHARDSON OFFICIALLY ADOPTED THE **SANDIA HAIRSTREAK** AS THE **STATE BUTTERFLY.** AS THE LEGISLATURE READS, THE SANDIA HAIRSTREAK BUTTERFLY,

"**SYMBOLIZES** THE **ABILITY** OF **NEW MEXICAN RESIDENTS** TO **THRIVE YEAR-ROUND** IN A **SEMIARID CLIMATE** WHERE DIFFERENT YEARS BRING **FLOODS** AND **DROUGHTS** AND WHERE THE **TERRAIN** IS **BEAUTIFUL** BUT **RUGGED.**"

THE SANDIA HAIRSTREAK WAS **DISCOVERED** IN **LA CUEVA CANYON** IN 1959 AND IT'S A **NATIVE** BUTTERFLY OF **NEW MEXICO.**

New York

NEW YORK STATE DESIGNATED THE NATIVE **NINE-SPOTTED LADYBUG** AS THE **STATE INSECT** IN 1989. PREVIOUSLY, THE **ASIAN LADY BEETLE,** A DIFFERENT SPECIES OF LADYBUG, HAD BEEN INTRODUCED IN THE **UNITES STATES** AS A **NATURAL PEST CONTROL.** THE ASIAN LADY BEETLE AND THE NINE-SPOTTED LADYBUG WERE **COMPETING** FOR THE **SAME FOOD,** BUT THE **ASIAN BEETLE** WAS MORE **SUCCESSFUL.** THIS DETERMINED THE **DISAPPEARANCE** OF THE **NINE-SPOTTED LADYBUG** FROM NEW YORK. WHEN LEGISLATORS REALIZED THIS, THEY **CHANGED** THE OFFICIAL STATE INSECT. THE **SPOTTED LADYBUG,** ANOTHER LADYBUG, HAS BEEN THE **OFFICIAL INSECT** SINCE JUNE 15, 2006.

North Carolina

THE **HONEYBEE** BECAME NORTH CAROLINA'S **OFFICIAL INSECT** IN 1973. SINCE NOVEMBER 2006, **HONEYBEES** HAVE BEEN **ABANDONING** THEIR **HIVES WORLDWIDE** FOR **NO APPARENT REASON.** A **HEALTHY COLONY** CAN SUDDENLY **DIE,** LEAVING ONLY THE **QUEEN** AND **FEW BEES.** THIS **PHENOMENON** IS CALLED **COLONY COLLAPSE DISORDER** (CCD) AND IT'S AFFECTING MANY **STATES.**

Ohio

THE **NEWS** THAT THE **BALTIMORE CHECKERSPOT BUTTERFLY** HAD BECOME THE **STATE INSECT** OF **MARYLAND** THROUGH THE EFFORT OF SOME **STUDENTS** INSPIRED THE **KIDS** OF LINCOLNSHIRE SCHOOL, TOLEDO, OHIO.

WITH THEIR TEACHER, **MRS. RUTH MICHAELIS,** THEY COLLECTED **4,000 SIGNATURES** ON THEIR **PETITION** TO ELECT THE **LADYBUG** AS **STATE INSECT** OF **OHIO.**

THEIR PETITION BECAME **LAW** IN 1975. THE **BILL** READS, "THE LADYBUG IS **TRULY EMBLEMATIC** OF OUR GREAT **STATE. . .**THE **QUEENLY LADYBUG** IS **SYMBOLIC** OF THE **PEOPLE** OF OHIO—SHE IS **PROUD** AND **FRIENDLY,** BRINGING **DELIGH**T TO **MILLIONS OF CHILDREN.**"

STATE INSECTS

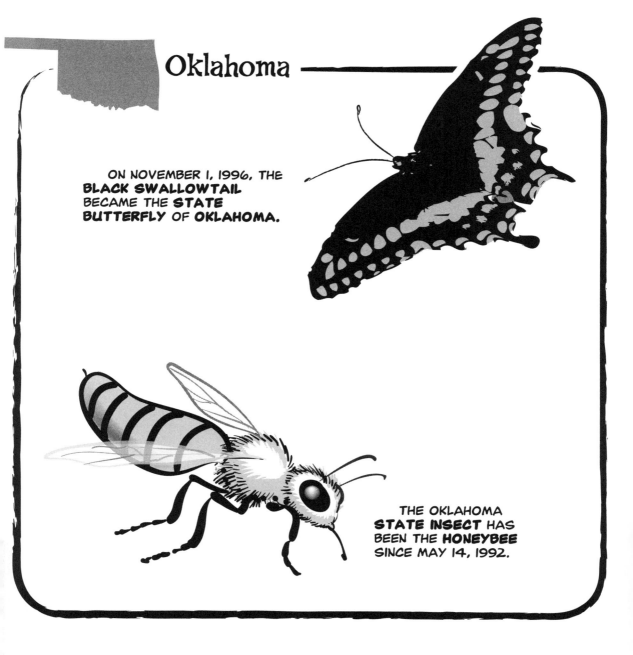

Oklahoma

ON NOVEMBER 1, 1996, THE **BLACK SWALLOWTAIL** BECAME THE **STATE BUTTERFLY** OF **OKLAHOMA.**

THE OKLAHOMA **STATE INSECT** HAS BEEN THE **HONEYBEE** SINCE MAY 14, 1992.

Oregon

THIS STATE ELECTED THE **OREGON SWALLOWTAIL** AS THEIR **OFFICIAL BUTTERFLY** IN **1979.**

THE OREGON SWALLOWTAIL WAS FEATURED ON A **U.S. POSTAL STAMP** IN 1977 (SEE MARYLAND AND CALIFORNIA). AT THE TIME, THE **STAMPS** COST **13 CENTS** EACH.

THE OREGON SWALLOWTAIL BUTTERFLY'S **SCIENTIFIC NAME** IS **PAPILIO OREGONIUS,** WHICH, IN LATIN, MEANS **"BUTTERFLY FROM OREGON."** THE FACT THAT THE WORD **OREGON** APPEARS **BOTH** IN THE **COMMON NAME** AND IN THE **SCIENTIFIC NAME** WAS **NOTED** ON THE **BILL** THAT DESIGNATED THIS BUTTERFLY AS **STATE INSECT.**

Pennsylvania

THE **FIREFLY** WAS DESIGNATED **STATE INSECT TWICE** IN **PENNSYLVANIA.** THE FIRST TIME WAS IN 1974. BECAUSE SOME PEOPLE CONFUSED **FIREFLIES** WITH **BLACK FLIES,** A COMMON **PEST,** A **SECOND BILL** WAS ISSUED ON DECEMBER 5, 1988.

TO **END** THE **CONFUSION,** THE **SECOND BILL** SPECIFIED THE FIREFLY'S **SCIENTIFIC NAME.** THIS IS **PHOTURIS PENNSYLVANICA DE GEER,** OR **"CHARLES DE GEER'S FIREFLY FROM PENNSYLVANIA."**

CHARLES DE GEER WAS A **SWEDISH ENTOMOLOGIST** WHO **DISCOVERED** AND **NAMED** THIS **FIREFLY** IN THE EIGHTEENTH CENTURY.

THERE ARE **EIGHT U.S. STATES** THAT DON'T HAVE AN OFFICIAL INSECT OR BUTTERFLY. THEY ARE **HAWAII, INDIANA, IOWA, MICHIGAN, NEVADA, NORTH DAKOTA, RHODE ISLAND,** AND **WYOMING.**

South Carolina

THE **STATE INSECT** OF **SOUTH CAROLINA** WAS NAMED THE **CAROLINA MANTIS** IN 1988. THE **BILL** RECOGNIZES THE MANTIS AS A **BENEFICIAL INSECT** THAT **PREYS** ON **PESTS**.

A STUDY CONDUCTED BY **DR. YEAGER** DISCOVERED THAT **MANTIS MALES HEAR** THE **HIGH-FREQUENCY NOISES** OF **BATS**, WHILE **FEMALES** ARE **DEAF**. MANTIS MALES **FLY** AT **NIGHT** LOOKING FOR **FEMALES**. THIS MAKES MALES IN **DANGER** OF **BEING EATEN** BY **BATS**. FEMALES DON'T HAVE THIS PROBLEM, SINCE THEIR **WINGS** ARE **TOO SHORT** FOR **FLIGHT**. THEY **HIDE** IN **BUSHES** WHERE BATS **CAN'T FIND** THEM.

IN **1587**, DURING HIS **THIRD TRIP** TO **AMERICA**, ENGLISH COLONIST **JOHN WHITE** PAINTED A **WATERCOLOR PICTURE** OF THE **EASTERN TIGER SWALLOWTAIL BUTTERFLY**. AT THAT TIME **CAMERAS** HADN'T BEEN INVENTED, SO PEOPLE MADE **DRAWINGS**. JOHN WHITE BROUGHT HIS DRAWINGS BACK TO **ENGLAND**, AND, FOR THE **VERY FIRST TIME**, PEOPLE COULD **ADMIRE** THE EASTERN TIGER SWALLOWTAIL.

SOUTH CAROLINA ALSO DESIGNATED A **STATE SPIDER**, THE **CAROLINA WOLF SPIDER**, IN 2000. **WOLF SPIDERS** ARE NAMED SO BECAUSE THEY **CHASE** THEIR **PREY**, LIKE **WOLVES** DO. THE CAROLINA WOLF SPIDER IS **NATIVE** TO **NORTH AMERICA** AND IS THE **BIGGEST SPIDER** WITHIN ITS GROUP.

South Dakota

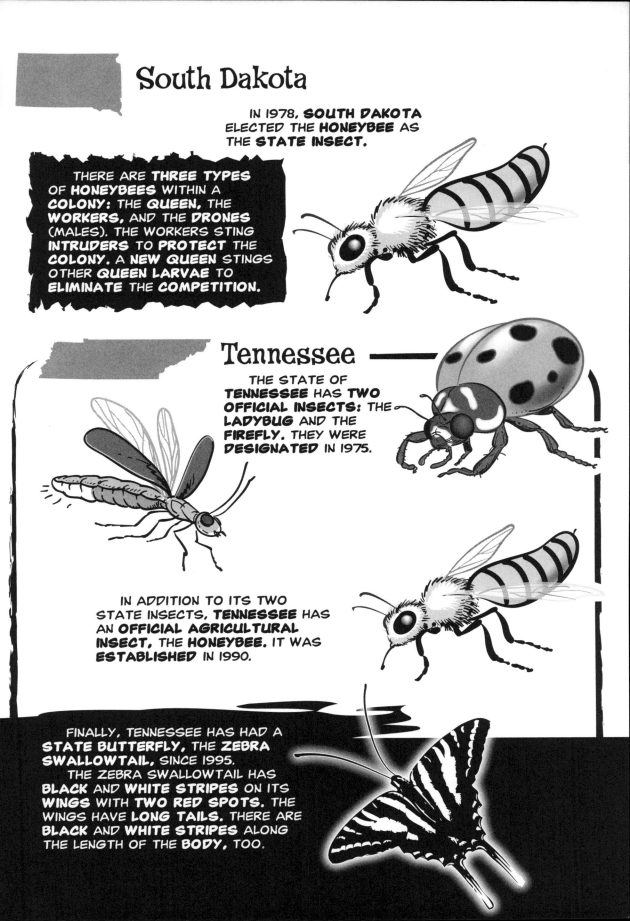

IN 1978, **SOUTH DAKOTA** ELECTED THE **HONEYBEE** AS THE **STATE INSECT**.

THERE ARE **THREE TYPES** OF **HONEYBEES** WITHIN A **COLONY**: THE **QUEEN**, THE **WORKERS**, AND THE **DRONES** (MALES). THE WORKERS STING **INTRUDERS** TO **PROTECT** THE **COLONY**. A **NEW QUEEN** STINGS OTHER **QUEEN LARVAE** TO **ELIMINATE** THE **COMPETITION**.

Tennessee

THE STATE OF **TENNESSEE** HAS **TWO OFFICIAL INSECTS**: THE **LADYBUG** AND THE **FIREFLY**. THEY WERE **DESIGNATED** IN 1975.

IN ADDITION TO ITS TWO STATE INSECTS, **TENNESSEE** HAS AN **OFFICIAL AGRICULTURAL INSECT**, THE **HONEYBEE**. IT WAS **ESTABLISHED** IN 1990.

FINALLY, TENNESSEE HAS HAD A **STATE BUTTERFLY**, THE **ZEBRA SWALLOWTAIL**, SINCE 1995.
THE ZEBRA SWALLOWTAIL HAS **BLACK** AND **WHITE STRIPES** ON ITS **WINGS** WITH **TWO RED SPOTS**. THE WINGS HAVE **LONG TAILS**. THERE ARE **BLACK** AND **WHITE STRIPES** ALONG THE LENGTH OF THE **BODY**, TOO.

STATE INSECTS

Texas

THE **MONARCH BUTTERFLY** HAS BEEN **TEXAS' OFFICIAL INSECT** SINCE 1995.

MONARCH **BUTTERFLIES** AND **CATERPILLARS** ARE **POISONOUS** AND **PREDATORS AVOID** THEM. THIS IS BECAUSE THEY **FEED** ON **MILKWEED,** A TOXIC PLANT. MONARCHS ARE **NOT SENSITIVE** TO THE **CHEMICALS** OF THE **MILKWEED,** BUT THEIR PREDATORS ARE.

Utah

FIFTH GRADERS OF RIDGECREST ELEMENTARY SCHOOL, COTTONWOOD HEIGHTS, UTAH, **LOBBIED** THEIR **LEGISLATORS** TO DESIGNATE THE **HONEYBEE** AS **STATE INSECT.** THEY SUCCEEDED IN **1983.**

THE **MORMON WORD** FOR HONEYBEE IS **"DESERET."** IT WAS **PROPOSED** AS THE **NAME** OF THE **STATE** OF **UTAH.** IT WAS **REJECTED** IN 1849.
UTAH'S **NICKNAME** IS THE **BEEHIVE STATE.**

Vermont

VERMONT'S OFFICIAL BUTTERFLY IS THE **MONARCH BUTTERFLY,** AS ESTABLISHED ON JUNE 8, 1987.

ON FEBRUARY 17, 1978, **VERMONT** DESIGNATED THE **HONEYBEE** AS **STATE INSECT.**

Virginia

THE **STATE INSECT** OF **VIRGINIA** IS THE **TIGER SWALLOWTAIL BUTTERFLY** AS OF 1991. THE **SCIENTIFIC NAME** OF THIS BUTTERFLY IS **PAPILIO GLAUCUS LINNAEUS.** IT MEANS THE **LIGHT BLUE** (GLAUCUS) **BUTTERFLY** (PAPILIO) OF LINNAEUS. **CARL LINNAEUS** WAS A **SWEDISH SCIENTIST** WHO INVENTED THE **RULES** FOR **NAMING ANIMALS** AND **SPECIES.** HE LIVED

STATE INSECTS

Washington

INSPIRED BY COLORADO STUDENTS, WHO MADE THE HAIRSTREAK BUTTERFLY THEIR STATE INSECT, **KIDS** IN **WASHINGTON STATE** STARTED A **CAMPAIGN.** THEY WANTED TO ELECT THE **GREEN DARNER DRAGONFLY** AS THEIR **OFFICIAL STATE INSECT.**

WITH THE HELP OF THEIR TEACHER, **MS. SHOL,** AND AN ENTOMOLOGIST, **DR. RICHARD ZACH,** THE KIDS OF CRESTWOOD ELEMENTARY SCHOOL NOMINATED THE **GREEN DARNER DRAGONFLY,** THE **GREEN LACEWING,** AND THE **LADYBUG.** A **VOTING POLL** INVOLVING **STUDENTS** ACROSS **WASHINGTON STATE** FOLLOWED. THE GREEN DARNER DRAGONFLY **WON** WITH MORE THAN **15,000 VOTES.**

THEN, THE STUDENTS **PETITIONED** THEIR **STATE REPRESENTATIVES,** AND IN 1997 THE GREEN DARNER DRAGONFLY BECAME **OFFICIAL INSECT.**

CRESTWOOD ELEMENTARY SCHOOL IS NOW KNOWN AS THE **HOME** OF THE **WASHINGTON STATE INSECT.**

West Virginia

WEST VIRGINIA DECLARED THE **MONARCH BUTTERFLY STATE INSECT** ON MARCH 1, 1995.

THE MONARCH BUTTERFLY ADULT AND CATERPILLAR WERE **FEATURED** ON THE **"INSECTS AND SPIDERS"** SET OF **U.S. POSTAL STAMPS** IN 1999.

WEST VIRGINIA DESIGNATED THE **HONEYBEE** AS **STATE INSECT** IN 2000.

THE **HEALING PROPERTIES** OF BEES' **HONEY** HAVE BEEN KNOWN FOR **THOUSANDS** OF **YEARS.** A **3,500 YEAR OLD PAPYRUS** FROM **EGYPT** DESCRIBES HOW TO CURE **SKIN BURNS** USING **HONEY.**

Wisconsin

THE **HONEYBEE** WAS DESIGNATED **STATE INSECT** OF **WISCONSIN** IN 1977.

THE HONEYBEE IS ONE OF THE **MOST BENEFICIAL INSECTS** FOR **HUMANKIND**. AS THE **U.S. DEPARTMENT OF AGRICULTURE** STATES, "**ONE-THIRD** OF THE **HUMAN DIET** IS DERIVED DIRECTLY OR INDIRECTLY FROM **INSECT-POLLINATED PLANTS**." THESE INSECTS INCLUDE, OF COURSE, **HONEYBEES**.

DOES YOUR STATE HAVE AN OFFICIAL BUG YET?!

NOT ALL THE **STATES** HAVE AN **OFFICIAL INSECT** OR **BUTTERFLY**, BUT SOME HAVE **BOTH**. IF YOUR STATE DOESN'T HAVE ONE OR BOTH, YOU SHOULD **LEAD** A **PETITION** TO GET YOUR **STATE LEGISLATORS** TO **DESIGNATE** ONE. ASK YOUR **TEACHER** HOW TO **WRITE** A **PETITION, COLLECT SIGNATURES,** AND **LOBBY** YOUR LEGISLATORS.

A **CANDIDATE** FOR **STATE INSECT** COULD BE A **BENEFICIAL BUG**. MANY STATES HAVE CHOSEN THE **LADYBUG**, BUT OTHERS, LIKE CONNECTICUT AND SOUTH CAROLINA, PREFERRED THE **MANTIS**. LADYBUGS AND MANTIDS ARE BENEFICIAL BECAUSE THEY KEEP **PEST POPULATIONS** IN CHECK BY **EATING HARMFUL INSECTS**.

ANOTHER **CANDIDATE** FOR **STATE INSECT** COULD BE A **BUG** THAT IS **NATIVE** TO YOUR **STATE**. FOR MARYLAND AND OREGON THIS WAS THE WAY TO GO. THEY DESIGNATED RESPECTIVELY THE **BALTIMORE CHECKERSPOT BUTTERFLY** AND THE **OREGON SWALLOWTAIL**.

A STATE INSECT **CANDIDATE** COULD BE AN **INSECT** THAT IS **IMPORTANT** TO THE **ECONOMIC DEVELOPMENT** OF YOUR STATE. MANY STATES CHOSE THE **HONEYBEE** FOR THIS REASON, BUT THERE ARE OTHER **BUGS** THAT IMPACT OUR **ECONOMY** IN A BENEFICIAL WAY.

IN STARTING YOUR PETITION, DON'T FORGET TO **ENROLL** THE HELP OF AN **EXPERT ENTOMOLOGIST**, POSSIBLY A PERSON **FAMILIAR** WITH THE **INSECTS** IN YOUR **AREA**, LIKE THE KIDS IN WASHINGTON STATE DID.

CHELICERATA

CHELICERATA IS ONE OF THE **GROUPS** OF **ANIMALS** BELONGING TO **ARTHROPODS**. CHELICERATA MEANS **"ANIMALS WITH CHELICERAE,"** OR **FANGS**. ALL ANIMALS IN THIS GROUP HAVE A **PAIR** OF **FANGS** NEAR THEIR **MOUTH**. THESE ANIMALS USE THEIR FANGS TO **GRAB** THEIR **PREY**, **CHEW** THEIR **FOOD** OR **INJECT VENOM** INTO THEIR **VICTIMS**.

BECAUSE **CHELICERATA** BELONG TO **ARTHROPODS**, THEY MUST HAVE ALL THE **CHARACTERISTICS** OF THE **ARTHROPODS**.

1 ALL **CHELICERATA** HAVE **JOINTED LEGS**.

2 **CHELICERATA** ARE **SYMMETRICAL**.

3 THEIR **BODIES** ARE **SEGMENTED**.

4 THEY HAVE AN **EXOSKELETON**.

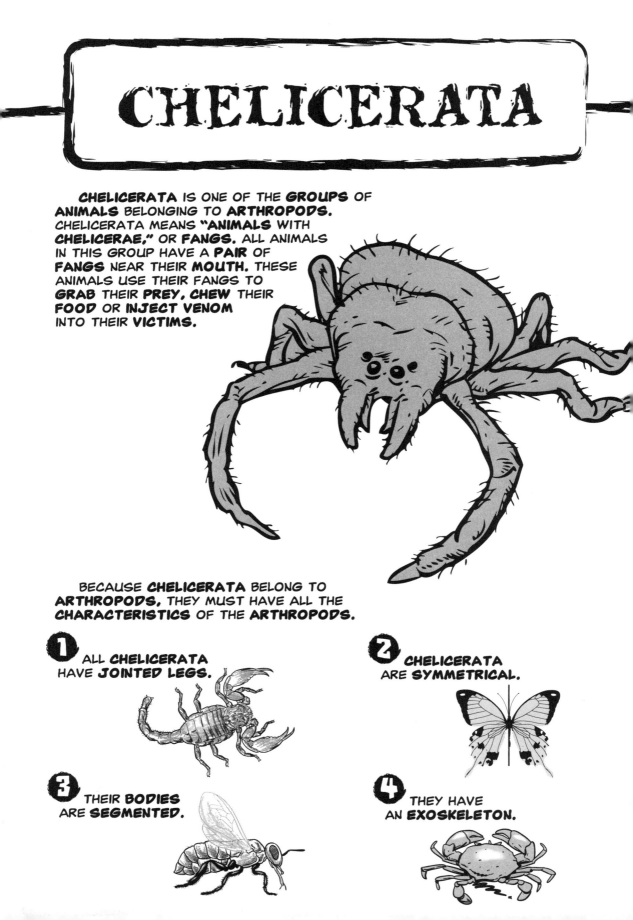

CHELICERATA INCLUDES THREE GROUPS: **ARACHNIDS**, **MEROSTOMATA**, AND **PYCNOGONIDA.**

ARACHNIDS

PSEUDOSCORPIONS

SCORPIONS

WHIP SCORPIONS

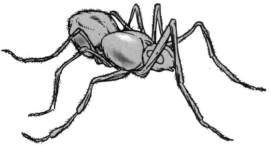

ARANEAE (SPIDERS)

ACARI (MITES AND TICKS)

SOLIFUGAE (WIND SCORPIONS)

OPILIONES
(HARVESTMEN, PHALANGIDS,
DADDY LONGLEGS)

MEROSTOMATA

PYCNOGONIDA

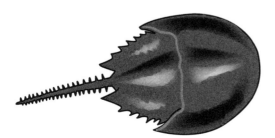

HORSESHOE CRABS

SEA SPIDERS

ARACHNIDS ARE A **GROUP** OF **ANIMALS** THAT BELONG TO THE **ARTHROPODS.** TO BE CALLED AN **ARACHNID,** AN ANIMAL MUST HAVE THE FOLLOWING **CHARACTERISTICS. . .**

THE BODY

THE **BODY** OF AN ARACHNID IS **DIVIDED** INTO **TWO PARTS:** THE **CEPHALOTHORAX** AND THE **ABDOMEN.** THESE TWO PARTS ARE UNITED BY THE **PEDICLE,** THE WAIST.

PEDICLE

LEGS

ARACHNIDS HAVE **EIGHT JOINTED LEGS.** ONLY THE **LARVAE** OF THE **MITES** HAVE **SIX LEGS.**

ARACHNIDS ARE MAINLY CARNIVOROUS (THEY EAT OTHER ANIMALS), BUT SOME FEED ON PLANTS. SOME SPECIES ARE CANNIBALISTIC. SOME ARACHNIDS ARE PARASITIC (THEY LIVE AT THE EXPENSE OF OTHER ANIMALS). MANY ARACHNIDS CAN INJECT POISON INTO THEIR VICTIMS.

ARACHNIDS DON'T HAVE ANTENNAE OR WINGS.

CHELICERAE

ARACHNIDS HAVE A PAIR OF CHELICERAE. CHELICERAE ARE TWO APPENDAGES POSITIONED ON EITHER SIDE OF THE ANIMAL'S MOUTH.

PEDIPALPS

ARACHNIDS HAVE ONE PAIR OF PEDIPALPS. THESE APPENDAGES ARE LOCATED NEAR THE MOUTH, AFTER THE CHELICERAE AND BEFORE THE FIRST PAIR OF LEGS. PEDIPALPS ARE SENSORY ORGANS ARACHNIDS USE TO TOUCH AND FEEL THEIR SURROUNDINGS AND, FOR SOME SPECIES, TO MATE.

BUG BITES

The cephalothorax is composed of the head (cephalon) and the thorax fused together.

WHIP SCORPIONS

Thelyphonida

WHIP SCORPIONS GET THEIR NAME FROM THE **WHIP-LIKE TAIL** AT THE **END** OF THEIR **ABDOMEN.** IT'S UNKNOWN EXACTLY WHAT THE TAIL IS **USED FOR.** SOME SCIENTISTS THINK THAT THE TAIL CAN **DETECT LIGHT.** WHIP SCORPIONS DON'T LIKE THE **SUNLIGHT** AND LIVE **UNDER ROCKS, DEAD LEAVES,** AND **BARK.**

THE **WHIP-LIKE TAIL** IS CALLED THE **FLAGELLUM.**

WHIP SCORPIONS DON'T HAVE A **POISONOUS STINGER** LIKE SCORPIONS, AND **CAN'T PRODUCE SILK** LIKE SPIDERS.

THEY USE ONLY **SIX LEGS** FOR WALKING. THE **FIRST TWO LEGS** ARE **MUCH THINNER** AND **LONGER** THAN THE **OTHER LEGS.** THEY ARE **SENSORY ORGANS,** LIKE ANTENNAE. THIS MEANS THAT WHIP SCORPIONS USE THEIR **FIRST PAIR** OF LEGS TO **FEEL** THEIR **SURROUNDINGS.**

WHEN WHIP SCORPIONS FEEL **THREATENED** BY A **PREDATOR**, THEY **SPRAY** AN **ACID** FROM THEIR **ANAL GLANDS**. THIS ACID IS **STINKY**. SOME SPECIES, CALLED **VINEGAROON**, SPRAY AN ACID THAT **SMELLS** LIKE **VINEGAR**. OTHERS SPRAY A **FLUID** THAT SMELLS LIKE **CHLORINE**. THE SMELL OF THE FLUID **REPELS ATTACKERS**, AND THE **ACID** CAN ACTUALLY **WOUND THEM**.

WHIP SCORPIONS ARE **CARNIVOROUS PREDATORS** AND **HUNT** AT **NIGHT**. THEY EAT **INSECTS, WORMS, SLUGS, ROACHES, CRICKETS,** AND **GRASSHOPPERS**.

WHEN THEY **CATCH** THEIR **PREY**, WHIP SCORPIONS **CRUSH** AND **CHEW** IT WITH THEIR **SAW-LIKE CLAWS**.

THE **CLAWS** ARE CALLED **PEDIPALPS**. WHIP SCORPIONS ALSO USE THEM TO **DIG HOLES**.

WHIP SCORPIONS HAVE **ONE PAIR** OF EYES ON THE **FRONT** OF THEIR **HEAD,** AND **THREE PAIRS** ON **EACH SIDE.**

WHEN IT'S TIME TO **LAY EGGS,** THE **WHIP SCORPION FEMALE** DIGS A **BURROW** IN THE GROUND. THEY LAY THEIR EGGS **INSIDE** A **SACK,** WHICH KEEPS THE EGGS **MOISTENED.** THE FEMALE **DOESN'T ABANDON** THE EGGS, AND **MAKES SURE** THAT THEY ARE **SAFE FROM PREDATORS.** WHEN THE EGGS HATCH, THE NEWBORNS **GLUE THEMSELVES** TO THE **BACK** OF THEIR **MOTHER.** WHEN THE **YOUNG WHIP SCORPIONS** HAVE GROWN **ENOUGH,** THEY **LEAVE** THEIR **MOTHER,** AND THEIR MOTHER **DIES.**

SPIDERS

Araneae

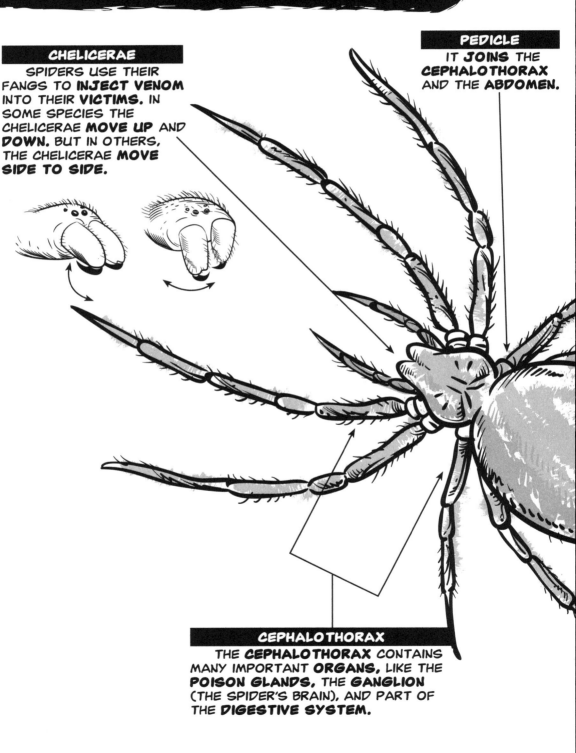

CHELICERAE

SPIDERS USE THEIR FANGS TO **INJECT VENOM** INTO THEIR **VICTIMS.** IN SOME SPECIES THE CHELICERAE **MOVE UP** AND **DOWN.** BUT IN OTHERS, THE CHELICERAE **MOVE SIDE TO SIDE.**

PEDICLE

IT **JOINS** THE **CEPHALOTHORAX** AND THE **ABDOMEN.**

CEPHALOTHORAX

THE **CEPHALOTHORAX** CONTAINS MANY IMPORTANT **ORGANS,** LIKE THE **POISON GLANDS,** THE **GANGLION** (THE SPIDER'S BRAIN), AND PART OF THE **DIGESTIVE SYSTEM.**

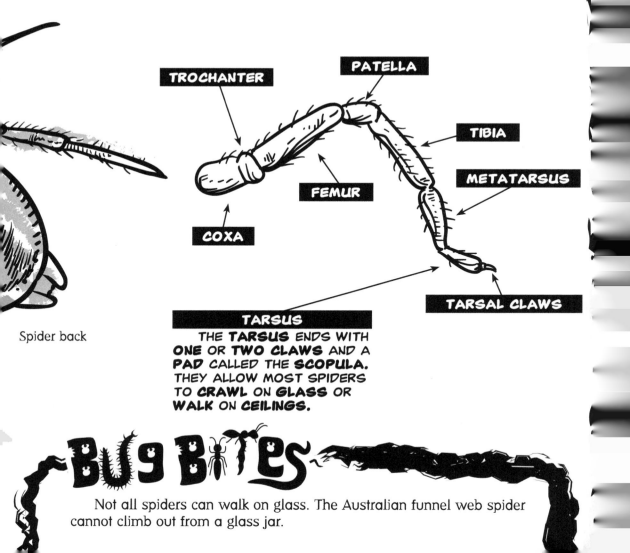

EYES

SPIDERS GENERALLY HAVE **SIX** OR **EIGHT EYES,** DEPENDING ON THEIR SPECIES. IN SPITE OF THIS ABUNDANCE OF EYES, ONLY THE **JUMPING SPIDERS** ARE BELIEVED TO HAVE **GOOD EYESIGHT.**

CHELICERAE

LEGS

SPIDERS HAVE **EIGHT JOINTED LEGS,** EACH MADE UP OF **SEVEN SEGMENTS.**

TROCHANTER

PATELLA

TIBIA

METATARSUS

FEMUR

COXA

TARSAL CLAWS

Spider back

TARSUS

THE **TARSUS** ENDS WITH **ONE** OR **TWO CLAWS** AND A **PAD** CALLED THE **SCOPULA.** THEY ALLOW MOST SPIDERS TO **CRAWL** ON **GLASS** OR **WALK** ON **CEILINGS.**

BUG BITES

Not all spiders can walk on glass. The Australian funnel web spider cannot climb out from a glass jar.

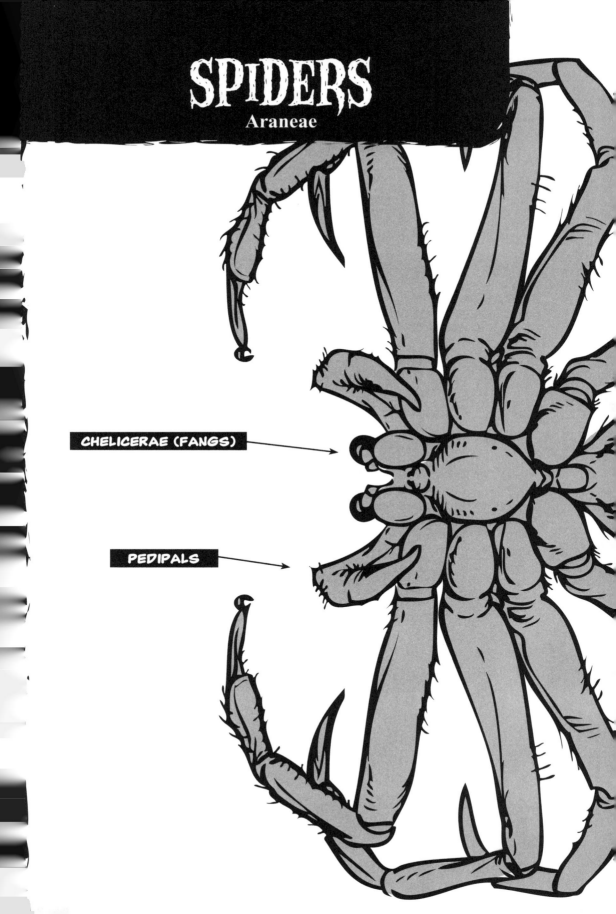

SPIDERS
Araneae

CHELICERAE (FANGS)

PEDIPALS

ABDOMEN

THE **ABDOMEN** CONTAINS MANY IMPORTANT **ORGANS,** LIKE THE **HEART,** THE **REPRODUCTIVE SYSTEM,** BOOK LUNGS, PART OF THE **DIGESTIVE SYSTEM,** AND THE **SILK GLANDS** (TO PRODUCE **SILK** FOR THE **WEB**).

BOOK LUNGS

SPIDERS BREATHE WITH THEIR **BOOK LUNGS.** THEY ARE LOCATED ON THE **BOTTOM** PART OF THE **ABDOMEN.** SPIDERS DON'T HAVE **NOSES,** LIKE HUMANS.

THE **SHAPE** OF THE BOOK LUNGS RESEMBLES THE **PAGES** OF A **BOOK,** FROM WHICH THEY GET THEIR NAME. THE BOOK LUNGS ARE FILLED WITH **HEMOLYMPH,** OR **SPIDER BLOOD.** THE **AIR** ENTERS THE BOOK LUNGS AND **ENRICHES** THE **BLOOD** WITH **OXYGEN.** THEN, THE BLOOD BRINGS THE **OXYGEN** TO ALL THE **ORGANS** OF THE SPIDER'S BODY.

Spider belly

SPINNERETS

THE SILK COMES OUT FROM THE **SPINNERETS,** WHICH ARE GLANDS IN THE ABDOMEN. WHEN IT FIRST COMES OUT, THE SILK IS **LIQUID,** BUT IT QUICKLY **HARDENS.**

BUG BITES

When the eggs hatch, the newborn spiders are called spiderlings.

THE AMAZING SPIDERWEBS!

The silk of spiderwebs is very elastic. The higher the humidity, the more elastic the silk gets. The silk is also very strong, and has been compared to steel. There is no man-made fiber that is able to be as elastic and as strong as spider's silk.

Many spiders spin webs, but not all of them do.

Female spiders use silk to create a sack, in which they deposit their eggs.

Often, spiders use their silk to wrap up their prey.

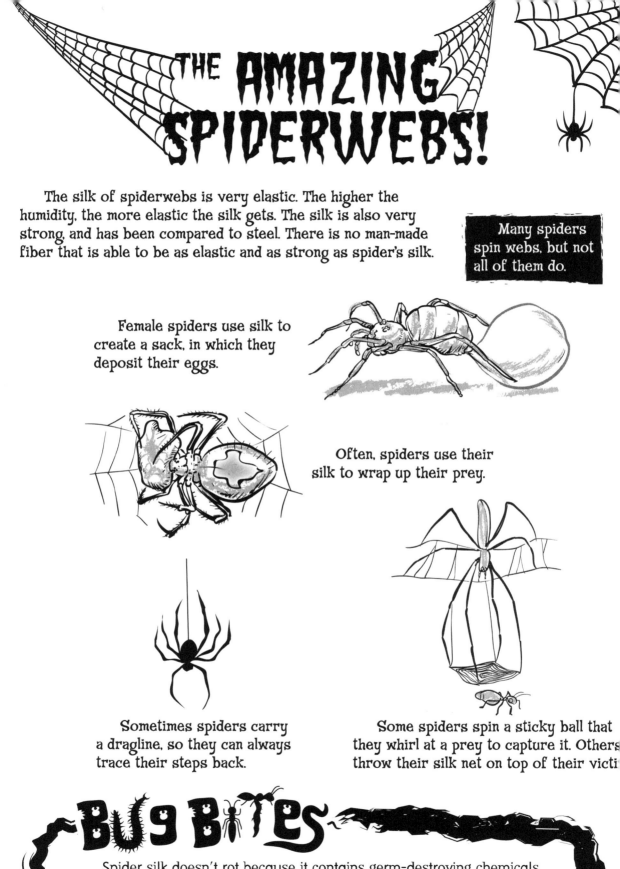

Sometimes spiders carry a dragline, so they can always trace their steps back.

Some spiders spin a sticky ball that they whirl at a prey to capture it. Others throw their silk net on top of their victi

BUG BITES

Spider silk doesn't rot because it contains germ-destroying chemicals that keep it clean and elastic.

By spinning a long thread of silk, some spiders get carried by the wind. While some might die, landing in the middle of an ocean for example, others can find new territories to conquer. In 1983, the volcano on the island of Krakatoa erupted, killing all life on the island. A few months later, scientists found that Krakatoa wasn't deserted anymore. The wind has brought life back carrying spiders for over 30 miles from the closest shore.

The water spider spends most of its life underwater. In order to breathe, it spins a bell of silk and anchors it to the underwater vegetation. When the spider dives into the water, air bubbles remain trapped in its very hairy body. The water spider deposits the air bubbles inside its silk dome, in which it inserts its abdomen. In this way, its book lungs, or respiratory organs, are exposed to the air.

Spiders have different kinds of glands, and can spin different kinds of silk, depending on what they want to do. For example, a specific gland is used to spin the silk for egg sacks, another is used for draglines, and another for sticky silk.

BUG BITES

Canadian scientists have been experimenting with putting spider genes into mammals, like cows, hamsters, and goats. They hope that these animals will produce silk proteins to create a fiber as strong and as flexible as spider's silk.

THE AMAZING SPIDERWEBS!

Some species of spiders can weave circular nests, or orb webs. To create an orb web, a spider spins a thread and lets the wind carry it to an anchor point. As this is the support for the whole web, the spider might strengthen this first line by adding more silk to it.

Next, the spider spins a loose thread.

Then, it anchors it. This Y-shaped frame is the basis of the orb web.

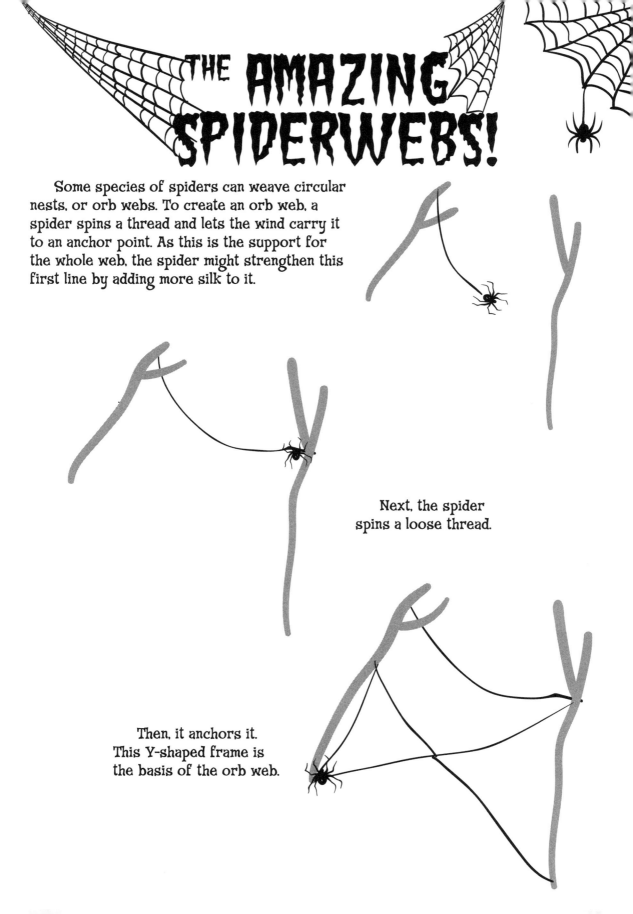

Radial threads
are added.

The spider spins a non-sticky,
spiral-like thread. This will help
the spider to lay the sticky thread.

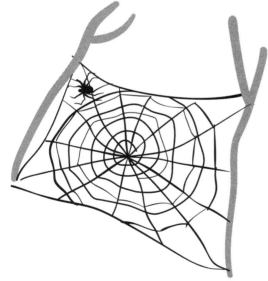

To avoid being stuck on its own
sticky thread, the spider walks on the
non-sticky thread. The thin lines indicate
non-sticky silk, while the thick lines
indicate sticky silk.

Spiders generally build or repair their webs
in the evening, so they are ready to hunt at night.

BUG BITES

Spiders can recycle their silk by eating it.

THE AMAZING SPIDERWEBS!

When a prey flies into the web, it gets caught by the sticky thread. The spider runs to its prey, wraps it up in more silk, and bites it. The spider's venom kills the prey. Sometimes spiders eat their prey right away, while other times they store it for later.

Some species of spiders don't build orb webs. Instead, they line their burrows with silk, creating a kind of a tube. Outside their nest, these spiders lay trip lines. Trip lines are threads of silk that vibrate when an unsuspecting prey walks on them. The spider feels the trip line vibrations and jumps out of its burrow to catch the prey.

Trap-door spiders also dig burrows in the ground and line them with silk. Then, by mixing dirt, dead leaves, and silk, they create a trap door for their nests. The trap door has hinges, also made of silk. The spider's nest is completely hidden by the trap door. When a victim passes by, the spider flings the trap door open and catches its prey.

Many other spiders don't use silk to hunt. Their techniques to catch prey vary. Some spiders camouflage themselves to blend with their environment, and victims spot them when it's too late. Others are expert jumpers, and land on their prey. And others are so quick at running that they chase their food.

BUG BITES

On August 2007, in Lake Tawakoni State Park, Texas, a massive spiderweb, over 200 yards long, was discovered. Scientists suggest that cobweb spiders were responsible for building the giant blanket of silk. This is because some species of cobweb spiders are social and live communally. But other scientists disagree. They had found several species of spiders, not just cobwebs, in the web. Also, cobweb spiders don't seem to be able to build such a large web.

THE BLACK WIDOW

THERE ARE **MANY SPECIES** OF **BLACK WIDOWS**. SOME ARE **BLACK** WITH **YELLOW, ORANGE,** OR **RED MARKS** ON THEIR **BELLY.** SOMETIMES THESE **MARKS** ARE IN THE **SHAPE** OF AN **HOURGLASS.** SOME BLACK WIDOWS ARE **DARK BROWN** OR SIMPLY **BLACK ALL OVER.** BLACK WIDOW **SPIDERLINGS** ARE **LIGHTER** IN COLOR AND GET **DARKER** AS THEY **GROW.**

BLACK WIDOW SPIDERS ARE VERY **SHY** AND PREFER TO **RUN** AND **HIDE** THAN TO **ATTACK** A POTENTIAL **AGGRESSOR.**

BLACK WIDOWS ARE **NOCTURNAL** AND **SPIN** THEIR **WEBS** IN **DARK** AND **QUIET PLACES.** AT NIGHT THEY **HANG** FROM THEIR WEBS **BELLY** UP.

THE GLOOMY NAME **BLACK WIDOW** COMES FROM THE BELIEF THAT THE **FEMALE** SPIDER **KILLS** AND **EATS** THE **MALE** AFTER MATING. BUT THIS **RARELY** HAPPENS.

FEMALES ARE 1/2 AN INCH **LONG,** INCLUDING THEIR LEGS, WHICH ARE LONG AND THIN. **MALES** ARE **MUCH SMALLER.**

BLACK WIDOWS EAT **INSECTS**, LIKE **COCKROACHES**, **CRICKETS**, **ANTS**, AND **OTHER SPIDERS**. BLACK WIDOWS CAN EAT **FIRE ANTS** AND **SCORPIONS**.

WHEN A PREY GETS **TANGLED** IN A BLACK WIDOW'S WEB, THE SPIDER QUICKLY **WRAPS IT UP TIGHTLY**. WHEN THE PREY IS **IMMOBILIZED**, THE BLACK WIDOW **PIERCES** IT WITH ITS **FANGS, POISONING** IT. AFTER A **FEW MINUTES**, THE **PREY DIES**. THE BLACK WIDOW OOZES **DIGESTIVE FLUIDS** FROM ITS **MOUTH** ONTO THE **PREY**. THEN, THE SPIDER **SUCKS** IN THE **PRE-DIGESTED PREY**, LEAVING ONLY THE HARD **EXOSKELETON**.

BLACK WIDOWS DEPOSIT THEIR **EGGS** IN A **ROUND POUCH** THEY CREATE WITH THEIR **SILK**. THEY CAN DEPOSIT **400 EGGS** OR MORE DURING THE **SUMMER**, BUT ONLY A **FEW SPIDERS** REACH **ADULTHOOD**. THE **SPIDERLINGS** HAVE A **CANNIBALISTIC** NATURE, AND END UP **EATING ONE ANOTHER**. ONLY A FEW OF THEM **SURVIVE**.

DANGER TO PEOPLE: VERY LOW

ALTHOUGH THE **VENOM** OF THE BLACK WIDOW IS **POWERFUL**, ONLY A VERY **SMALL AMOUNT** IS INJECTED INTO THE **VICTIM**. THE **NEUROTOXINS** CONTAINED IN THE VENOM ATTACK THE PERSON'S **NERVOUS SYSTEM**, AND CAN CAUSE **CRAMPS, FEVER**, AND **NAUSEA** THAT CAN LAST FOR **DAYS**. IN **RARE CASES**, THE VENOM CAN CAUSE **BREATHING PROBLEMS**.
HUMAN **DEATH RATE** FROM A **BLACK WIDOW SPIDER'S** BITE: LESS THAN 1%.

THE TARANTULA

THERE ARE OVER **800 SPECIES** OF **TARANTULA SPIDERS** ON **EVERY CONTINENT** EXCEPT THE **POLES**.

TARANTULAS ARE **BIG SPIDERS** COVERED WITH **HAIR**. THEY ARE MOSTLY **GREY** OR **BLACK**. SOME TARANTULAS ARE **IRIDESCENT BLUE**, OR HAVE **ORANGE** AND **BLACK STRIPES**.

THE NAME **TARANTULA** COMES FROM THE ITALIAN CITY OF **TARANTO**. IN THE **MIDDLE AGES** IT WAS BELIEVED THAT PEOPLE **BITTEN** BY A TARANTULA WOULD BECOME **INFECTED** WITH A **DEADLY DISEASE**. THE ONLY **CURE** WAS **DANCING** A **FAST-PACED DANCE** CALLED THE **TARANTELLA**. IT TURNED OUT THAT THERE WERE NO **TARANTULAS** IN **TARANTO**, BUT ONLY **WOLF SPIDERS**. WOLF SPIDERS ARE OFTEN **CONFUSED** WITH TARANTULAS BECAUSE THEY ARE BOTH **VERY HAIRY**. BOTH THE **WOLF SPIDER** AND THE **TARANTULA'S** BITE ARE **NOT DANGEROUS** TO HUMANS.

TARANTULAS **LIVE ALONE** AND COME IN **CONTACT** WITH OTHER TARANTULAS ONLY FOR **MATING**. AFTER MATING, THE **FEMALE MIGHT** ACTUALLY **EAT** THE **MALE** IF SHE'S **HUNGRY** AND HE DOESN'T **LEAVE** QUICKLY ENOUGH.

SOME SPECIES OF TARANTULA DIG **BURROWS** IN THE GROUND, AND **LINE** THEM WITH THEIR **WEB**. TARANTULAS **HIDE** IN THEIR BURROWS, **AMBUSHING** UNAWARE **PREY** PASSING BY. OTHER SPECIES OF TARANTULAS ARE **ARBOREAL**. THIS MEANS THAT THEY **LIVE ON TREES**.

THE **GOLIATH BIRDEATER** IS THE **BIGGEST TARANTULA** AND THE **BIGGEST SPIDER** IN THE WORLD. IT CAN MEASURE **13 INCHES**, INCLUDING THE LEGS.

BUG BITES

Tarantulas are considered a delicacy in Cambodia, where they are served fried, and in Venezuela, where people prefer them roasted.

MANY PEOPLE HAVE **FEMALE TARANTULAS** AS **PETS**. THESE SPIDERS AREN'T **NOISY, MESSY,** OR **EXPENSIVE** AS COMMON PETS, LIKE CATS AND DOGS, CAN BE. A FEMALE TARANTULA CAN LIVE FOR OVER **20 YEARS IN CAPTIVITY.** A **MALE TARANTULA** CAN LIVE FROM A **FEW DAYS** TO **TWO YEARS,** DEPENDING ON THE SPECIES.

TARANTULAS FEED ON MANY KINDS OF **INSECTS** AND **ARTHROPODS,** INCLUDING OTHER TARANTULAS. SOME TARANTULAS ARE **BIG ENOUGH** TO **KILL** AND **EAT SMALL MICE, LIZARDS, SMALL SNAKES,** AND EVEN **FISH.** THE **GOLIATH BIRDEATER** CAN ACTUALLY **KILL** AND **EAT BIRDS,** AS ITS NAME SUGGESTS.

DANGER TO PEOPLE: VERY LOW

OFTEN PEOPLE **BITTEN** BY **TARANTULAS** SUFFER MORE FROM AN **ALLERGIC REACTION** TO THE **VENOM,** THAN FROM THE **VENOM ITSELF.** THE **BITE** OF SOME **ASIAN SPECIES** CAN INDUCE A **FEVER.** TARANTULAS OFTEN **DEFEND THEMSELVES** WITH **DRY BITES.** THESE ARE **WARNING BITES** AND THE VICTIM IS **NOT INJECTED** WITH **VENOM.**

SOME SPECIES OF TARANTULAS USE A **DIFFERENT DEFENSE STRATEGY.** WHEN THIS SPIDER FEELS THREATENED, IT **SHOOTS** THE **HAIR** OF ITS **ABDOMEN** AGAINST ITS **AGGRESSOR.** THE HAIRS ARE **BARBED** AND **IRRITATING,** AND OFTEN **DISCOURAGE** THE **ATTACKER.**

THE BROWN RECLUSE

THE **BROWN RECLUSE** IS A **COMMON SPIDER** FOUND IN THE **SOUTHERN MIDWEST STATES.** BROWN RECLUSE SPIDERS PREFER **QUIET** AND **DARK SPOTS** AROUND THE **HOUSE,** IN THE **ATTIC** OR THE **BASEMENT,** OR OUTSIDE THE HOUSE, IN A **TOOLSHED** OR IN A **GARAGE.**

BROWN RECLUSES HAVE VERY **LONG LEGS** AND A **HAIRY BODY.** THEY ONLY HAVE **SIX EYES,** ARRANGED IN **THREE SECTIONS OF TWO.**

BROWN RECLUSES ARE **LIGHT** TO **DARK BROWN.** SOME MAY HAVE A **VIOLIN-SHAPED SPOT** ON THE **BACK.** FOR THIS REASON, **BROWN RECLUSES** ARE ALSO KNOWN AS **FIDDLEBACKS.**

THE **VENOM** OF A BROWN RECLUSE IS **MORE POWERFUL** THAN THAT OF A **RATTLESNAKE'S.** THE DIFFERENCE IS THAT THE **AMOUNT** OF **VENOM** THE BROWN RECLUSE IS ABLE TO **INJECT** IS **MUCH SMALLER** THAN THE **RATTLESNAKE.** THIS AMOUNT IS **NOT ENOUGH** TO **KILL** A **PERSON,** BUT THE BROWN RECLUSE'S VENOM CONTAINS **TOXINS** THAT CAUSE THE **DEATH** OF **SKIN** AND **TISSUE.** THIS IS CALLED **NECROSIS.**

BROWN RECLUSES ARE NOT **AGGRESSIVE** AND BITE ONLY IF **PROVOKED** OR FEEL **THREATENED.** THEY **SPIN** AN **IRREGULAR WEB,** BUT, AT **NIGHT,** THEY **WANDER AROUND** IN SEARCH OF **FOOD.** SOMETIMES THEY GET **TANGLED** IN **CLOTHES** OR **BED SHEETS,** AND THAT'S WHEN PEOPLE **ACCIDENTALLY** COME INTO CONTACT WITH THESE **SPIDERS.**

DANGER TO PEOPLE: MEDIUM
PEOPLE OFTEN DON'T REALIZE THEY HAVE BEEN BITTEN UNTIL THEY START **REACTING** TO THE BROWN RECLUSE'S **BITE.** A NORMAL REACTION IS **NAUSEA, VOMITING,** AND **INTENSE PAIN** NEAR THE **WOUND.** THE WOUND AND SURROUNDING AREA BECOME **SWOLLEN** AND **BLUE,** WHICH ARE **SIGNS** OF **NECROSIS.** THE WOUND CAN TAKE **MONTHS** TO **HEAL,** AND SOMETIMES THE NECROSIS CAN LEAVE A **SCAR.**

THE AUSTRALIAN FUNNEL WEB SPIDER

THERE ARE FEWER THAN **40 SPECIES** OF **AUSTRALIAN FUNNEL WEB SPIDERS**. THE **MOST DANGEROUS**, THE **SIDNEY FUNNEL WEB**, IS FOUND MAINLY IN AND AROUND **SYDNEY**, AUSTRALIA.

ONE OF THE **MOST AGGRESSIVE**, THE AUSTRALIAN FUNNEL WEB SPIDER WILL **ATTACK** RATHER THAN RETREAT. THEY HAVE THE **MOST POWERFUL FANGS**, AND CAN **PIERCE** THROUGH **TOENAILS** AND **SHOES**.

WHILE THE **TOXINS** CONTAINED **IN** THIS **SPIDER'S VENOM** CAN BE **LETHAL** TO **HUMANS**, THEY HAVE **NO EFFECTS** ON **OTHER MAMMALS**, LIKE CATS AND DOGS.

FUNNEL WEB SPIDERS **NEST** IN **BURROWS**. THEY SPIN **UNDERGROUND WEBS** IN THE **SHAPE** OF A **FUNNEL** AND **SURROUND** THE **ENTRANCE** WITH **TRIP LINES**. THESE ARE **STRANDS OF SILK** THAT **VIBRATE** WHEN A **PREY** WALKS ON THEM, **ALERTING** THE SPIDER THAT **QUICKLY ATTACKS** ITS **VICTIM**.

IN THE PAST, THE **SIDNEY FUNNEL WEB SPIDER** CAUSED **13 DEATHS**. FORTUNATELY, IN 1981, AN **ANTIDOTE** WAS **CREATED**. SINCE THEN, ALL TREATED VICTIMS HAVE **SURVIVED** THE **BITE** OF THIS SPIDER.

THE **AUSTRALIAN FUNNEL WEB SPIDER** IS BLACK OR **DARK BROWN**, WITH **GLOSSY LEGS** AND **CEPHALOTHORAX**.

DANGER TO PEOPLE: HIGH

PEOPLE'S IMMEDIATE **REACTION** TO THE BITE IS **INTENSE PAIN**. THE VICTIM CAN SUFFER FROM **ABDOMINAL CRAMPS** AND **MUSCLE SPASMS**, WITH **SWEATING** AND **VOMITING**. THIS CAN BE FOLLOWED BY **PULMONARY EDEMA** (ACCUMULATION OF FLUIDS IN THE LUNGS), **HYPERTENSION** (HIGH BLOOD PRESSURE), AND SOMETIMES **COMA**. AN UNTREATED VICTIM MIGHT DIE **WITHIN HOURS** OF BEING BITTEN.

THE BANANA SPIDER
OR THE BRAZILIAN WANDERING SPIDER

THIS IS A **VERY AGGRESSIVE, SOUTH AMERICAN SPIDER** NOT TO BE CONFUSED WITH THE **NORTH AMERICAN GOLDEN SILK SPIDER**. THE NORTH AMERICAN GOLDEN SILK SPIDER IS ALSO KNOWN AS THE **BANANA SPIDER** DUE TO THE **COLOR** AND **SHAPE** OF ITS **BODY**. THESE SPIDERS ARE **HARMLESS** TO **HUMANS**.

THE **SOUTH AMERICAN BANANA SPIDER** IS OFTEN FOUND UNDER **BANANA LEAVES** AND IN **CRATES** OF **BANANAS**. THIS SPIDER IS ALSO KNOWN AS THE **BRAZILIAN WANDERING SPIDER**. THIS IS BECAUSE IT **DOESN'T SPIN** A WEB AND PREFERS **TO WANDER AROUND** HUNTING FOR PREY. THESE SPIDERS ARE **DANGEROUS** TO **HUMANS**.

BRAZILIAN WANDERING SPIDERS ARE **VERY FAST** BECAUSE THEY **CHASE THEIR PREY**. THEY HUNT AT NIGHT.

BRAZILIAN WANDERING SPIDERS ARE **BIG**, AND, DEPENDING ON THE SPECIES, CAN MEASURE UP TO **FIVE INCHES**.

IT HAS BEEN REPORTED THAT, WHEN THREATENED, THE BRAZILIAN WANDERING SPIDER **WARNS** ITS **ATTACKER** BY **POINTING** ITS **FIRST TWO SETS** OF **LEGS UP, SHOWING OFF** ITS **FANGS,** AND **MOVING** ITS BODY FROM **SIDE TO SIDE.**

BRAZILIAN WANDERING SPIDERS LIVE IN THE **RAINFORESTS** OF **CENTRAL** AND **SOUTH AMERICA,** WANDERING ON THE **GROUND** OR IN **TREES.** THEY ARE ALSO FOUND IN **HOMES.**

AN **ANTIDOTE** TO THE BRAZILIAN WANDERING SPIDER'S **VENOM** WAS **CREATED** BY NOBEL PRIZE CANDIDATE **CARLOS CHAGAS,** A **BRAZILIAN PHYSICIAN.**

DANGER TO PEOPLE: HIGH

MOST OF THE **BRAZILIAN WANDERING SPIDER'S BITES** ARE **DRY,** OR DON'T CONTAIN **ENOUGH VENOM** TO **ENDANGER** A **PERSON.** BUT THE **VENOM** OF THIS SPIDER IS **POWERFUL,** AND CAN BE **LETHAL.** PEOPLE BITTEN BY THIS SPIDER CAN EXPERIENCE AN **IRREGULAR HEARTBEAT, PULMONARY EDEMA** (FLUID IN THE LUNGS), AND EVEN **DEATH.**

THERE ARE OVER **1,000 SPECIES** OF SCORPIONS
IN THE WORLD, ALL OF THEM **VENOMOUS.**
THEY CARRY **VENOM** IN THEIR **STINGER.**
SCORPIONS USE THEIR VENOM TO
KILL THEIR **PREY.**
   SCORPIONS LIVE IN
**FORESTS, RAIN FORESTS,
CAVES, DESERTS,** AND
MOUNTAINS. THOSE THAT
LIVE ON THE **ALPS** OR IN THE
ANDES GO INTO
HIBERNATION DURING THE
COLD MONTHS. SCORPIONS
LIVING IN THE **DESERTS** DIG
HOLES IN THE **SAND** TO AVOID
THE **HOT SUN.**

SCORPIONS **HUNT** MOSTLY AT **NIGHT.** THEY **CAN'T SEE** VERY WELL,
BUT ARE ABLE TO **SENSE** THE **PRESENCE** OF THEIR **PREY** FROM **OVER A
FOOT AWAY.** THEY DO SO WITH THEIR **SENSORY ORGANS,** LIKE THE
PECTINES AND THE **HAIR** ON THEIR **LEGS** AND **PEDIPALPS.**
   WHEN A SCORPION FINDS A **PREY,** IT **GRABS** IT WITH ITS **PEDIPALPS.**
IF THE **PREY** IS **SMALL** ENOUGH, THE SCORPION IS ABLE TO **KILL** IT WITH
ITS **CLAWS.** BUT IF THE PREY IS **BIG,** THE SCORPION **STINGS** IT WITH ITS
TAIL AND EITHER **PARALYZES** OR **KILLS** IT. THEN, THE SCORPION
CRUSHES AND **CHEWS** ITS VICTIM USING ITS **CHELICERAE.** AT THE SAME
TIME, THE SCORPION **VOMITS DIGESTIVE FLUIDS** ONTO ITS PREY. WHEN
THE **PREY** IS REDUCED TO **LIQUID FORM,** THE SCORPION **SUCKS** IT **UP**
WITH ITS **MOUTH,** LEAVING ONLY **INDIGESTIBLE PARTS.**

THE **BIGGEST LIVING SCORPION** IS THE **AFRICAN SCORPION**, WHICH MEASURES **EIGHT INCHES LONG**. THERE ARE SOME **EXTINCT SCORPIONS** THAT MEASURED OVER **THREE FEET IN LENGTH**!

SCORPIONS EAT **SPIDERS, CENTIPEDES, SNAILS,** AND **INSECTS.** SOMETIMES THEY EAT OTHER **SCORPIONS.** THEY CAN BE **CANNIBALISTIC,** EATING **SCORPIONS** OF THEIR **OWN SPECIES.** THEY CAN EVEN EAT **SMALL LIZARDS** AND **MICE.**

DURING MATING, THE **MALE SCORPION** GRABS THE **FEMALE** BY HER **PEDIPALPS** AND LEADS HER TO A **COURTSHIP DANCE.** SOMETIMES, THE MALE **STINGS** THE FEMALE. THE STING **DOESN'T KILL** THE FEMALE, BUT IT SEEMS TO **CALM** HER. THIS IS PROBABLY BECAUSE THE FEMALE **MIGHT EAT** THE MALE RIGHT AFTER MATING.

SCORPION FEMALES ARE **VIVIPAROUS,** AND GIVE **BIRTH** TO **LIVE SCORPLINGS.** AS SOON AS THEY ARE BORN, THE SCORPLINGS **CRAWL** ONTO THEIR **MOTHER'S BACK** AND **STAY THERE** UNTIL THEIR **FIRST MOLT.** AFTER THAT, THE YOUNG SCORPIONS **DON'T NEED** THE **PROTECTION** OF THEIR MOTHER AND ARE STRONG ENOUGH TO **HUNT.**

SCORPIONS

Scorpionidae

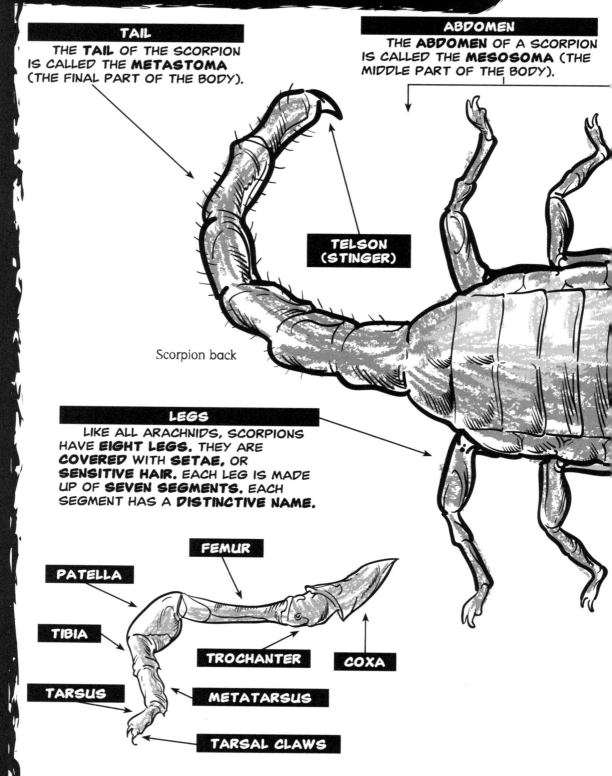

TAIL

THE **TAIL** OF THE SCORPION IS CALLED THE **METASTOMA** (THE FINAL PART OF THE BODY).

ABDOMEN

THE **ABDOMEN** OF A SCORPION IS CALLED THE **MESOSOMA** (THE MIDDLE PART OF THE BODY).

TELSON (STINGER)

Scorpion back

LEGS

LIKE ALL ARACHNIDS, SCORPIONS HAVE **EIGHT LEGS**. THEY ARE **COVERED** WITH **SETAE**, OR **SENSITIVE HAIR**. EACH LEG IS MADE UP OF **SEVEN SEGMENTS**. EACH SEGMENT HAS A **DISTINCTIVE NAME**.

FEMUR

PATELLA

TIBIA

TROCHANTER

COXA

TARSUS

METATARSUS

TARSAL CLAWS

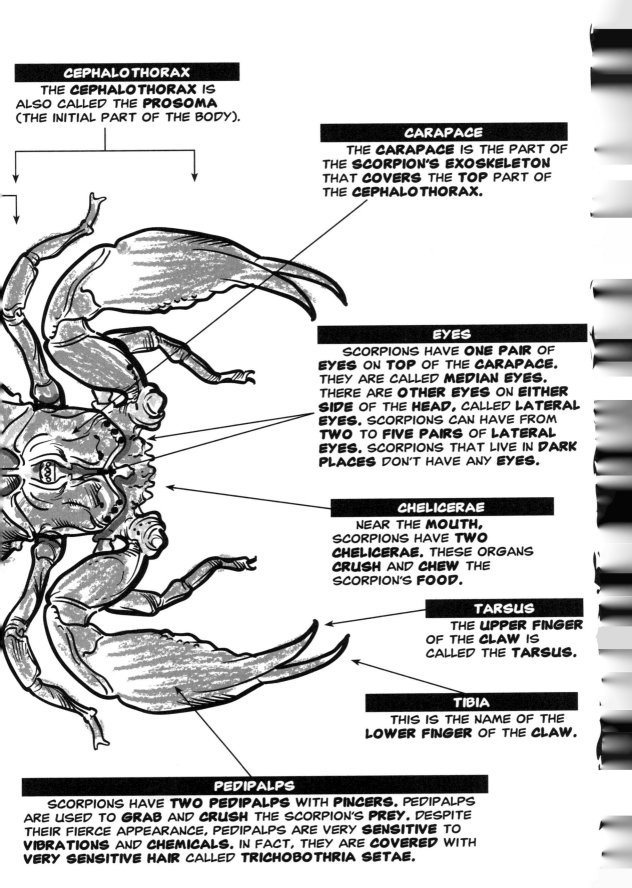

CEPHALOTHORAX
THE **CEPHALOTHORAX** IS ALSO CALLED THE **PROSOMA** (THE INITIAL PART OF THE BODY).

CARAPACE
THE **CARAPACE** IS THE PART OF THE **SCORPION'S EXOSKELETON** THAT **COVERS** THE **TOP** PART OF THE **CEPHALOTHORAX**.

EYES
SCORPIONS HAVE **ONE PAIR** OF **EYES** ON **TOP** OF THE **CARAPACE**. THEY ARE CALLED **MEDIAN EYES**. THERE ARE **OTHER EYES** ON **EITHER SIDE** OF THE **HEAD**, CALLED **LATERAL EYES**. SCORPIONS CAN HAVE FROM **TWO** TO **FIVE PAIRS** OF **LATERAL EYES**. SCORPIONS THAT LIVE IN **DARK PLACES** DON'T HAVE ANY **EYES**.

CHELICERAE
NEAR THE **MOUTH**, SCORPIONS HAVE **TWO CHELICERAE**. THESE ORGANS **CRUSH** AND **CHEW** THE SCORPION'S **FOOD**.

TARSUS
THE **UPPER FINGER** OF THE **CLAW** IS CALLED THE **TARSUS**.

TIBIA
THIS IS THE NAME OF THE **LOWER FINGER** OF THE **CLAW**.

PEDIPALPS
SCORPIONS HAVE **TWO PEDIPALPS** WITH **PINCERS**. PEDIPALPS ARE USED TO **GRAB** AND **CRUSH** THE SCORPION'S **PREY**. DESPITE THEIR FIERCE APPEARANCE, PEDIPALPS ARE VERY **SENSITIVE** TO **VIBRATIONS** AND **CHEMICALS**. IN FACT, THEY ARE **COVERED** WITH **VERY SENSITIVE HAIR** CALLED **TRICHOBOTHRIA SETAE**.

SCORPIONS

Scorpionidae

CEPHALOTHORAX

STERNUM

IT'S WHERE THE **COXAE MEET.** THE COXAE ARE THE **FIRST JOINTS** OF THE SCORPION'S **LEGS.**

REPRODUCTIVE ORGANS

THE **REPRODUCTIVE ORGANS** ARE IN THE **FIRST SEGMENT** OF THE ABDOMEN.

PECTINES

IN THE **SECOND SEGMENT,** SCORPIONS HAVE **TWO PECTINES,** OR **COMBS.** THESE ARE **TWO SENSORY ORGANS** THAT **TOUCH** THE **GROUND.** PECTINES DETECT **HUMIDITY, CHEMICALS,** AND **GROUND VIBRATIONS.** THIS INFORMATION **ALERTS** THE **SCORPION** OF MANY THINGS, LIKE IF A **PREY** IS **CLOSE BY,** IF THERE'S A **MATE** IN THE **AREA,** OR IF THERE ARE **PREDATORS** ON THE **HUNT.**

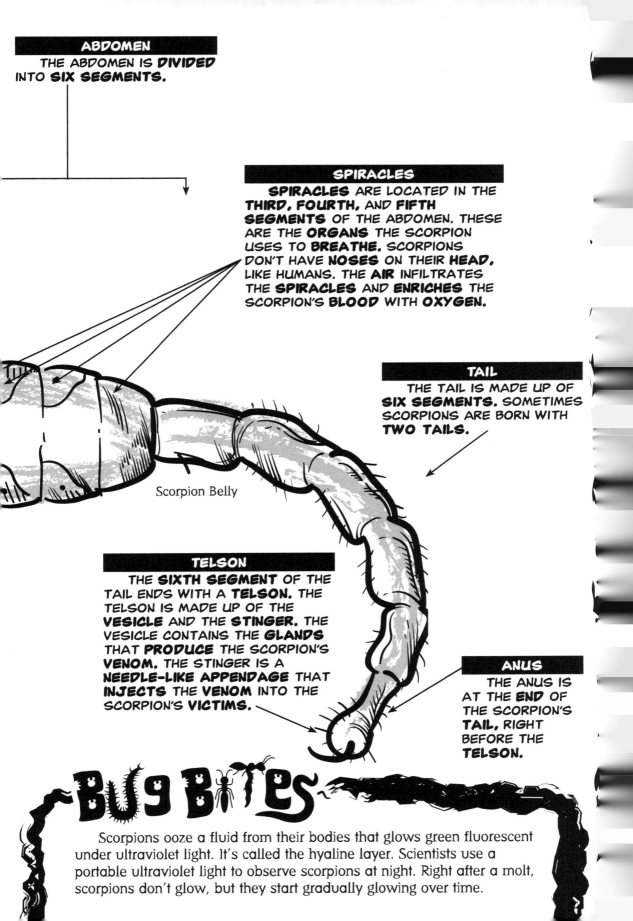

ABDOMEN

THE ABDOMEN IS **DIVIDED** INTO **SIX SEGMENTS.**

SPIRACLES

SPIRACLES ARE LOCATED IN THE **THIRD, FOURTH,** AND **FIFTH SEGMENTS** OF THE ABDOMEN. THESE ARE THE **ORGANS** THE SCORPION USES TO **BREATHE.** SCORPIONS DON'T HAVE **NOSES** ON THEIR **HEAD,** LIKE HUMANS. THE **AIR** INFILTRATES THE **SPIRACLES** AND **ENRICHES** THE SCORPION'S **BLOOD** WITH **OXYGEN.**

TAIL

THE TAIL IS MADE UP OF **SIX SEGMENTS.** SOMETIMES SCORPIONS ARE BORN WITH **TWO TAILS.**

Scorpion Belly

TELSON

THE **SIXTH SEGMENT** OF THE TAIL ENDS WITH A **TELSON.** THE TELSON IS MADE UP OF THE **VESICLE** AND THE **STINGER.** THE VESICLE CONTAINS THE **GLANDS** THAT **PRODUCE** THE SCORPION'S **VENOM.** THE STINGER IS A **NEEDLE-LIKE APPENDAGE** THAT **INJECTS** THE **VENOM** INTO THE SCORPION'S **VICTIMS.**

ANUS

THE ANUS IS AT THE **END** OF THE SCORPION'S **TAIL,** RIGHT BEFORE THE **TELSON.**

BUG BITES

Scorpions ooze a fluid from their bodies that glows green fluorescent under ultraviolet light. It's called the hyaline layer. Scientists use a portable ultraviolet light to observe scorpions at night. Right after a molt, scorpions don't glow, but they start gradually glowing over time.

SCORPIONS

Scorpionidae

SCORPIONS SEEM TO BE RELATED TO THE **EXTINCT EURYPTERIDS.** EURYPTERIDS WERE **ARTHROPODS** THAT FIRST APPEARED IN THE **ORDOVICIAN PERIOD,** **490 MILLION YEARS AGO.**

EURYPTERIDS WERE **SO SIMILAR** TO TODAY'S **SCORPIONS** THAT THEY'RE KNOWN AS **SEA SCORPIONS.** THEY HAD A **PAIR** OF **CHELICERAE** AND A **STINGER.** DEPENDING ON THEIR SPECIES, THEY HAD **THREE PAIRS** OF **LEGS** AND A **PAIR** OF **PADDLES,** OR **FOUR PAIRS** OF **LONG LEGS.**

FOSSILIZED TRACKS OF A **300 MILLION-YEAR-OLD** SEA SCORPION, **HIBBERTOPTERUS SCOULERI,** WERE FOUND IN **SCOTLAND.** THESE TRACKS SHOW A **GREAT DIFFERENCE** BETWEEN **MODERN SCORPIONS** AND **SOME ANCIENT ONES:** THEIR **SIZE.** HIBBERTOPTERUS SCOULERI IS BELIEVED TO HAVE BEEN **SIX FEET TALL** AND OVER **THREE FEET WIDE!**

This is how big you'd look if you were to meet an eurypterids!

IT SEEMS THAT **SEA SCORPIONS** LIVED IN **ANCIENT SEAS** AROUND THE WORLD, BUT **ADAPTED** TO **THRIVE** IN **SHALLOW WATERS** AND **LAGOONS.** EVENTUALLY, **SOME** OF THEM **CRAWLED** ONTO **LAND,** ALTHOUGH STILL DEPENDING ON **WATER** FOR THEIR **SURVIVAL.**

ANOTHER MONSTER FROM THE PAST WAS THE **BRONTOSCORPIO ANGLICUS.** ITS NAME MEANS THE **"THUNDER SCORPION** FROM **ENGLAND."** THIS SEA SCORPION LIVED IN THE **SILURIAN PERIOD,** ABOUT **420 MILLION YEARS AGO,** AND WAS ALMOST **FOUR FEET LONG.**

BUG BITES

It was thought that scorpions stung themselves to death if surrounded by fire. This is not true. If the heat is too strong, a scorpion can start twitching and may look like it's stinging itself. Even if it did, the scorpion would not die because scorpions are invulnerable to their own venom.

FAT TAILED SCORPION

THIS SCORPION LIVES IN THE **NORTHERN** PART OF **AFRICA**, IN THE **MIDDLE EAST,** AND **SOUTHERN ASIA.**

FAT TAILED SCORPIONS THRIVE IN **DESERTS** AND HIDE UNDER THE **SAND** OR **ROCKS** TO **PROTECT** THEMSELVES AGAINST THE **HEAT.**

THE FAT TAILED SCORPION IS **YELLOW** AND MEASURES UP TO **FOUR INCHES.**

IN GENERAL, **SCORPIONS** ARE **SHY.** WHEN THEY FEEL **THREATENED,** THEY EITHER **RUN AWAY** OR **REMAIN MOTIONLESS,** WAITING FOR THE ATTACKER TO LEAVE. BUT SOMETIMES SCORPIONS USE THEIR **STINGER** AGAINST AN **ATTACKER.**

SCORPIONS THAT ARE **DANGEROUS** BECAUSE OF THEIR **VENOM** HAVE A **VERY BIG TAIL** AND **SMALL PEDIPALPS.** SCORPIONS WITH **WEAKER VENOM** HAVE **BIGGER PINCERS.**

 DANGER TO PEOPLE: HIGH

DEATH STALKER

THIS SCORPION LIVES IN THE **NORTHERN** AND **EASTERN** PART OF **AFRICA**, AND IN THE **MIDDLE EAST**. THE DEATH STALKER **LIVES** IN **ROCKY DESERTS**. IT'S UP TO **FOUR INCHES LONG** AND HAS A **YELLOW COLOR**.

IN MOST SPECIES THE **VENOM** IS **NEUROTOXIC**. THIS MEANS THAT THE VENOM ACTS ON THE **NERVE CELLS, PARALYZING** THE **VICTIM**. IN SOME SPECIES, THE VENOM IS **CYTOTOXIC**, CAUSING **NECROSIS**, OR THE **DEATH** OF THE **CELLS**. AFTER BEING STUNG BY A DANGEROUS SCORPION, A PERSON FEELS **SEVERE PAIN** AND **NUMBNESS**. THERE CAN BE **CONVULSIONS, DIFFICULTY BREATHING**, AND **CHANGES** IN THE **HEARTBEAT RATE**. SOME PEOPLE MIGHT **DIE** OF **ANAPHYLAXIS**, AN **EXTREME ALLERGIC REACTION** TO THE VENOM. RARELY, PEOPLE DIE BECAUSE OF THE SCORPION'S VENOM ITSELF.

ALTHOUGH ARMED WITH **POWERFUL VENOM**, THESE DANGEROUS SCORPIONS **CANNOT INJECT ENOUGH** OF IT TO **KILL** A HEALTHY PERSON.

 DANGER TO PEOPLE: HIGH

MITES AND TICKS
Acari

ACARI ARE A GROUP OF **ANIMALS** BELONGING TO THE **ARTHROPODS.** IN ADDITION TO HAVING ALL THE **ARTHROPODS'** **CHARACTERISTICS,** ACARI HAVE SOME **TRAITS** THAT **DISTINGUISH** THEM FROM ALL THE **OTHERS.**

ACARI ARE THE **BIGGEST GROUP** OF ALL THE **ARTHROPODS.** THERE ARE ABOUT **50,000** KNOWN **SPECIES.** IT'S ESTIMATED THAT THIS REPRESENTS ONLY **5%** OF ALL THE **ACARI SPECIES,** WHICH MIGHT BE ABOUT **ONE MILLION!**

THE ACARI ARE DIVIDED INTO **TWO MAIN GROUPS: MITES** AND **TICKS.**

THE ACARUS' **BODY** IS CALLED THE **IDIOSOMA.**

THE ACARUS' **CEPHALOTHORAX** AND THE **ABDOMEN** ARE NOT SEPARATED.

THERE ARE **NO SEGMENTS** ON THE ACARUS' **BODY.**

MANY SPECIES ARE **BLIND.**

MANY SPECIES HAVE **CHELICERAE.**

NOT ALL ACARI HAVE **EIGHT LEGS;** SOME SPECIES HAVE **LESS.**

DURING THE **LARVAL STAGE,** SOME SPECIES OF ACARI HAVE **SIX LEGS.** THE **FOURTH** AND **LAST PAIR** APPEARS DURING THE **NYMPHAL STAGE.**

SOME ACARUS SPECIES, LIKE **TICKS**, CAN BE **PARASITIC** AND CAN CARRY **DANGEROUS DISEASES.** SOME SPECIES CAN **DAMAGE CROPS,** LIKE THE **SPIDER MITE.** OTHER SPECIES ARE **BENEFICIAL** BECAUSE THEY **FEED ON PESTS** AND **FUNGI.**

MANY ACARI GO THROUGH **FOUR STAGES** TO BECOME **ADULTS,** BUT NOT ALL SPECIES DO.

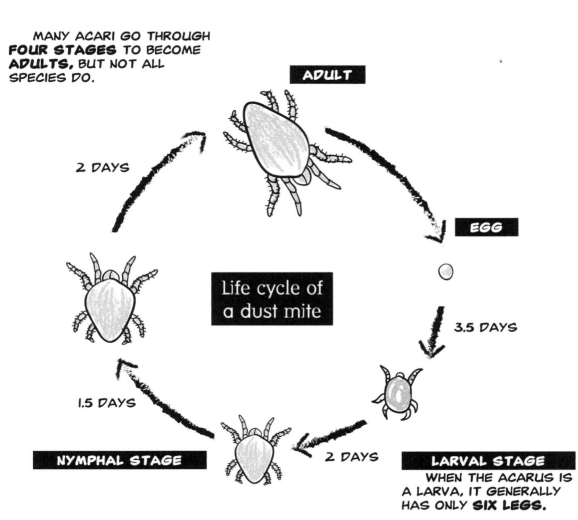

ADULT

2 DAYS

EGG

Life cycle of a dust mite

3.5 DAYS

1.5 DAYS

2 DAYS

NYMPHAL STAGE

LARVAL STAGE
WHEN THE ACARUS IS A LARVA, IT GENERALLY HAS ONLY **SIX LEGS.**

ACARI HAVE ADAPTED TO **THRIVE** IN **EVERY ENVIRONMENT.** THERE ARE SPECIES LIVING AT THE **POLES.** OTHERS LIVE IN **GEOTHERMAL SPRINGS** WHERE THE **WATER** REACHES **TEMPERATURES** OF OVER **100 DEGREES.** SOME ACARI LIVE AT **DEPTHS** OF **5,000 FEET** AT THE **BOTTOM** OF THE **OCEANS.**

MITES

MITES ARE OFTEN SO SMALL THAT THEY CAN BE SEEN ONLY WITH A MICROSCOPE.

MANGE IS A CONDITION CAUSED BY A SMALL MITE THAT LIVES IN THE HAIR FOLLICLES OF DOGS AND CAUSES ITCHINESS, LOSS OF FUR, AND INFECTION.

THERE'S ANOTHER TYPE OF MITE THAT CAUSES SARCOPTIC MANGE, ALSO KNOWN AS SCABIES. THESE MITES LIVE ON AND IN THE SKIN OF ANIMALS. GENERALLY THE FEMALE MITES BURROW IN THE SKIN AND DEPOSIT THEIR EGGS. MALES RARELY BURROW. THERE ARE SOME SPECIES OF MITES THAT CAUSE SCABIES IN HUMANS.

ONE OF THE **MOST COMMON SPECIES** IS THE **DUST MITE**. DUST MITES LIVE IN **CLOSE CONTACT** WITH **PEOPLE**. THEY PREFER **WARM, HUMID,** AND **DARK PLACES**. DIRECT SUNLIGHT **KILLS** DUST MITES.

DUST MITES FEED ON **DEAD SKIN CELLS** THAT PEOPLE **SHED** AND OTHER PARTICLES. DUST MITES ARE OFTEN FOUND IN **BEDS, MATTRESSES,** AND **CLOTHING,** WHERE THEY CAN FIND **FOOD** AND **WARMTH.**

DUST MITES PRODUCE **FECAL PELLETS.** THESE ARE BASICALLY DUST MITES' POOP. MANY PEOPLE CAN DEVELOP **ALLERGIC REACTIONS** AND **ASTHMA** TO THE FECAL PELLETS.

CHIGGERS ARE THE **LARVAE** OF **HARVEST MITES.** THEY FEED ON THE **SKIN** OF **ANIMALS,** INCLUDING **PEOPLE.** CHIGGERS MAKE A **HOLE** IN THE **SKIN** AND **FEED** ON **SKIN CELLS.** CHIGGERS CAUSE **ITCHING** AND **SMALL INFECTIONS.**
ONCE THEY MOLT INTO **NYMPHS** AND THEN **ADULTS,** HARVEST MITES **FEED** ON **PLANTS.**

TICKS

TICKS ARE **HEMATOPHAGOUS PARASITES.** THIS MEANS THAT THEY LIVE AT THE **EXPENSE** OF A **HOST,** SUCKING ITS **BLOOD. TICKS' HOSTS** CAN BE **MAMMALS** (RATS, DEER, HUMANS, ETC.), **BIRDS,** AND **REPTILES,** BUT **NOT FISH.**

TICKS GO THROUGH **THREE STAGES** TO BECOME **ADULTS.**

THE **FIRST STAGE** IS THE **EGG. EGGS HATCH** ON THE **GRASS.**

ADULTS LOOK FOR A **HOST.** ON THE THIRD AND **FINAL HOST,** TICKS **MATE.** FEMALE TICKS **FEED** ON THE HOST AND **FALL** ON THE **GRASS,** WHERE THEY **DEPOSIT** THEIR **EGGS.**

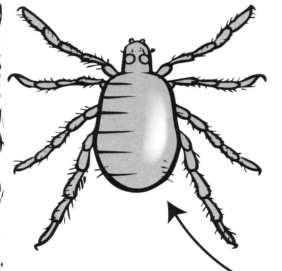

THE **LARVAE** NEED TO **FIND** A **HOST,** OR THEY **DIE.** AFTER A LARVA FINDS A HOST AND **FEEDS,** IT **DETACHES** ITSELF AND **FALLS** ONTO THE **GRASS** AGAIN.

LARVAE **MOLT** INTO **NYMPHS.** JUST LIKE LARVAE, NYMPHS NEED TO **FEED.** AFTER HAVING FED ON **ANOTHER HOST,** THE NYMPHS **FALL** ONTO THE **GRASS** AND **MOLT** INTO THE **ADULT TICK.**

SOMETIMES **MALE TICKS** FEED ON THE **FEMALES,** BECOMING **PARASITES** OF PARASITES!

TICKS **CAN'T FLY, JUMP,** OR **DROP FROM TREES.** THEY **CRAWL** TO THE **TOP** OF **GRASS** AND **WAIT** FOR A **HOST** TO **WALK BY.** THEY CAN **DETECT** THE **BODY HEAT** AND **BREATHING** OF AN APPROACHING HOST. THEY HAVE BEEN OBSERVED **HANGING** FROM **GRASS** WITH THEIR **HIND LEGS** AND **"WAVING"** THEIR **FORELEGS,** READY TO **ATTACH** THEMSELVES TO A **PASSERBY.**

WHEN A TICK **FINDS** A **HOST,** IT **CUTS** THE HOST'S **SKIN** WITH ITS **CHELICERAE** AND INSERTS ITS **HYPOSTOME** INTO THE HOST. THE **HYPOSTOME** IS A PART OF THE **TICK'S MOUTH** THAT LOOKS LIKE A **BARBED NEEDLE.** FOR THIS REASON IT'S **VERY HARD TO REMOVE** A TICK. TICKS **SUCK** THE **BLOOD** OF THEIR HOST WITH THE HYPOSTOME. ONCE THEY HAVE GORGED THEMSELVES, TICKS **LET GO** OF THEIR HOST AND **FALL** ONTO THE **GRASS.**

A TICK'S BODY **BLOATED** WITH **BLOOD** CAN GET **100% BIGGER!**

IN ORDER **NOT TO BE DETECTED** BY THEIR HOST, TICKS **OOZE** MANY **FLUIDS** LIKE **ANTICOAGULANTS** (FLUIDS THAT DON'T LET THE BLOOD CLOSE THE WOUND), **IMMUNOSUPRESSIVE** (FLUIDS THAT REPEL THE HOST'S ANTIBODIES), **VASODILATORS** (FLUIDS THAT MAKE THE VEINS OPEN UP, SO MORE BLOOD PASSES THROUGH), AND **ANTI-INFLAMMATORIES** (FLUIDS THAT PREVENT INFLAMMATION).

TICKS **SECRETE** A **SUBSTANCE** THAT **HARDENS,** SO THEY CAN GET **CEMENTED** TO THEIR **HOST.**

TICKS CAN CARRY **DISEASES** DANGEROUS FOR HUMANS. THEY CAN SPREAD **LYME DISEASE, TICK TYPHUS, ROCKY MOUNTAIN SPOTTED FEVER, EHRLICHIOSIS, BABESIOSIS,** AND MANY MORE.

THE BEST WAY TO **REMOVE** A **TICK** IS TO **PULL** IT OUT WITH **TWEEZERS** AS **SOON AS POSSIBLE.** THIS IS BECAUSE THE **CHANCE** OF BEING **INFECTED** WITH **BACTERIA** FROM THE TICK **INCREASES** WITH **TIME.**

IT'S **NOT RECOMMENDED** TO **CRUSH** THE TICK, OR **SUFFOCATE** IT WITH PETROLEUM JELLY, OR **BURN** IT WITH A MATCH. THIS IS BECAUSE THE **DYING TICK** MIGHT **REGURGITATE** INTO THE **WOUND.** MANY **BACTERIA,** ESPECIALLY **LYME DISEASE,** LIVE IN THE TICK'S **STOMACH** AND MIGHT **END UP** RIGHT **INSIDE** A **PERSON'S BLOOD STREAM.**

PSEUDOSCORPIONS

Pseudoscorpionidae

PSEUDOSCORPIONS ARE **ANIMALS** THAT **LOOK LIKE SCORPIONS.** THE NAME PSEUDOSCORPION MEANS **"FALSE SCORPION."** JUST LIKE TRUE SCORPIONS, PSEUDOSCORPIONS HAVE **EIGHT LEGS** AND **BIG PEDIPALPS,** OR **PINCERS.** UNLIKE SCORPIONS, PSEUDOSCORPIONS **DON'T HAVE** EITHER **TAIL** OR **STINGER.**

PSEUDOSCORPIONS ARE **VERY SMALL,** ABOUT 1/8 OF AN **INCH.** THERE ARE **OVER 2,000 SPECIES** DESCRIBED SO FAR.

PSEUDOSCORPIONS LIKE **HUMID** AND **DARK PLACES,** LIKE THE **UNDERGROWTH, DEAD LEAVES,** BARK, AND **STONES,** OR IN THE **HOUSE,** IN BASEMENTS AND BATHROOMS.

PSEUDOSCORPIONS ARE SOMETIMES FOUND LIVING ALONGSIDE **BEETLES** OR **ANTS,** EATING THEIR **PARASITE MITES.**

PSEUDOSCORPIONS **CAN'T WALK** FOR **LONG DISTANCES** BECAUSE THEY ARE **VERY SMALL.** IN ADDITION, THEY **CAN'T FLY.** TO CONQUER NEW TERRITORIES, PSEUDOSCORPIONS **ATTACH** THEMSELVES TO THE **LEGS** OF **FLYING ANIMALS,** LIKE **BEETLES, WASPS,** AND, LESS OFTEN, **BIRDS.** THIS WAY OF "HITCHHIKING" IS CALLED **PHORESY.**

PSEUDOSCORPIONS ARE **CARNIVOROUS** AND **EAT PESTS** LIKE **BOOKLICE, MITES, FLIES, SPRINGTAILS,** AND **CATERPILLARS.** TO **CATCH** THEIR **PREY,** PSEUDOSCORPIONS EITHER **AMBUSH** IT OR **CHASE** IT. PSEUDOSCORPIONS ARE **BENEFICIAL** AND THEIR **VENOM** IS **NOT DANGEROUS** TO PEOPLE.

AFTER **CAPTURING** A **PREY** WITH ITS **PINCERS** AND **INJECTING** IT WITH ITS **VENOM,** THE PSEUDOSCORPION **POKES** A **HOLE** THROUGH IT. THEN, IT **INJECTS** THE PREY WITH **DIGESTIVE FLUIDS** AND **SUCKS** THE **DIGESTED INSIDES,** LEAVING AN EMPTY EXOSKELETON.

PSEUDOSCORPIONS ARE ALSO KNOWN AS **BOOK SCORPIONS.** THIS IS BECAUSE THEY ARE SOMETIMES **FOUND NEAR BOOKS,** PROBABLY **HUNTING** FOR **BOOKLICE,** ONE OF THEIR PREY.

FEMALE PSEUDOSCORPIONS **DEPOSIT** ABOUT **20 EGGS, TWICE** DURING THE **SUMMER.** ONCE THEY HATCH, THE **NEWBORNS CRAWL** ONTO THE **BACK** OF THEIR **MOTHER** WHERE THEY **REMAIN** FOR A **FEW DAYS.** THE YOUNG PSEUDOSCORPIONS **MOLT THREE TIMES** BEFORE BECOMING **ADULTS.** ADULT PSEUDOSCORPIONS LIVE FOR ABOUT **THREE YEARS.**

PSEUDOSCORPIONS CAN **WALK FORWARD** AND **BACKWARD.** SOME MOVE **SIDEWAYS.**

FOSSILS OF PSEUDOSCORPIONS ARE OVER **380 MILLION YEARS OLD,** FROM THE **DEVONIAN PERIOD.** ALTHOUGH LOOKING MORE LIKE SCORPIONS, PSEUDOSCORPIONS ARE THOUGHT TO **DESCEND** FROM **SPIDERS.**

PSEUDOSCORPIONS

Pseudoscorpionidae

CEPHALOTHORAX

THE **CEPHALOTHORAX** IS THE **FIRST PART** OF THE **BODY.** ALL THE **APPENDAGES** (CHELICERAE, PEDIPALPS, AND LEGS) ARE **ATTACHED** TO THE **CEPHALOTHORAX,** NOT TO THE ABDOMEN.

CHELICERAE

NEAR THE MOUTH, PSEUDOSCORPIONS HAVE **TWO CHELICERAE.** THESE ORGANS **PRODUCE SILK.**

ABDOMEN

THE **ABDOMEN** IS DIVIDED INTO **12 SEGMENTS.** THERE'S **NO TAIL** AT THE END OF THE ABDOMEN.

PSEUDOSCORPIONS **BREATHE** THROUGH **SPIRACLES,** OR **OPENINGS,** POSITIONED **ALONG** THE **ABDOMEN.**

SILK

PSEUDOSCORPIONS USE THEIR **SILK** TO **BUILD** A **COCOON** WHERE THEY SPEND THE **COLDER MONTHS.** THEY ARE **ACTIVE** DURING THE **SPRING** AND THE **SUMMER.**

FEMALE PSEUDOSCORPIONS **WEAVE** A **SACK** IN WHICH THEY **LAY** THEIR **EGGS.** THE **EGG SACK** HANGS FROM THE **FEMALE ABDOMEN** UNTIL THE **EGGS HATCH.**

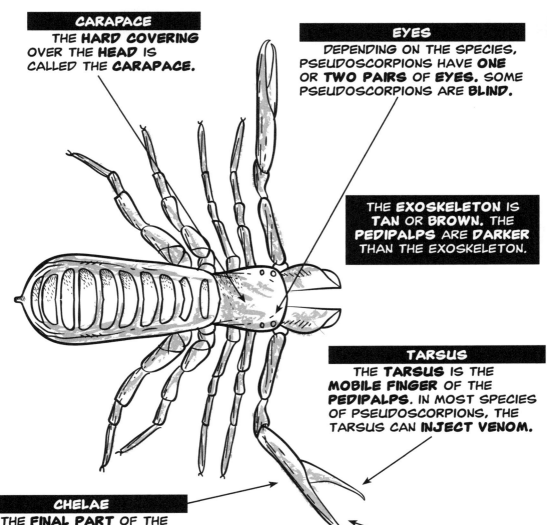

CARAPACE
THE **HARD COVERING** OVER THE **HEAD** IS CALLED THE **CARAPACE.**

EYES
DEPENDING ON THE SPECIES, PSEUDOSCORPIONS HAVE **ONE** OR **TWO PAIRS** OF **EYES.** SOME PSEUDOSCORPIONS ARE **BLIND.**

THE **EXOSKELETON** IS **TAN** OR **BROWN.** THE **PEDIPALPS** ARE **DARKER** THAN THE EXOSKELETON.

TARSUS
THE **TARSUS** IS THE **MOBILE FINGER** OF THE **PEDIPALPS.** IN MOST SPECIES OF PSEUDOSCORPIONS, THE TARSUS CAN **INJECT VENOM.**

CHELAE
THE **FINAL PART** OF THE **PEDIPALP** IS CALLED THE **CHELA.** IT'S MADE UP OF **TWO FINGERS,** THE **TARSUS** AND THE **METATARSUS.**

METATARSUS
THE **METATARSUS** IS THE **FIXED FINGER** OF THE **PEDIPALPS.**

PEDIPALPS
PSEUDOSCORPIONS HAVE **TWO BIG PEDIPALPS,** OR **PINCERS.** THE PEDIPALPS ARE USED TO **GRAB** AND **STING** THE **PREY.** PSEUDOSCORPIONS DON'T RELY ON THEIR **EYESIGHT** TO **HUNT,** BUT THEY ARE **GUIDED** BY THEIR **PEDIPALPS.** PEDIPALPS ARE KEEN **SENSORY ORGANS** COVERED WITH **SENSITIVE HAIR.** THEY CAN SENSE THE **APPROACH** OF OTHER **ANIMALS,** LIKE PREY OR ATTACKERS.

WIND SCORPIONS

Solifugae

SOLIFUGAE IS THE SCIENTIFIC NAME OF A GROUP OF **ARTHROPODS** WITH **MANY COMMON NAMES.** ONE OF THEM IS THE **WIND SCORPION,** BECAUSE THEY ARE **VERY FAST** AND CAN RUN "LIKE THE WIND." BUT THESE ANIMALS ARE **NOT SCORPIONS.** ANOTHER COMMON NAME IS THE **SUN SPIDER** OR THE **CAMEL SPIDER,** PROBABLY BECAUSE THEY LIVE IN **ARID PLACES** LIKE **DESERTS.** BUT THESE ANIMALS ARE **NOT SPIDERS,** EITHER.

THE SCIENTIFIC NAME **SOLIFUGAE** MEANS **"SUN FLEEING,"** BECAUSE MOST SPECIES ARE **NOCTURNAL** AND **"RUN AWAY"** FROM THE **SUN.**

THERE ARE **OVER 1,000 SPECIES** OF WIND SCORPIONS DESCRIBED SO FAR.

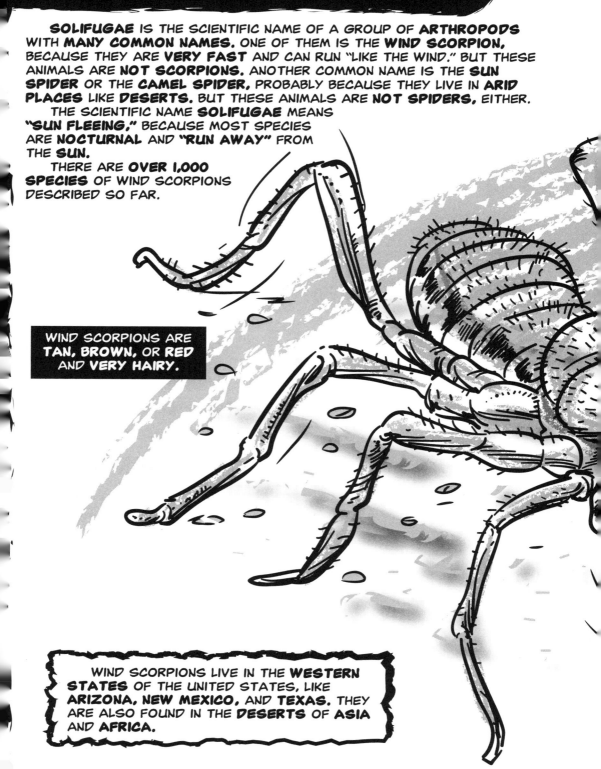

WIND SCORPIONS ARE **TAN, BROWN,** OR **RED** AND **VERY HAIRY.**

WIND SCORPIONS LIVE IN THE **WESTERN STATES** OF THE UNITED STATES, LIKE **ARIZONA, NEW MEXICO,** AND **TEXAS.** THEY ARE ALSO FOUND IN THE **DESERTS** OF **ASIA** AND **AFRICA.**

WIND SCORPIONS MEASURE BETWEEN **1/4** OF AN **INCH** TO **THREE INCHES,** DEPENDING ON THE SPECIES. THE **BIGGEST** ONES MEASURE **SIX INCHES** INCLUDING THE LEGS.

WIND SCORPIONS ARE **EXTREMELY VORACIOUS** AND **EAT ANYTHING** THEY CAN **PUT THEIR PEDIPALPS ON.** WIND SCORPIONS ARE CARNIVOROUS, **VERY AGGRESSIVE,** AND **VERY ACTIVE.**

PEDIPALP

ONCE THE WIND SCORPION **CATCHES** ITS **PREY,** IT **CRUSHES** IT WITH ITS **CHELICERAE.** THEN, THE WIND SCORPION **EATS** IT BY **SECRETING DIGESTIVE FLUIDS** OVER IT AND **SUCKING** IN THE **LIQUEFIED PREY.**
WIND SCORPIONS EAT **INSECTS** (LIKE **ROACHES, TERMITES,** AND **BEES**), OTHER **ARTHROPODS** (LIKE **SCORPIONS**), AND **SMALL LIZARDS** AND **MICE.**

PEDIPALP

WIND SCORPIONS
Solifugae

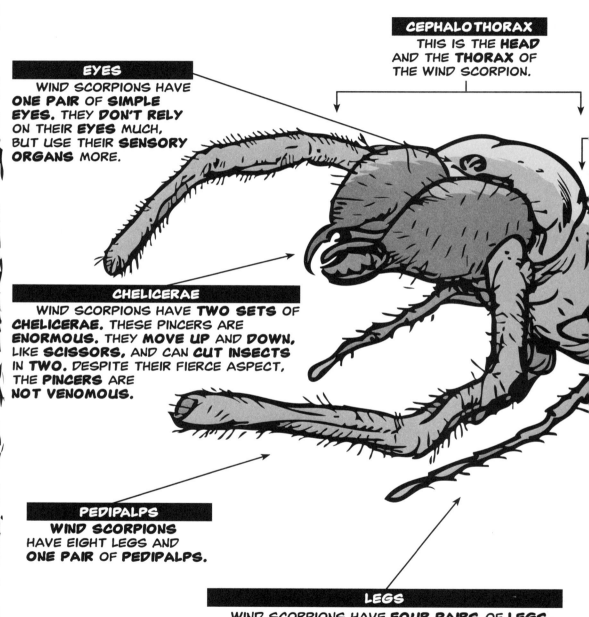

CEPHALOTHORAX
THIS IS THE **HEAD** AND THE **THORAX** OF THE WIND SCORPION.

EYES
WIND SCORPIONS HAVE **ONE PAIR** OF **SIMPLE EYES.** THEY **DON'T RELY** ON THEIR **EYES** MUCH, BUT USE THEIR **SENSORY ORGANS** MORE.

CHELICERAE
WIND SCORPIONS HAVE **TWO SETS** OF **CHELICERAE.** THESE PINCERS ARE **ENORMOUS.** THEY **MOVE UP** AND **DOWN,** LIKE **SCISSORS,** AND CAN **CUT INSECTS** IN **TWO.** DESPITE THEIR FIERCE ASPECT, THE **PINCERS** ARE **NOT VENOMOUS.**

PEDIPALPS
WIND SCORPIONS HAVE EIGHT LEGS AND **ONE PAIR** OF PEDIPALPS.

LEGS
WIND SCORPIONS HAVE **FOUR PAIRS** OF **LEGS,** BUT THE **FIRST PAIR,** THE ONE CLOSEST TO THE HEAD, IS USED AS A **SENSORY ORGAN** JUST LIKE THE PEDIPALPS.
UNDER THE **FOURTH PAIR** OF **LEGS,** WIND SCORPIONS HAVE **SENSORY ORGANS** CALLED **RACQUET ORGANS** OR **MALLEOLI.** WITH THESE ORGANS WIND SCORPIONS CAN **SENSE CHEMICALS** TO **LOCATE MATES, PREY,** AND **ATTACKERS.**

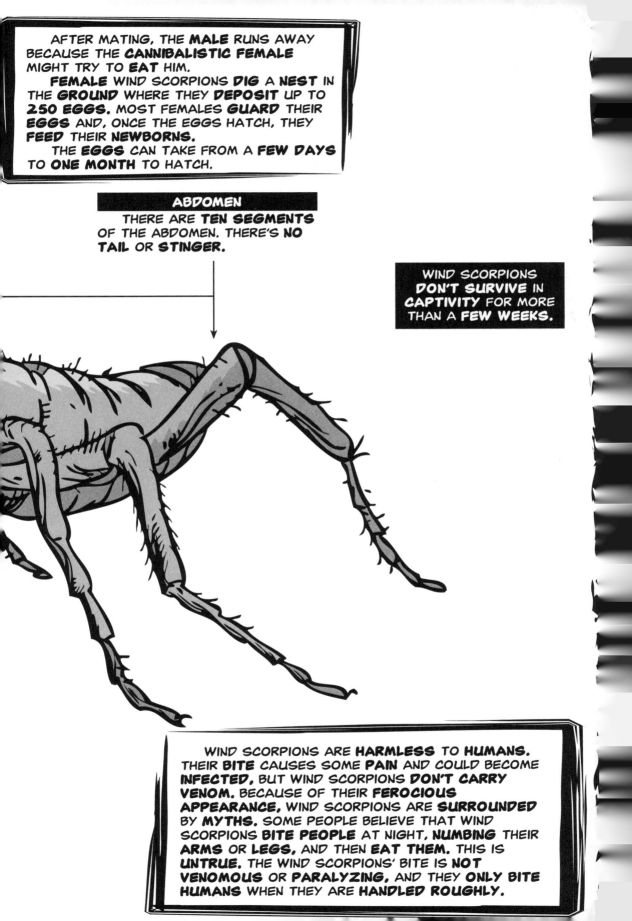

AFTER MATING, THE **MALE** RUNS AWAY BECAUSE THE **CANNIBALISTIC FEMALE** MIGHT TRY TO **EAT** HIM.

FEMALE WIND SCORPIONS **DIG** A **NEST** IN THE **GROUND** WHERE THEY **DEPOSIT** UP TO **250 EGGS.** MOST FEMALES **GUARD** THEIR **EGGS** AND, ONCE THE EGGS HATCH, THEY **FEED** THEIR **NEWBORNS.**

THE **EGGS** CAN TAKE FROM A **FEW DAYS** TO **ONE MONTH** TO HATCH.

ABDOMEN

THERE ARE **TEN SEGMENTS** OF THE ABDOMEN. THERE'S **NO TAIL** OR **STINGER.**

WIND SCORPIONS **DON'T SURVIVE** IN **CAPTIVITY** FOR MORE THAN A **FEW WEEKS.**

WIND SCORPIONS ARE **HARMLESS** TO **HUMANS.** THEIR **BITE** CAUSES SOME **PAIN** AND COULD BECOME **INFECTED,** BUT WIND SCORPIONS **DON'T CARRY VENOM.** BECAUSE OF THEIR **FEROCIOUS APPEARANCE,** WIND SCORPIONS ARE **SURROUNDED** BY **MYTHS.** SOME PEOPLE BELIEVE THAT WIND SCORPIONS **BITE PEOPLE** AT NIGHT, **NUMBING** THEIR **ARMS** OR **LEGS,** AND THEN **EAT THEM.** THIS IS **UNTRUE.** THE WIND SCORPIONS' BITE IS **NOT VENOMOUS** OR **PARALYZING,** AND THEY **ONLY BITE HUMANS** WHEN THEY ARE **HANDLED ROUGHLY.**

DADDY LONGLEGS

Opiliones

OPILIONES IS THE SCIENTIFIC NAME OF A GROUP OF **ARTHROPODS** COMMONLY KNOWN AS **DADDY LONGLEGS** OR **HARVESTMEN**.

THE NAME **OPILIONES** COMES FROM THE LATIN WORD **OPILIO**, WHICH MEANS "**SHEPHERD**." **SHEPHERDS** USED TO **STAND ON STILTS** TO BETTER **GUARD** THEIR **FLOCKS**. MANY SPECIES OF OPILIONES, OR HARVESTMEN, HAVE **VERY LONG LEGS**, AS IF THEY WERE **WALKING ON STILTS**.

NOT ALL THE HARVESTMEN HAVE **LONG LEGS**. MANY SPECIES HAVE **SHORT LEGS** AND LOOK MORE **LIKE MITES**.

PEOPLE CALL THESE ANIMALS **HARVESTMEN** PROBABLY BECAUSE THEY **NOTICED** THEM **DURING** THE **FALL**, AT THE **TIME** OF **HARVEST**.

IN SOME SPECIES, THE **LEGS** ARE **SO LONG**, THEY ARE **40 TIMES LONGER** THAN THE **BODY**. IF PEOPLE HAD **LEGS LIKE THAT**, THEY WOULD BE **OVER 100 FEET TALL**!

THERE ARE OVER **6,000 SPECIES** OF HARVESTMEN, BUT THERE ARE PROBABLY **MORE** THAN **10,000** NOT YET DISCOVERED.

HARVESTMEN LIVE FOR ABOUT **ONE YEAR**. THEY ARE MOSTLY **ACTIVE** IN THE **WARM MONTHS**, AND **DIE** IN THE **WINTER**.

HOW TO RECOGNIZE A DADDY LONGLEGS (HARVESTMAN) FROM A DADDY LONGLEGS SPIDER

DADDY LONGLEGS SHOULDN'T BE CONFUSED WITH **DADDY LONGLEGS SPIDERS**. **DADDY LONGLEGS** ARE **NOT SPIDERS**.

THE **BODY** LOOKS LIKE AN **OVAL** BECAUSE THE **HEAD** AND THE **ABDOMEN** ARE **FUSED TOGETHER**.

DADDY LONGLEGS (HARVESTMEN) **DON'T PRODUCE SILK**.

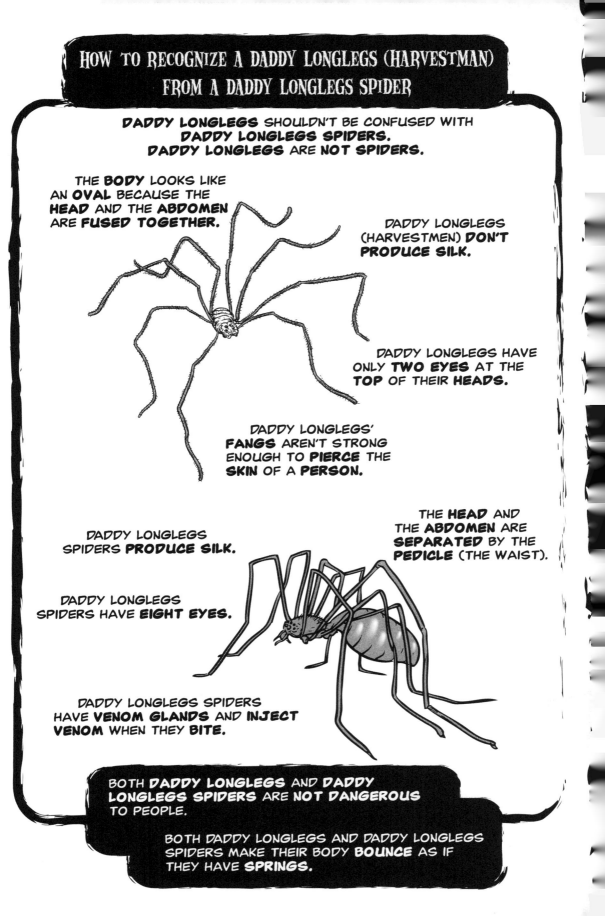

DADDY LONGLEGS HAVE ONLY **TWO EYES** AT THE **TOP** OF THEIR **HEADS**.

DADDY LONGLEGS' **FANGS** AREN'T STRONG ENOUGH TO **PIERCE** THE **SKIN** OF A **PERSON**.

DADDY LONGLEGS SPIDERS **PRODUCE SILK**.

THE **HEAD** AND THE **ABDOMEN** ARE **SEPARATED** BY THE **PEDICLE** (THE WAIST).

DADDY LONGLEGS SPIDERS HAVE **EIGHT EYES**.

DADDY LONGLEGS SPIDERS HAVE **VENOM GLANDS** AND **INJECT VENOM** WHEN THEY **BITE**.

BOTH **DADDY LONGLEGS** AND **DADDY LONGLEGS SPIDERS** ARE **NOT DANGEROUS** TO PEOPLE.

BOTH DADDY LONGLEGS AND DADDY LONGLEGS SPIDERS MAKE THEIR BODY **BOUNCE** AS IF THEY HAVE **SPRINGS**.

DADDY LONGLEGS
Opiliones

BODY
THE **HEAD, THORAX,** AND **ABDOMEN** ARE ALL **FUSED TOGETHER.**

SPIRACLES
HARVESTMEN HAVE **TWO SPIRACLES,** EACH PLACED **BEHIND** THE **FOURTH LEG.** HARVESTMEN USE THESE **SPIRACLES** TO **BREATHE.**

LEGS
HARVESTMEN HAVE **EIGHT LEGS.** THE **SECOND PAIR** OF LEGS IS **LONGER** THAN ALL THE OTHERS. THIS IS BECAUSE HARVESTMEN USE THEM AS IF THEY WERE **ANTENNAE,** OR **SENSORY ORGANS.**

SOMETIMES HARVESTMEN **DON'T HAVE** ALL THEIR **LEGS.** THIS HAPPENS WHEN A PREDATOR **CATCHES** THEM BY ONE OF THEIR LEGS. THE HARVESTMAN PREFERS TO **CUT OFF** ITS **LEG** THAN **LOSE** ITS **LIFE.** THIS IS CALLED **AUTOTOMY,** OR **SELF-AMPUTATION.**

OZOPORES
OZOPORES ARE **GLANDS** LOCATED IN THE CEPHALOTHORAX AND SECRETE **DISGUSTING CHEMICALS.** WHEN THE HARVESTMAN FEELS **THREATENED,** IT **OOZES** CHEMICALS FROM ITS OZOPORES TO KEEP **PREDATORS** AWAY.

EYES

MOST HARVESTMEN HAVE ONLY **TWO EYES**, EACH POINTING TO ONE SIDE. SOME HARVESTMEN ARE **BLIND**.

TUBERCLE

THE **EYES** ARE POSITIONED ON **TOP** OF A **TUBERCLE**, OR **BUMP**, ON THE **HEAD** OF THE HARVESTMAN.

CHELICERAE

THESE ARE THE HARVESTMAN'S **JAWS**. THEY **CUT** AND **CHEW** THE **FOOD**. HARVESTMEN CAN SWALLOW **SMALL CHUNKS** OF **FOOD**, UNLIKE **SPIDERS** THAT CAN ONLY SUCK **LIQUEFIED PREY**.

PEDIPALPS

PEDIPALPS ARE **SENSORY ORGANS** THAT HARVESTMEN USE TO **TOUCH** AND **FEEL** THEIR **SURROUNDING SPACE**, A LITTLE BIT LIKE HUMAN HANDS. IN SOME SPECIES, THE PEDIPALPS ARE ABLE TO **GRAB PREY** AND **CARRY** IT TO THE **MOUTH**.

goin' buggy!

19.

WHAT DOES A **SPIDER** LIKE ABOUT **BASEBALL?**

-THE **FLY**-BALLS!

20.

WHAT'S THE **OPPOSITE** OF AN **INSECT?**

-AN **OUT**-SECT!

21.

WHAT'S A **DUNG BEETLE'S** FAVORITE **CHARACTER?**

-WINNIE THE **POOH!**

22.

WHY WAS THE **PLUMBER MOTH** EMBARRASSED?

-BECAUSE, WHEN HE BENT, HIS **BUTT-ER FLY** WAS SHOWING!

23.

WHAT IS A **SPIDER'S** FAVORITE GAME?

-CRICKET!

24.

WHAT BUG IS WORTH ONLY **ONE PENNY?**

-A **CENT**-IPEDE!

MYRIAPODS

MYRIAPODS ARE A GROUP OF ANIMALS BELONGING TO THE ARTHROPODS. THEY SHARE ALL THE ARTHROPODS' TRAITS, LIKE HAVING JOINTED LEGS, A SEGMENTED AND SYMMETRICAL BODY, AND AN EXOSKELETON.

THE WORD MYRIAD COMES FROM THE GREEK AND MEANS "COUNTLESS." MYRIAPOD MEANS "ANIMALS WITH A LOT OF LEGS." SOME SPECIES HAVE ONLY TEN LEGS, BUT OTHERS CAN HAVE MORE THAN 750!

MYRIAPODS HAVE A PAIR OF ANTENNAE ON THEIR HEADS.

FOSSIL RECORDS SEEM TO INDICATE THAT ANCIENT MYRIAPODS WERE THE FIRST ANIMALS TO WALK ON LAND, OVER 400 MILLION YEARS AGO.

BECAUSE THEIR EXOSKELETON DRIES UP, MYRIAPODS MAINLY LIVE IN HUMID PLACES, LIKE UNDER DEAD LEAVES IN FORESTS, UNDER THE BARK OF TREES, OR IN CAVES.

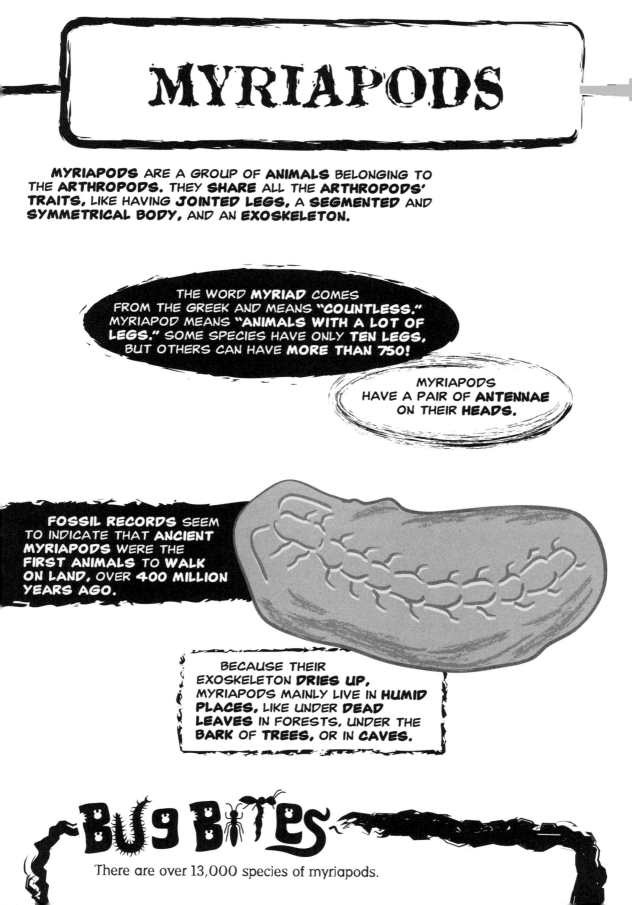

BUG BITES

There are over 13,000 species of myriapods.

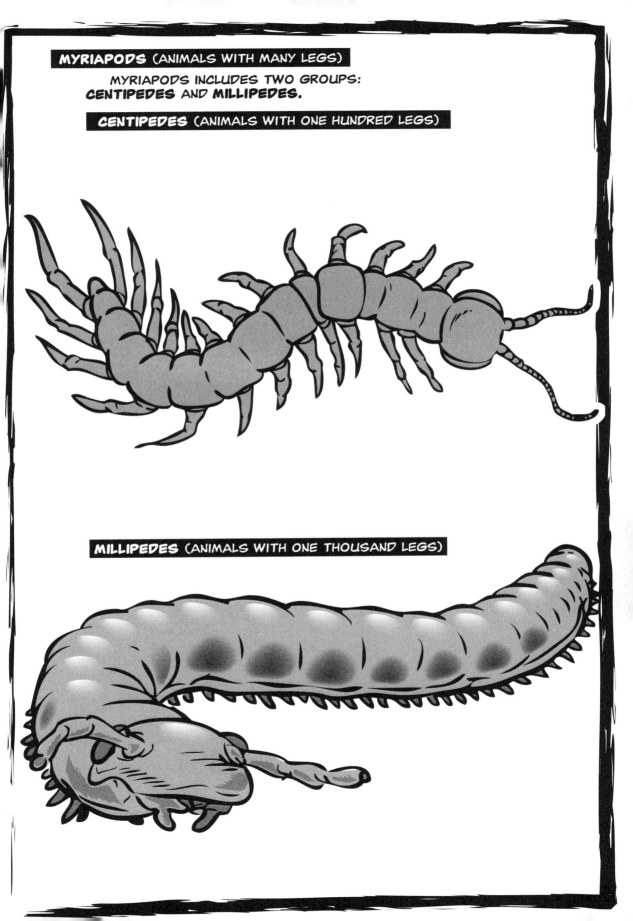

MYRIAPODS (ANIMALS WITH MANY LEGS)

MYRIAPODS INCLUDES TWO GROUPS:
CENTIPEDES AND **MILLIPEDES.**

CENTIPEDES (ANIMALS WITH ONE HUNDRED LEGS)

MILLIPEDES (ANIMALS WITH ONE THOUSAND LEGS)

CENTIPEDES

THE WORD **CENTIPEDE** COMES FROM THE LATIN WORDS **CENTI**, WHICH MEANS **"ONE HUNDRED,"** AND **PEDES**, WHICH MEANS **"FEET."** MOST CENTIPEDES HAVE ONLY **30 FEET.** SOME CENTIPEDES HAVE **OVER 300!**

CENTIPEDES HAVE A **LONG, THIN,** AND **FLATTENED BODY,** DIVIDED INTO **SEGMENTS.** EACH **SEGMENT** OF THE BODY BEARS **ONE PAIR OF LEGS,** EXCEPT FOR THE SEGMENT RIGHT **AFTER THE HEAD** AND THE **TAIL SEGMENT.** THESE TWO SEGMENTS **DON'T BEAR ANY LEGS.**

CENTIPEDES ARE MOSTLY **NOCTURNAL.** THEY ARE VERY **AGGRESSIVE** AND **CARNIVOROUS PREDATORS.** THEY HUNT **INSECTS** AND **EARTHWORMS.**

CENTIPEDES HAVE A PAIR OF **FANGS UNDER** THEIR **HEAD.** THESE FANGS CAN **INJECT VENOM** INTO THEIR VICTIM, **KILLING** OR **PARALYZING** IT.

MOST **CENTIPEDES** ARE ONLY **ONE INCH LONG.** BUT THERE'S **ONE CENTIPEDE** THAT MEASURES **OVER ONE FOOT!** IT'S CALLED THE **AMAZONIAN GIANT CENTIPEDE,** AND LIVES IN **SOUTH AMERICA.** THE AMAZONIAN GIANT CENTIPEDE IS SO BIG THAT IT CAN KILL **RATS, LIZARDS,** AND **FROGS.** THIS CENTIPEDE HAS DEVELOPED A **HUNTING TECHNIQUE** TO CATCH **BATS TOO.** IT **CRAWLS** TO THE **TOP** OF A **CAVE** WHERE BATS LIVE. THEN, IT **HANGS UPSIDE DOWN,** HOLDING ONTO THE CEILING WITH ITS **BACK LEGS.** WHEN A BAT **FLIES BY,** THE AMAZONIAN GIANT CENTIPEDE **GRABS IT** AND **INJECTS** IT WITH ITS **VENOM.** THE BAT **QUICKLY DIES,** AND THE GIANT ENJOYS ITS **MEAL.**

CENTIPEDES HAVE **TWO EYES**, BUT MANY CENTIPEDES ARE **BLIND** AND **GUIDED BY** THEIR **ANTENNAE.**

THE **HOUSE CENTIPEDE** LIVES IN **PEOPLE'S HOMES.** IT'S A **QUICK** AND **EXPERT HUNTER,** AND IT'S **HARD** FOR PEOPLE TO **CATCH.** IN SPITE OF BEING **QUITE REPULSIVE,** HOUSE CENTIPEDES ARE **BENEFICIAL** BECAUSE THEY EAT HOUSE PESTS, LIKE **COCKROACHES** AND **HOUSEFLIES.**

BUG BITES

The number of the body segments of a centipede is always odd.

MILLIPEDES

MILLIPEDES HAVE **LONG, ROUNDED BODIES,** DIVIDED INTO **SEGMENTS.** EACH SEGMENT HAS **TWO PAIRS** OF **LEGS,** EXCEPT FOR THE FIRST SEGMENT **AFTER THE HEAD,** WHICH **DOESN'T BEAR ANY LEGS.**

WHILE **CENTIPEDES** ARE MOSTLY **CARNIVOROUS** AND **FAST, MILLIPEDES** ARE MOSTLY **HERBIVOROUS** AND MOVE **QUITE SLOWLY.**

WHEN **THREATENED,** THE **PILL MILLIPEDE** ROLLS ITSELF UP INTO A **SPIRAL.** IN THIS WAY, IT **EXPOSES** ONLY ITS **HARD EXOSKELETON** TO ITS ENEMIES.

THE **PILL MILLIPEDE** IS OFTEN **CONFUSED** WITH THE **WOODLICE,** OR **PILL BUG,** WHICH ALSO ROLLS ITSELF UP IN A **BALL** WHEN **THREATENED.** THE **PILL BUG** HAS **SEVEN PAIRS** OF LEGS, WHILE THE **PILL MILLIPEDE** HAS MORE THAN **22.** ALSO, PILL MILLIPEDES ARE **SHINIER** THAN PILL BUGS.

MANY SPECIES OF MILLIPEDES CAN **SECRETE CHEMICALS** WHEN DISTURBED. ALTHOUGH THESE CHEMICALS ARE **NOT DANGEROUS** TO PEOPLE, THEY ARE VERY **EFFECTIVE** AGAINST THE MILLIPEDES' NATURAL **ENEMIES**, LIKE **ANTS**. IN MADAGASCAR **LEMURS** USE THE MILLIPEDE CHEMICALS TO **RID THEMSELVES OF PESTS**. THEY DO SO BY **RUBBING MILLIPEDES** ALL OVER THEIR **BODIES**. THE MILLIPEDES **RELEASE** THEIR CHEMICALS, **KILLING PESTS** LIVING ON THE **LEMURS**.

IN JANUARY OF 2003, IN SCOTLAND, **MIKE NEWMAN**, A BUS DRIVER AND FOSSIL HUNTER, FOUND A **FRAGMENT** OF A **FOSSILIZED MILLIPEDE**. THE FRAGMENT IS ONLY **HALF AN INCH LONG**. BUT IT WAS **ENOUGH** FOR SCIENTISTS TO FIGURE OUT THAT THIS MILLIPEDE LIVED **428 MILLION YEARS AGO**. IT WAS ONE OF THE **FIRST CREATURES** THAT HAD ADAPTED TO **LIVE** ON **LAND**. THE MILLIPEDE WAS NAMED **PNEUMODESMUS NEWMANI**, IN HONOR OF MIKE NEWMAN.

300 MILLION YEAR OLD FOSSILS OF **EUPHOBERIA** SHOW THAT THIS EXTINCT MILLIPEDE WAS ABOUT **THREE** AND A **HALF FEET LONG!**

BUG BITES

The African giant black millipede is often kept as a pet. It's very docile and can live to be eight years old. African giant black millipedes can be one foot long.

GLOSSARY

ABORIGINE
A NATIVE PERSON OF AUSTRALIA.

ANAMORPHIC DEVELOPMENT
A PROCESS IN WHICH AN INSECT'S ABDOMINAL SEGMENTS GROW IN NUMBER AS THE INSECT BECOMES AN ADULT.

ANAPHYLAXIS
AN EXTREME ALLERGIC REACTION THAT CAN BE FATAL.

ANESTHETIC
A NUMBING SUBSTANCE.

ANTIBACTERIAL
PREVENTING OR KILLING BACTERIA.

ANTICOAGULANT
A SUBSTANCE THAT PREVENTS BLOOD FROM CLOTTING.

ANTI-INFLAMMATORY
A SUBSTANCE THAT CURES INFLAMMATION.

ANTIOXIDANT
A SUBSTANCE THAT PRESERVES FRESHNESS.

ANTISEPTIC
A SUBSTANCE THAT PREVENTS INFECTION.

APOSEMATIC COLORATION
A COMBINATION OF BRIGHT COLORS ARTHROPODS DISPLAY TO WARN THEIR PREDATORS THAT THEY ARE TOXIC.

ASTHMA
A DISEASE THAT CAUSES COUGHING, WHEEZING, AND DIFFICULTY IN BREATHING.

BEEKEEPER
A PERSON WHO BREEDS HONEYBEES.

BIOLUMINESCENCE
A PROCESS IN WHICH AN ANIMAL CAN PRODUCE LIGHT.

BROOD
A GROUP OF LARVAE HATCHED AT ABOUT THE SAME TIME.

CANNIBAL
AN ANIMAL THAT EATS ANIMALS OF ITS OWN SPECIES.

CAMOUFLAGE
TO DISGUISE ONESELF IN THE ENVIRONMENT.

CARBON DIOXIDE
A GAS THAT ANIMALS EXHALE WHEN THEY BREATHE.

CARCASS
THE BODY OF A DEAD ANIMAL.

CARNIVORE (CARNIVOROUS)
AN ANIMAL THAT EATS OTHER ANIMALS.

CARRION
ROTTING FLESH.

CASTE
A GROUP OF INSECTS THAT LIVE IN A COLONY AND THAT PERFORM SPECIFIC TASKS.

CAUDAL FILAMENT
A HAIR-LIKE APPENDAGE LOCATED AT THE TIP OF THE ABDOMEN.

CCD (COLONY COLLAPSE DISORDER)
A PHENOMENON IN WHICH MOST OF THE WORKERS ABANDON THE BEEHIVE FOR NO APPARENT REASON. THE REMAINING QUEEN AND WORKERS ARE TOO FEW TO BE ABLE TO SUPPORT THE COLONY, WHICH SOON DIES.

CELLULOSE
THE MAIN COMPONENT OF PLANT FIBER.

CRUSTACEANS
A GROUP OF ARTHROPODS WITH A HARD SHELL, LIKE CRABS AND SHRIMP.

CYTOTOXIN
A POISON THAT AFFECTS THE CELLS CAUSING NECROSIS.

DARWIN, CHARLES ROBERT (1809 - 1882)
ENGLISH NATURALIST. HE CONCEIVED THE IDEA THAT ONE ANCESTOR SPAWNED ALL CREATURES, WHICH SURVIVE IF THEY ADAPT TO THEIR ENVIRONMENT. DARWIN'S THEORY IS CALLED NATURAL SELECTION.

DEVELOPMENTAL BIOLOGY
THE SCIENCE THAT STUDIES HOW ANIMALS DEVELOP FROM A FERTILIZED EGG.

DIURNAL
ACTIVE DURING THE DAY.

ECDYSIS (OR MOLTING)
A PROCESS DURING WHICH AN ARTHROPOD SHEDS ITS OLD EXOSKELETON.

ELYTRON (PLURAL, ELYTRA)
THE HARDENED FOREWING OF A BEETLE.

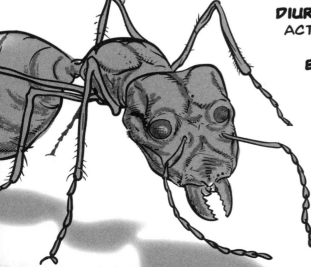

ENTOMOLOGIST
A SCIENTIST WHO STUDIES INSECTS.

FAO (THE FOOD AND AGRICULTURE ORGANIZATION)
AN AGENCY OF THE UNITED NATIONS THAT LEADS INTERNATIONAL EFFORTS TO DEFEAT WORLD HUNGER.

FERTILIZED EGG
AN EGG THAT IS FUSED TO A MALE REPRODUCTIVE CELL.

FOLLICLE
A SMALL OPENING WITH HAIR ON THE SKIN.

FORAGER
A BEE THAT SEARCHES FOR AND COLLECTS FOOD.

FORENSIC ENTOMOLOGY
A SCIENCE THAT STUDIES THE BEHAVIOR OF INSECTS FOR LEGAL PURPOSES.

GANGLION (PLURAL, GANGLIA)
A NERVE CENTER, LIKE THE BRAIN.

GANGRENE
THE DEATH OF BODY TISSUE CAUSED BY LOSS OF BLOOD FLOW.

GENETICS
THE SCIENCE THAT STUDIES HEREDITY.

GEOTHERMAL SPRING
A HOT SPRING.

GILLS
THE ORGANS THAT AQUATIC ANIMALS USE TO BREATHE.

HEMATOPHAGOUS
AN ANIMAL THAT FEEDS ON BLOOD.

HEMOLYMPH
THE ARTHROPODS' BLOOD.

HERBIVORE (HERBIVOROUS)
AN ANIMAL THAT EATS PLANTS.

HEXAGONAL
A SIX-SIDED SHAPE.

HIBERNATE
TO SLEEP OR BECOMING INACTIVE DURING THE WINTER.

IMAGO
THE FOURTH STAGE OF THE ENDOPTERYGOTA INSECTS'
METAMORPHOSIS, ALSO KNOWN AS ADULT.

IMMUNOSUPPRESSIVE
A SUBSTANCE THAT PREVENTS HEALING.

INSECTICIDE
A SUBSTANCE THAT KILLS INSECTS.

INVERTEBRATES
ANIMALS WITHOUT A BACKBONE, LIKE WORMS, ARTHROPODS, SEA
URCHINS, JELLYFISH, ETC.

JUSTINIAN I (482 - 565)
EMPEROR OF THE BYZANTINE EMPIRE. HE ATTEMPTED TO RECREATE
THE ROMAN EMPIRE AND BUILT THE HAGIA SOPHIA.

MAMMAL
A WARM-BLOODED ANIMAL
WITH MAMMARY GLANDS
AND SKIN COVERED WITH
HAIR.

MANDIBLES
JAWS.

MEDICI
AN ITALIAN NOBLE FAMILY THAT
LIVED IN THE 15TH CENTURY.

METAMORPHOSIS
THE DEVELOPMENT OF AN INSECT, FROM THE EGG TO ADULT, WHICH
CONSISTS OF AN EXTREME TRANSFORMATION.

MIGRATE
TO MOVE FROM ONE PLACE TO ANOTHER AND THEN BACK AGAIN.

MOLTING
SEE ECDYSIS.

MUTUALISM
A RELATIONSHIP THAT BENEFITS ALL THE ORGANISMS INVOLVED.

NAIAD
THE SECOND STAGE OF THE METAMORPHOSIS OF EXOPTERYGOTA
INSECTS THAT SPEND THEIR LARVAL STAGE UNDERWATER.

NASA (NATIONAL AERONAUTICS AND SPACE ADMINISTRATION)
A U.S. AGENCY IN CHARGE OF SPACE EXPLORATION AND RESEARCH.

NECROSIS
THE DEATH OF BODY TISSUE CAUSED BY POISON OR DISEASE.

NECTAR
A SUGARY LIQUID SECRETED BY FLOWERS AND PLANTS.

NEUROTOXIN
A POISON THAT AFFECTS THE NERVES AND BRAIN.

NOCTURNAL
ACTIVE AT NIGHT.

NYMPH
THE SECOND STAGE OF THE METAMORPHOSIS OF EXOPTERYGOTA
INSECTS THAT SPEND THEIR LARVAL STAGE ON LAND.

OMNIVORE (OMNIVOROUS)
AN ANIMAL THAT EATS BOTH PLANTS AND ANIMALS.

OOTHECA
A CONTAINER OF EGGS.

PANDEMIC
A DISEASE THAT SPREADS TO THE WHOLE WORLD.

PARASITISM
A RELATIONSHIP THAT BENEFITS ONE ORGANISM AT THE EXPENSE
OF ANOTHER, CALLED A HOST.

PATHOGENS
A MICROORGANISM THAT CAUSES DISEASE. IT CAN BE A
BACTERIUM, A WORM, A VIRUS, OR A FUNGUS.

POISONOUS
HARMFUL TO EAT.

POLLEN
THE MALE REPRODUCTIVE CELL OF FLOWERS.

PORE
A SMALL OPENING ON THE SKIN.

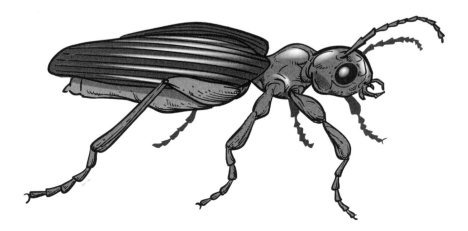

PRESERVATIVE
A SUBSTANCE THAT PREVENTS
FOOD FROM BECOMING ROTTEN.

SCAVENGER
AN ANIMAL THAT EATS DEAD
ANIMALS.

SCORPLING
A NEWBORN SCORPION.

SENSORY RECEPTOR
AN ORGAN CAPABLE OF
SENSING AN IMPULSE, LIKE A
HAND OR AN ANTENNA.

SERICULTURE
THE RAISING OF SILK WORMS.

SPIDERLING
A NEWBORN SPIDER.

STERILE
UNABLE TO REPRODUCE.

STRIDULATE
TO MAKE A SOUND BY SCRATCHING TOGETHER TWO PARTS OF
THE BODY. CRICKETS STRIDULATE.

SUBIMAGO
A STAGE IN WHICH INSECTS ARE NOT PUPAE ANYMORE, BUT
THEY ARE NOT YET ADULTS (IMAGO).

SYNTHETIC
MADE WITH CHEMICALS, NOT NATURAL.

TEGMEN (PLURAL, **TEGMINA**)
A HARDENED FOREWING.

TIMBAL
A DRUM-LIKE ORGAN USED BY CICADAS TO MAKE THEIR "SONG."

TOXIC
POISONOUS.

TROPHALLAXIS
THE EXCHANGE OF NUTRIENTS FROM THE ADULT INSECT'S MOUTH
OR ANUS TO THE LARVA'S MOUTH.

TUSCAN
FROM TUSCANY, A REGION IN ITALY.

ULTRAVIOLET LIGHT
A PART OF THE LIGHT SPECTRUM BEYOND THE VIOLET. PEOPLE
CANNOT SEE THIS LIGHT, BUT MANY ARTHROPODS DO.

VASODILATOR
A SUBSTANCE THAT ENLARGES THE VEINS TO FACILITATE BLOOD
FLOW.

VENOMOUS
AN ANIMAL THAT CAN INJECT POISON.

WINGSPAN
THE DISTANCE BETWEEN THE TIPS OF WINGS OF AN ARTHROPOD
WHEN KEPT OUTSTRETCHED.

XI LING SHI (CIRCA 2700 B.C.)
WIFE OF HUANG TI, OR THE YELLOW EMPEROR OF CHINA. SHE IS BELIEVED TO
HAVE INVENTED SERICULTURE AND SILK WEAVING.